KU-188-314

Laws in Nature

What are the laws of nature? Do they control the actions and movements of the other things that exist in our world? Is there a sense in which such laws are real things?

Both scientists and philosophers have been attracted by the view that the world contains laws of nature. It is such laws that dictate the behaviour of particulars, rather than any of those things' intrinsic or internal forces. In this book Stephen Mumford argues against this popular view. He shows that no adequate account has been produced of what such laws in nature would be, or how they would perform the work that has been required of them. In their place, he argues that there are other necessary connections in nature that can do all the work for which we thought laws were needed.

This book offers a holistic and connected account of reality in which the world's elements do not need to be activated or controlled by laws. It is not possible that these elements behave other than they do. The world is more of a jigsaw than a mosaic: its pieces can form only one picture, and laws are no part of it.

Stephen Mumford is Reader in Metaphysics in the Department of Philosophy at the University of Nottingham. He is the author of *Dispositions* (1998) and various papers in metaphysics. He is editor of *Russell on Metaphysics* (2003) and *Powers* by the late George Molnar (2003).

Routledge studies in twentieth-century philosophy

Laws in Nature

Stephen Mumford

NOTTINGHAM UNIVERSITY LIBRARY

Routledge
Taylor & Francis Group

LONDON AND NEW YORK

100407276X T

First published 2004
by Routledge
2 Park Square, Milton Park, Abingdon, Oxfordshire OX14 4RN

Simultaneously published in the USA and Canada
by Routledge
29 West 35th Street, New York, NY 10001

Routledge is an imprint of the Taylor & Francis Group

© 2004 Stephen Mumford

Typeset in Baskerville by Wearset Ltd, Boldon, Tyne and Wear
Printed and bound in Great Britain by MPG Books Ltd, Bodmin

All rights reserved. No part of this book may be reprinted or
reproduced or utilized in any form or by any electronic, mechanical,
or other means, now known or hereafter invented, including
photocopying and recording, or in any information storage or
retrieval system, without permission in writing from the publishers.

British Library Cataloguing in Publication Data
A catalogue record for this book is available from the British Library

Library of Congress Cataloging-in-Publication Data
Mumford, Stephen.
 Laws in nature / Stephen Mumford.
  p. cm.
 Includes bibliographical references and index.
 1. Law (Philosophy) 2. Power (Philosophy) 3. Philosophy of nature.
I. Title.
 B105.L3M86 2004
 117–dc22

                                                    2004000286

ISBN 0-415-31128-4

Contents

Illustrations

Preface

Both philosophers and scientists speak of laws of nature. They quantify over laws and can use the term as a count noun. Hence, they may speak of *a* law of nature, *three* laws of motion, *the* laws of nature (meaning the set of them all), and the laws of thermodynamics (meaning a particular subset of all the laws). If we endorse the view that to quantify over something is to accept an ontological commitment to it, then it would seem that these expressions indicate the view that there exist individuable things or entities called the laws of nature. Should we commit to such existents, it would be reasonable to suppose that we could provide some positive description of them, say what they are like, and what they consist in. Instantly, however, the issues become murky. Are laws of nature substances, in the philosophical sense of substance, meaning independent existences? Could a law exist though no other substances exist (following Hoffman and Rosenkrantz's, 1997, criterion of substance)? This would look strange, for what would such a law govern if there were no other substance in the world? If laws are not substances, are they collective existents like a pile of stones? If so, then what are they collections of? Are they collections of events? If they are, in what way do they qualify as laws? How can they govern that from which they are constituted? These are simple questions and yet few simple answers are to be found. There is a conspicuous absence of clarity even with such basics. The notion of a law of nature is commonly invoked, especially in the sciences, yet rarely are we given a clear and credible account of the nature of such laws.

It is plausible to suppose that many different senses of law of nature are in common usage. Such diversity would make it impossible to extrapolate a single theory that conveys what everybody means by a law. This book, therefore, focuses on one issue and one sense of law. The issue is reification: are laws real and distinct existents? The sense of law is duly a metaphysical one and the main question: what in the world is a law? Others may have a different sense of law and be concerned with different issues. They may say that laws are just summaries of observed regularities, which can be projected to unobserved cases by induction. Some may say that a law is merely an empirically justified inference rule of science. With these senses of law, the issue of reification is less controversial. One could hardly deny that there are summaries of observed regularities or rules of inference. The distinctly metaphysical concern of this book, however, is whether there are any real existents in nature that could correctly be called laws. Perhaps they would be the basis for the world's regularities and our inferences. In this case, both the positive and negative answers to the question of reification seem sensible options, even though only one of them can be true. This appears to be a meaningful and worthwhile debate in metaphysics, therefore.

A little while ago I thought that a realism about dispositions would allow us to dispense with laws of nature as an irreducible ontological category. I set out the basics of an account in the last chapter of my 1998a work, rhetorically titled 'Laws of nature outlawed'. At the time I was optimistic that I would be able to work out the detail of the account and produce a new book on laws within a year or so. This would have presented an anti-realism about laws as metaphysical existents. Things didn't turn out to be so simple or easy, however. I became tempted in time by a more realist view of laws, prompted by an interest in the account of E. J. Lowe (1980, 1982, 1987a, 1987b and 1989: Chs 8–10). Some of my published papers showed a little leaning in this direction (2000a, 2001, 2004), though I was still pondering what strange things real laws in nature would have to be. However, subsequently reading a number of things averted my conversion to a metaphysics of laws.

First, I was privileged to become closely involved with George Molnar's *Nachlass*, culminating in a finished version of his book on *Powers* (Molnar 2003). Molnar had a vision that was even more realist about dispositions than mine. The book is a major contribution to the case against Humeanism. This gave me more confidence that the world's particulars were, as Rom Harré (2001) would say, powerful actors rather than impotent patients.

Second, I was delighted by the appearance of Brian Ellis's *Scientific Essentialism* (2001), which was the end product of a number of years of his work. This book contained a damaging critique of the Humean metaphysic, yet it also contained a theory of laws that I thought looked redundant. If there really are powers, it seemed to me that laws were altogether the wrong way of talking about the world. Law-talk looked, at best, purely metaphorical. But it was not even a harmless metaphor. Laws go hand in hand with the Humean metaphysic that Ellis had so effectively attacked. They are a putative solution to the inadequacies of Humeanism, which looks like a way of salvaging something of the old view. Real laws seemed to be a way that some hoped to activate the otherwise inactive Humean world. But, in accepting that laws did this, one was accepting the metaphysics of discrete, inanimate particulars that created the problem in the first place. If one sees the world's particulars as connected and active, one never needs laws. To accept laws, seems to me, is to accept the problem they 'solve'. Better, then, to accept neither them nor what spawns them.

Third, I seriously read van Fraassen (1989) for the first time. I did not agree with all of it. It showed me, however, that to attack the idea of there being real laws in nature was not to attack science. Arguably, science makes no attempt to reify laws. One may think that science never seriously invokes laws at all. But if it does, it remains metaphysically neutral as to their nature. This made me think that science could fairly easily get along if there were no real laws in nature, though Harré and Madden (1975) had already argued this and Giere (1999) has done so since. Harré and Madden thought instead that science appealed to causal powers. Van Fraassen disagrees with this. There is no necessity, no modal facts, in his accounts of things. On this issue, I side with Harré and Madden.

Fourth, I came to understand better the ideas of Nancy Cartwright (1983, 1989, 1999). This was important because I realized that of all the stances previously taken on the relation between laws and powers, hers is the closest to mine. However, I think we reach that stance via very different paths. Cartwright builds an argument that is scientifically informed. I wanted an argument that was metaphysically compelling. I think that metaphysics has something important to contribute to our understanding of laws and related phenomena. I concede that a full understanding of laws would be both philosophical and empirical (see §1.2). But I was searching primarily for an account of the world that was metaphysically motivated and metaphysically adequate. I take it that philosophy has a distinctive approach to knowledge of the world that other disciplines cannot provide. This means that I am not prepared always to defer to science over the nature of the world. I want something, therefore, that has more in its favour than merely being scientifically informed.

The upshot of these influences was that, by a circuitous route, I became once again a convinced anti-realist about laws. The position I argue in this book is perhaps even more radical than the claims in 'Laws of nature outlawed'. The position there could be described as a reductive one. I hoped that in place of every law, I might put a disposition. Now, I am even more against the notion of a law. I advocate a stance, therefore, that can better be described as eliminativist. Others have recommended something similar. But unlike Harré and Madden, Cartwright, van Fraassen, and Giere, who argue against laws on broadly epistemological grounds, I argue that a lawless view is (also) metaphysically plausible. This contrasts with van Fraassen who argues that the notion of a law of nature is a metaphysical creation, as if all metaphysicians will want to support it (van Fraassen 1989: Ch. 1, §3, 'The end of metaphysics?'). Metaphysicians such as I do not support the notion of a law, and for metaphysical reasons. I am not even the first metaphysician to argue this. I suggest, in Part I, that Humean metaphysics is a lawless metaphysics. My metaphysics, however, is anti-Humean because I accept, while Humeanism denies, necessary connections in nature. This leaves me with a position that can be called *realist lawlessness*: realism about necessary connections but not about laws. Because I am arguing for the metaphysical plausibility of this view, I hope that I am being sufficiently original to justify another addition to the literature.

Acknowledgements

This book has had a difficult birth. Rather than taking one or two years, it has taken five or six. I could not have made it through without the support of a number of people. General support and encouragement have been the crucial counter to my tendency to pessimism and despondency. I must therefore give thanks to those who persuaded me that I had something worthwhile to say. I can think of David Armstrong, Alexander Bird, Nancy Cartwright, Eros Corazza, Alice Drewery, Bill Fish, Jonathan Lowe, Hugh Mellor, Peter Menzies, Alexander Miller, Jean-Maurice Monnoyer, Johannes Persson, Stathis Psillos and Claudine Tiercelin. I give some more specific philosophical acknowledgements in Chapter 11. Further, I would like to thank the University of Lund for the invitation that permitted me a week of uninterrupted reflection; the pan-European Metaphysics in Science group for welcoming me into the fold; Routledge for showing confidence in this project at an early stage, when all the ideas were not yet together; my Department at Nottingham for allowing me study leave, and the AHRB for providing a matching grant to ensure that the book was finished.

When the first draft was complete, I wanted to get some good quality critical feedback. I was very fortunate that three outstanding philosophers agreed to read and comment on the draft. I approached them because they were very likely to disagree with me and would be candid enough to say so. Two were Humeans and one was a realist about laws. They were Stephen Barker, Stathis Psillos and David Armstrong. They provided hundred of comments and objections for me. I thought hard about them and very much hope that I have done them justice. I am convinced that the book is a far stronger one for their input. That they should aid an opponent in such an enthusiastic manner is an incontrovertible demonstration of their intellectual integrity.

Finally, I thank my family, Maggie, William and Oliver. Among many other inconveniences, they had to forego a holiday in the hot Summer of 2003 so that I could get the first draft finished before the start of the new term. For their sake, and for all those people named, I hope it has all been worth it.

1 Laws in science and philosophy

1.1 Laws and explanations

It is a common thought that the world is regular and orderly to a high degree. Because it is so orderly, we are able to make many predictions about its future course that, for most practical purposes, are reliable. Is there a reason why there is such regularity? Some philosophers have said not.[1] But there is a relatively recent response that differs. Philosophers and scientists alike have been tempted by the idea that there are things called the laws of nature.[2] Such laws are considered to be very closely related to the regularities that we are able to find. They are supposed to explain the world's order, according to some views.

Examples of regularities are not hard to find. When water is heated to 100°C it boils and turns to steam. When a ray of light reflects from a surface, the angle of reflection to the surface is equal to the angle of the incident, reflected ray. When members of a species produce offspring, the offspring are of the same species as the parents. Objects are (gravitationally) attracted to each other, the degree of attraction being a function of their masses and distances apart.

The theory of laws is that the world contains certain fundamental truths, facts or things that, on many views, explain why there are such regularities. It is no accident that water boils at a certain temperature as there is a law of nature that it does so. This is a law about water but it is a specific -instance of a more general law about the boiling points of all liquids. Light reflects from surfaces in a uniform manner because there are laws of reflection. The law concerning angle of reflection is usually quoted as the second law of reflection (Isaacs 2000: 414). In this case, however, there appears to be a more fundamental law concerning light that explains the reflection law. This is Fermat's principle (after Pierre de Fermat), which says that the path of a light beam between two points minimizes the travel time for the light. As well as explaining the law of reflection, Fermat's principle also explains Snell's law concerning light refraction (Trefil 2002: 166). The laws concerning the propagation of species came to be understood much later than we knew about the regularity of such propagation.

Biologists now know much about the structure of DNA and the workings of chromosomes. This eventual success might lead us to be optimistic that in other cases where we have an unexplained regularity, underlying explanatory laws will eventually be found if we continue searching. The explanation of attraction has also been one of the great successes of science. The law of gravitation states that objects with masses M_1 and M_2, and having distance apart d, are attracted with force $F = GM_1M_2/d^2$. This equation involves the constant G – the gravitational constant – which has a value of $6.67259(85) \times 10^{-11}\,\mathrm{N}\,\mathrm{m}^2\mathrm{kg}^{-2}$.[3] The law is so successful because it explains so much, not just why apples fall to the ground. Kepler's three laws of planetary motion, for example, can be explained by the more fundamental law of gravitation. There is, however, another law of attraction, which in form and origin has similarities to gravity but which concerns electrostatic attraction. Coulomb's law states that the force between two charged particles is a function of their charges and distance apart. We can state the law as $F = KQ_1Q_2/d^2$, where Q_1 and Q_2 are the two charges of two particles and d their distance apart. Again, the law is stated with a constant, K, which is best explained in the first of Maxwell's equations (after James Clerk Maxwell, 1864). The form of Coulomb's law resembles the law of gravitation and there is a putative common explanation for the two laws. Quantum theory says that electrical and gravitational forces are generated by the exchanges of massless particles. The particles are called the photon in the case of electrical forces and the graviton in the case of gravitational forces. Quantum theory seems, therefore, to offer an explanation even more fundamental than those offered by such seemingly basic laws as Coulomb's.

A regularity is usually thought of as universal, holding for every instance, but it might not always be. A law sometimes explains why there is a regularity but sometimes a law explains why a regularity is less than universal. Water does not always boil when its temperature reaches 100°C. It usually does, in normal background conditions, but the background conditions are not always normal. There is a theory of boiling that explains why this is so and allows us to retain the idea that the world is regular. A liquid boils when the saturated vapour pressure is equal to the external atmospheric pressure. The external atmospheric pressure can vary. We assume a standard atmospheric pressure of 760 mmHg = 101325 Pa, therefore, when we quote boiling points. The claim that offspring are of the same species as the parents is inconsistent with the theory of evolution as the theory allows that, through a chain of ancestry over time, a descended individual could be of a different species from a distant ancestor. But the theory of DNA has allowed us to understand more precisely what it is that is inherited from ancestors. The commonly understood regularity has, in this case, been succeeded by something more accurate. Even the regularity of electrostatic attraction is not of universal scope. Maxwell's equations do not apply at the Planck scale because there are quantum mechanical effects at work (Psillos 2002: 186). In such cases, the world contains a less than universal degree of regularity. For practical purposes, what is a regularity in most standard conditions will suffice for our explanations and predictions.

The relations between regularities in the world and the laws of nature that are thought to explain them are not, therefore, entirely straightforward. However, in each instance the law might be thought of as in some sense a basis or ground, and thereby explanation, of the regularity; in the more complex instances, a basis or explanation for a regularity in a certain class of regularities. This raises a first philosophical question. How, and in what way, would a law of nature explain something else in the world? Specifically, how can a law explain the existence of a regularity or the existence of the instances of a regularity?

To provide a solution to this problem we need to consider again how a law stands in relation to a regularity. In the first place, we can note that the key intuitive difference between a true and a false explanation is to be found in a metaphysical fact. The best account of explanation, in the current case, would be that the true explanation is one that invokes some kind of entity or existent that is a metaphysical grounding of our explanans. The epistemic role of laws is thus parasitic on their metaphysical role. Laws play a role in truthful explanation if and only if they exist and, in some way, determine that which they explain. On this view, therefore, laws must be real and must really make, or be responsible for, the regularities to which they are related. This view contrasts sharply with those that take the status of a law to be determined entirely by epistemic concerns.[4] On such views, a statement is a law if and only if it occupies a certain central position within a theory or is that which licenses inferences and provides explanations. Epistemology is prior to metaphysics, in these accounts.

On the other hand, there is a philosophical view of laws that considers a law to be entirely constituted by, or exhausted by, its instances. There is nothing that *makes it* that water usually boils at 100°C, on such views. Indeed, it is regarded as a mistake to reify a law: it is a category mistake to treat a law as an object in its own right. Rather, a law is simply the fact *that* water boils at 100°C in every instance, for example. A major problem with this view is that the credentials of laws to explain their instances are thrown into doubt. A law cannot non-trivially explain the regularity if it is nothing more than the regularity, for that would be a case of something explaining itself.[5] We might try to say instead that the law does not explain the regularity, as a whole, but only the instances of the regularity. But this would not be a very enlightening explanation as it would be an explanation only of the form that this instance is one particular part, or fact, of the whole that constitutes the law. The sense in which a whole explains one of its parts would then have to be made clear.

However, the proponent of this view might point out that the reification of laws appears to provide a better explanation only through making the above-mentioned category mistake and, further, the realist about laws invokes the existence of something for which we have no evidence. The scientific approach is not to go beyond the observable phenomena whereas those who believe in laws are positing an unknown cause behind that which is known. A deflationary account is less metaphysically ambitious, one might argue.

This is only a beginning to the philosophical consideration of natural laws. But it has not yet been shown that philosophy has anything useful to contribute to this subject, especially as it is a subject of which science already has such intimate knowledge. Can the role of philosophy, specifically metaphysics, in this debate be justified? Should metaphysics, instead, abdicate responsibility for the theory of laws of nature to physics?

1.2 Apology for metaphysics

Both physics and metaphysics includes the study of laws and, it might be thought, physics studies laws in a more thorough and better-informed way. This raises a challenge for philosophy: does metaphysics have anything useful to contribute to the understanding of laws of nature? If one tends to the view that metaphysics has little to contribute, then one might think that it should always defer to the better empirical understanding of laws that is provided by science. The study and discovery of the laws of nature are, after all, two of the major tasks of science. How could philosophers possibly hope to be able to tell the scientists anything?

If one thought that, ultimately, physics could solve all the problems about laws, there would be no point to this book at all. However, this does not seem to be the case and arguably there is a role for philosophy. There would be a number of problems to face if one were to defend a 'physics-only' approach to this subject matter. These problems suggest that there is at least some role for a metaphysical study of the laws of nature, of the kind this book attempts.

First, one might be tempted to defer to physics on this subject because physics can discover facts that are certain, whereas philosophical results are always provisional or uncertain. Many who begin to study philosophy are often frustrated by its apparent failure to deliver final conclusions. There is always, it seems, scope for further argument in philosophy. Science, in contrast, is seen as a realm of comforting certainty where to ascertain indubitable facts about the world one need only consult the relevant authority. However, just a little understanding of the history and philosophy of science reveals that things are not quite so clear-cut. We know that science has been subject to a number of revolutions where the whole framework within which it was working was overturned.[6] This might undermine faith in the certainty of current scientific beliefs, as previous beliefs, which are now rejected, were once thought just as certain. Philosophers of science have questioned science not just on its historical failures, however, but also on a more abstract level, examining concerns around theories, evidence, objectivity and knowledge (Popper 1959; Lakatos 1970; Feyerabend 1977).[7] This merely reaffirms a persistent epistemological theme, however, that certain empirical knowledge is not as easy to acquire as the philosophically untutored might have believed. Over-simplification must be avoided, however. I am not arguing in favour of scepticism nor for the pessimistic meta-induction (Ladyman 2002: 230–1) but nor should we adopt an unquestioning naïve realism about science.[8]

(If one adopts a more considered view on the epistemic status of science, the view that science has all the facts, and philosophy should give way, loses its attraction. Furthermore, it is possible to argue that the status of science bears resemblances with that of philosophy. Hence, while the claims of philosophy always seem provisional and conditional, one can say something analogous of science. Its own claims remain provisional. They must be open to empirical refutation. There is always the possibility of some new theory (or argument) that will overthrow the received view. Like philosophy, scientific investigation never ends but merely settles for interim conclusions. One may think that science is progressing to a grand unified theory that answers all scientific questions (Davies 1986: vii), but this seems just as optimistic as a claim that philosophy might finally arrive at an all-encompassing final theory. As long as it remains possible to question the truth of any particular claim of science, a certainly true, finished theory of everything remains an extremely remote possibility. The view that metaphysics should defer to science because science deals in fact while metaphysics deals in speculation should be rejected.)

There is a second reason why it would be problematic if metaphysics abdicated responsibility for the understanding of laws. Even in the credible theories of science, the nature and role of laws seem uncertain. It is by no means obvious, therefore, that the idea of laws of nature is better understood in science than it is in metaphysics. Physics has offered an account of how forces work, for example, in the form of a field theory. Laws then appear as ways of describing operations of the field. But there is never a full and general account, provided by science, of what it is for something to be a law and what, if anything, a law of nature is supposed to do. Such accounts that we have been given seem to be metaphysically inadequate. One authoritative account, for instance, says that a law is 'a descriptive principle of nature that holds in all circumstances' (Isaacs 2000: 260). If by a 'descriptive principle' a statement or proposition is intended, then this would be inadequate as our subject is what *in nature* is a law.[9] If something in nature is intended, on the other hand, it is difficult to see how 'principle of nature' is any more enlightening, or anything different at all, from 'law of nature'. A reason for this apparent failing, on the part of science, may be that the questions I am asking are specifically philosophical ones. For example: does a law determine nature or is a law entirely exhausted by its instances? Is a law of nature anything like a moral or legal law? If these are specifically philosophical questions, we could hardly expect science to answer them. Despite their expertise in some areas, we cannot expect scientists to be better at answering metaphysical questions than are the metaphysicians. The above questions look more metaphysical than scientific.

The third reason why philosophy must be involved in the issue of laws is that there is a specific role for philosophy that science cannot fill. Arguably, it has to be the role of metaphysics to tell us if laws exist and, if so, what they are. Science, it can be argued, deals always and only with the phenomena. Admittedly, its subject matter is phenomena in a wide sense, as many things are discussed first when they are theoretical. But this means that although such entities cannot be observed currently, it is at least theoretically possible that some observation is able to confirm the existence of such things. Hence, theoretical entities are in principle observable even if they are not yet actually observable. Science deals only with the phenomena in the sense that its subject matter is constituted by the things that are either actually or in-principle observable. By contrast, it is metaphysics, and only metaphysics, that tells us what ultimately exists.[10] This may seem an odd, even incredible, claim. It seems that it is physics that tells us that up quarks exist and biology that tells us that there are black swans. Observation might be thought to deliver the authoritative verdict on what there is. But metaphysics is far more general than this and considers questions of far bigger scope. If science is about observation of the phenomena, it cannot consider, without itself moving into meta-physics, questions such as whether those phenomena constitute things in the world, are merely caused by things, or bear no relation to reality at all.[11] If science were to reject the validity of the phenomena, it would thereby reject its own foundations. Metaphysics asks what really exists. It may well conclude that the phenomena are real, or a reliable and truthful representation of what there is, but to maintain so would remain a dis-tinctly philosophical claim that is outside the remit of science.

Marc Lange illustrates the differences in approach, between physics and metaphysics, on the question of the existence of electric fields. He raises some of the following issues:

> Take the remark 'The electric field here has an intensity of 100 dynes per statcoulomb' ... Should this remark be interpreted *literally*, as aiming to describe a certain entity (the electric field) that exists in just the way that tables and chairs exist? ... Or should a remark about the electric field be interpreted *non-literally*, so that its truth does not require that any such thing as a field *really exist*? For instance, perhaps the sentence 'The electric field here has an intensity of 100 dynes per statcoulomb' simply means that were a charged particle to find itself here, then it would feel an electric force of 100 dynes for every stat-

coulomb of charge it possesses. In that case, the remark about the electric field may be true when no charged particle is here – even if there is no such thing as an electric field.

(Lange 2002a: xi–xii)

He then relates his disappointment with his education in physics. It failed to answer the sorts of questions to which he wanted answers. One textbook gave him the following unhelpful response:

> Perhaps you will still want to ask, what *is* an electric field? Is it something real, or is it merely a name for a factor in an equation which has to be multiplied by something else [a body's electric charge] to give the numerical value of the force [on the body] we measure in an experiment? ... [S]ince it works, it doesn't make any difference. This is not a frivolous answer, but a serious one.

(Purcell 1965: 17, quoted in Lange 2002a: xii–xiii)

Partly because this response was so unenlightening, Lange swapped physics for philosophy.

The present book is asking this sort of question, concerning real existence, in the case of laws. Science can describe cases where something holds in all circumstances. It may assert that sophisticated universal equations are an adequate description of what is always the case. It may even employ referring expressions, speaking of electrons, fields and quarks. But if we want to know whether there really are things called laws in nature, perhaps that account for the truth of these equations, then we have moved beyond the phenomena: beyond physics into metaphysics.

There is a fourth and final reason I offer for why we need metaphysics in addition to physics. The history of ideas suggests that thinking often develops through an interplay of ideas between science and metaphysics. There is a role for both as the best thoughts will often be a result of the exploratory and abstract interacting with the concrete and empirical. Some of the big ideas of science may begin more in the character of a metaphysical speculation. There may be no available empirical evidence to confirm or refute the theory. But something abstract could fuel or inspire a more concrete version of the same idea: a theory that does expose itself to empirical scrutiny. If this is plausible, then the question of whether physics or metaphysics comes first would be seen as mistaken. Science and metaphysics occur in parallel and can inform each other.

This interplay of kinds of thinking has been acknowledged in the philosophy of science. Popper and Kuhn, for instance, distinguish the context of discovery from the context of justification. In the case of discovery, anything goes. Hence, an idea, such as the idea of there being laws in nature, may begin as a metaphysical speculation but it may nevertheless inform scientific thinking and, in turn, be informed by it. Occasionally, the two types of thinking, metaphysical and scientific, may occur in the same mind. Einstein seemed at times able to think as a physicist and at times as a metaphysician. The four-dimensional insight, that space and time are a single manifold, is a philosophical as much as scientific theory.[12]

These considerations suggest that there is a quite significant and distinctive purpose in the philosophical consideration of laws of nature. Metaphysics might be able to say something about the subject that physics cannot say. It might then make a vital contribution to a full understanding of laws.

1.3 Laws in nature

Why laws *in* nature? The title of this book is meant to convey the true subject of the enquiry. The search is for something in nature that might count as a law. The intention is to exclude two types of things that others have thought of as laws.

First, the intention is to exclude laws as nothing more than regularities or, on more sophisticated accounts, parts of a systematization and axiomatization of the world's history. Accounts such as these do not count as theories of laws *in* nature as I rule that a systematization of history is not naturally occurring nor governing. Rather, such accounts are theories of why there are no laws in nature. The world contains just a series of events, on this account. Sometimes we find a pattern in the series but, according to well-known Humean arguments, there is nothing that has made the · pattern. The pattern has just occurred. There is no necessity in nature.

Second, I wish the exclude the accounts that take laws to be nothing more than statements or a certain class of statements, such as Ayer's (1963) view. There is, of course, a perfectly reasonable sense in which both regularities and statements are in nature. They occur in the natural world of space and time. Why are they not *laws in nature*? The reason I wish to exclude both these cases from my enquiry is that there is no metaphysically enlightening enquiry to be undertaken about them. If laws just are these things, then of course they exist. Of course, there are patterns in nature and, of course, there are statements. These are simple empirical facts. But recalling what Lange said of fields, we want to know whether there is really something in the world that could count as a law. There are, thus, two things something must be to count as a law in nature, namely, being in nature and being a law. If we find such things, perhaps they would be the things that would make there be a pattern in the world's events or perhaps they would be the truthmakers of the true law statements. If we found that there were such things, they would be in a strong position to play the explanatory role we originally thought they had. By contrast, neither regularities nor statements would be in a good position to fill the explanatory role, for reasons we have already touched upon. Regularities cannot explain that of which they are constituted. Statements cannot explain why something in the world happens.[13] So while regularities and statements have a claim to being in nature, they do not have a good claim to being laws in nature.

This book is an attempt to tackle some well-trodden territory: the metaphysics of natural laws or laws of nature. One of the key questions is realism about laws. Do laws, as conceived by philosophers, and sometimes by scientists, really exist? The accounts of laws as regularities and as statements have confused and hindered this investigation. They have obscured the question of what it would be for laws to have fully existent status. To take an example that will be discussed in more detail later, the Mill–Ramsey–Lewis theory is often spoken of as one of the theories of laws.[14] But I am looking whether laws can exist in nature itself. Are they, in contrast, things that exist purely in minds or in theories about the world? The Mill–Ramsey–Lewis theory takes laws to be axioms (or theorems) of the best possible systematizations of the world's total history, where such a history is a history of events or facts. Many people support this view of laws. Earman (1993: 416) cites it, for instance, as a counter to van Fraassen's (1989) 'no-laws' view. But are the laws of such systematizations really laws in nature? I think not and give my reasons in Chapter 3. Earman would be wrong, therefore, to use the Ramsey–Lewis theory (as it is usually called) as a response to the lawless view of van Fraassen. The Ramsey–Lewis theory is not a theory of laws. Rather, I take it to be a theory in which there are no metaphysically real laws. At best, the axioms of the best systematizations are the surrogates of laws in a lawless world. Similar things can be said of the so-called regularity view of laws.

The second source of possible confusion, concerning what is intended by a law, is the distinction between laws and law statements. John Carroll (1994) has said that laws are *true*. Throughout his book, laws are clearly understood as statements. He is not alone in seeing laws this way. There has been a tradition that has tried to find a linguistic, syntactical or semantic, criterion of laws. A law, for instance, was said to be a universally quantified conditional containing empirical, projectible and non-local predicates. This approach has not been faring too well, however, as statements have been produced that have all these features and yet still do not seem to be laws.[15] If some philosophers really have believed that laws are statements, then this book has a wholly different starting point. Any laws, worthy of the name, would be things in the world – in non-linguistic reality – rather than a class of statements. There are certainly law statements, some of which may be capable of truth, but it is the thing in the world – that which would make true law statements true, in truthmaker theory – that is the focus of this study.[16]

Laws in nature would be the metaphysically real, worldly truthmakers of the true law statements. While people and their languages are certainly part of the natural world, the search is for laws that are what they are whatever we may think about them. They would be the kind of laws that would have existed from the start of the universe, or quite soon after the beginning, and would continue to exist unthought-of and undiscovered. They would be, it seems, some kind of fact or state of affairs that occurs naturally without our intervention.

However, later in this book, some scepticism will be apportioned to the idea of there being such laws. It will be scepticism from a realist perspective, which is not a common combination and will have to be outlined and explained in greater detail later. But given this professed scepticism, why, it might be thought, should one start with such a strong sense of laws? Might it be that the target has been made too small, and too difficult to achieve, that it is no wonder that the case is found against laws? Might we be able to defend the view that there are laws if we weaken the sense of laws? Of course there can be laws, if by 'law' we mean something much less than what was originally intended by the term. A number of weaker senses of law have been developed, but I argue that these should be viewed as the surrogate laws that have been mentioned already. Nothing can be said against such things *per se*, except that they are not the laws that some philosophers and scientists have believed that we uncover.

George Molnar has said of causation that we are never just describing 'the concept we have' (2003: 190). All philosophical theories are to an extent revisionary. Concepts can change by undergoing a process of justified evolution. But in the study of metaphysics, as opposed to conceptual analysis, this should not matter quite so much. The concept of a law of nature might well be fully appropriated, given time, by those who argue for laws in the weakened sense, the surrogate laws. But the fundamental, metaphysical question of this study would remain even if it would have to be rephrased. That question would be whether there are any universal governing or controlling features in nature, features which, in some original sense of law, could be described as laws. It is this question to which I have a sceptical response. The response is, I hope, an interesting kind of scepticism. Many features are to be found in nature that involve regularity, universality and modality. Are there laws besides? Or, are laws just exactly these features? I answer both questions in the negative. This leaves me with a position not too far from those who accept only surrogate laws. There are not laws in nature, in the strong and, we might claim, original sense of law. So any laws that there are could only be of the surrogate kind. What I will be at pains to emphasize, however, is that these are not the real laws in nature that some have sought.

1.4 Laws in science

It is far from clear that science, if there is a single thing called science, accepts the reality of laws in nature in the strong sense described above.[17] Science restricts itself to the phenomena and cannot go beyond the patterns it finds. Hence, it is not clear that, by a law, science means something in nature that produces a pattern or regularity. Instead, the law might just be the regularity. Feynman suggests both views. First:

> There is also a rhythm and a pattern between the phenomena of nature which is not apparent to the eye, but only to the eye of analysis; and it is these rhythms and patterns which we call Physical Laws.
>
> (Feynman 1965: 13)

But, shortly after, he speaks of a law not simply as the pattern in nature but as something that nature is obeying when it is patterned: 'I am interested not so much in the human mind as in the marvel of nature which can obey such an elegant and simple law as the law of gravitation' (ibid. 14). I will not attempt to reconcile these two views. Rather, I take it as symptomatic of a reluctance on the part of science to go beyond the phenomena and consider the metaphysical nature of its laws, yet also a grudging acknowledgement that some truth beyond the phenomena exists. Is the law just the pattern or something underlying and producing the pattern? As Lange observed in the case of fields, for science this question doesn't really matter and isn't answered. Feynman realizes this. Later (1965: 50–3) he describes three different formulations of the law of gravity: Newton's, the local field method and the minimum principle. How do we decide which, between them, is the true formulation? Scientifically, we cannot. They have the same scientific – that is mathematical – consequences in that they all entail that $F = GM_1M_2/d^2$. Having this mathematical consequence is sufficient to make the three formulations scientifically equivalent.

Feynman's idea puts in mathematical terms what van Fraassen expresses by the idea of empirical adequacy (van Fraassen 1980). In the position that van Fraassen calls constructive empiricism, science can continue successfully without invoking any underlying entities behind the phenomena. This is not to deny that there may be such unobservable entities, only that science has any interest in them. Hence, van Fraassen describes his position thus: 'Science aims to give us theories which are empirically adequate: and acceptance of a theory involves as belief only that it is empirically adequate' (1980: 12). And 'the belief involved in accepting a scientific theory is only that it "saves the phenomena", that is that it correctly describes what is observable' (ibid: 4). These apparently simple claims by van Fraassen conceal hidden difficulties, when intended as a complete and thorough account of science.[18] However, I would not want to challenge it as a general and rough account of the nature and aims of science. Indeed, the fact that constructive empiricism seems incomplete, because it declines to consider metaphysical entities, need not entail that it is an inadequate account of science. Science declines to consider metaphysical entities, so it is also, in this sense, an incomplete account of the world.

From this brief and no doubt superficial account of the aim of science, the lesson with respect to laws seems to be that science considers primarily the patterns and regularities to be found in the world. It does not enter into the metaphysical debate about the grounds of such regularities. In place of metaphysics, epistemological concerns are to the fore. Hence, the difference between a law and a hypothesis is given in a definitive source (Isaacs 2000: 260) in terms of an epistemic attitude. There may be doubt about a hypothesis but not about a law. Lange (1993 and 2000) also has argued that something is a law in virtue of its epistemic role. Trefil (2002: ix–xxi) describes various epistemic stages that are to be gone through before something is judged by science to be sufficiently certain to be lawful. We begin with observations of regularities, form hypotheses, make predictions, then tests, revise the hypothesis, and so on. However, Trefil also acknowledges how relatively little it means to science to bestow the title *Law of Nature* on one of its discoveries:

> Scientists are remarkably sloppy about their use of the word 'law'. In a book devoted to the elucidation of laws of nature, this is an issue that needs to be addressed. It would be very convenient if there were a simple rule about how words like 'theory', 'principle', 'effect', and 'law' were used in the sciences. It would be nice, for example, if something that had been verified a thousand times was called an 'effect', something verified a million times a 'principle', and something verified 10 million times a 'law', but things just don't work that way. The use of these terms is based entirely on historical precedent and has nothing to do with the confidence scientists place in a particular finding.
>
> (ibid.: xiii)

Having argued that metaphysics has a role to play in the understanding of laws, it seems that we are justified in complementing this with another claim. Science has little role to play in the metaphysical understanding of what laws really are. Science tells us what the particular, observable patterns in the world are, usually expressed in mathematical form. It does not tell us in more general terms what it is to be a law of nature, what a law does and by what means it conducts its business. In 'saving the phenomena', science gives these metaphysical concerns a wide berth. What matters, for science, is the epistemic integrity of the discovered pattern, explicated in terms of explanation, sustaining of counterfactuals and supporting of inductive inference.

The remainder of this book (with the exception of Chapter 8) will be ignoring much of what science says about laws. Notwithstanding an earlier point, that ideas often develop though parallel philosophical and empirical investigation, it seems to have been sufficiently established that the present concerns about laws are specifically metaphysical concerns, about which science has little to say. The relatively little science in this book is, I hope, justified on these grounds.

1.5 Lawlessness

The metaphysics that will be advanced in this book will be a lawless metaphysics. This will be a denial of the view that there are real laws in nature that are responsible for nature's regularities. It will be, therefore, against a position that can be called nomological realism: realism about laws. Nomological realism, it could be argued, would be a view that is suggested by a naïve interpretation of science, which is not to suggest that nomological realism is a naïve theory. For the reasons given in the previous section, I hesitate to call this interpretation an orthodox view of science, held by scientists themselves. Scientists are careful not to go beyond the phenomena but they may, like Feynman above, occasionally speak of nature 'obeying' laws when they are in a more speculative mood. Nomological realism is more a metaphysical view that is held by philosophers. Two recent examples would be Armstrong's (1983) theory and John Carroll's (1994) primitivist position if it is of laws, not statements.

An obvious point about these instances is that nomological realism is a relatively new theory in metaphysics. Laws have been denied before, and there is a far richer history of lawless metaphysics. Laws do not appear in Aristotle's metaphysics, for example, and it wasn't until Descartes (1644: Pt 2, §§37–45) and Newton (1687) that laws entered the intellectual mainstream. Hume and his followers have a lawless metaphysics, which comes from the denial of necessary connection in nature. Any such necessity we find is only a projection onto the world of our own, metaphysically misled, thinking about it. This view has continued through the empiricist tradition in Russell (1927b: Ch. 11) and Ayer (1963). In contemporary philosophy its best representative is David Lewis (1973: 72–7, 1986a). He argues that while there may be modal truths in our world, there are no intrinsic (intra-world) modal facts that make them true. Rather, they are made true only by our world's relations of similarity with other worlds. Our own world contains no intrinsic necessity in nature. It consists merely of a vast mosaic of unconnected, local matters of fact (1986b: ix). Another empiricist has also been advocating a lawless view of the world. Bas van Fraassen's (1989) denial of laws comes from his epistemological commitment, which was described above. He sees laws as nothing more than a class of important features of a model. They are not even the most important features, as symmetry principles occupy a more fundamental place in a model. However, science is not looking for models that are true so we cannot accurately say that there are true laws in nature. Rather, science aims only for empirical adequacy. A final example of lawlessness is worthy of note as it is the position closest to the one of this book, namely the position advocated by Nancy Cartwright (1983, 1989, 1999). Cartwright argues against laws on the basis that most law claims are not true. They assert that a regularity holds universally but the regularities to be found in the world will almost always hold only *ceteris paribus*. Cartwright thinks this is indicative of the fact that it is dispositions or capacities that are doing the real work. Only in the artificial conditions created by nomological machines do we see the real manifestation of a capacity in a strict regularity.

While wishing to acknowledge these previous lawless positions, however, the stance of this book differs from all of them in at least some respect. A major difference is in general approach. All the above lawless views reach their conclusion via epistemological considerations. The argument of this book will be metaphysical throughout, which, I am convinced, is the safest way to achieve a reliable metaphysical conclusion. Second, there is a difference with all but Cartwright over the status of modality. The empiricists deny necessary connections in nature. The stance in this book will be to affirm it. The position of this book deserves the name *modal realism* better than David Lewis's directly opposite view that also uses it.[19]

The denial of intrinsic modality – necessity in things – might be viewed historically as a key step in the establishment of laws. This is a rather perverse claim as Humeans deny all necessity in nature and therefore think that there are no laws. The problem seems to have been, however, that those who have felt a need to argue for laws have done so because they have already accepted that a world without laws would be lacking in modal facts. It would be composed of non-modal, intrinsically unrelated and discrete units. Laws are supposed to be somehow the things that activate the world: the things that add the necessity and possibility to it and thereby make events happen. But, I will argue, laws are a solution to a problem that was misconceived in the first place. Only if you think that the world would be otherwise inactive or inanimate, do you have the need to add laws to your ontology. Instead, I advance an ontology in which some of the main things out of which the world is composed, its properties, are already modally involved. They already have necessary connections with other properties. When they are instantiated in natural objects in the world, there is necessity in nature. There is no further, vacant role that laws might play. There is no gap in the world that they are needed to fill. To add to the case against laws, however, I will also have an argument for why laws could not play the requisite role. It has not been shown, by those who believe in laws, how laws do their work.

Because my position is realist about modal facts, it is important that I distinguish it from the Humean and other empiricist forms of lawlessness. I will give the empiricist view the name Humean lawlessness and my own position the rather ugly yet accurately descriptive title *realist lawlessness*. The position sides with the Humeans in denying the existence of laws yet sides with the nomological realists in accepting the reality of modal facts. The three positions can helpfully be represented as in Figure 1.1.

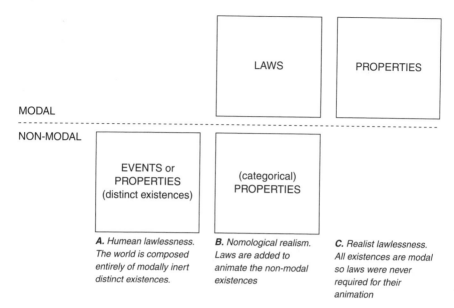

Figure 1.1 The three metaphysics.

The position depicted in C, realist lawlessness, is closest to Cartwright, as remarked above, particularly in her 1993 work. I think there is a need for the present book, however, as I think a much more powerful, directly metaphysical, argument can be made. Cartwright correctly points out the modally-laden nature of our language. But I do not take this as a proof of a modally-laden world. A metaphysical argument would be better. In her 1999 work, Cartwright argues against laws on the basis that they would all need to be *ceteris paribus* qualified: all regularities hold only if 'all else is equal'. But I agree with Lange (2002b) in the view that we needn't reject laws just because they are *ceteris paribus* qualified. *Ceteris paribus* laws could still be laws, depending on your theory of laws.[20] Hence, I think a better, directly metaphysical argument against laws is needed. I will attempt to produce such an argument.

1.6 Overview of the book

The remaining section of this introductory chapter gives a rough overview of the structure of the book as a whole. The structure is dictated by the three positions depicted in Figure 1.1.

Part I contains an examination and eventual rejection of Humean lawlessness. Hume does not discuss laws directly. His argument concerns necessary connections in nature and his conclusion is that there are none or, at the very least, that we have no good reason to believe in them. It is safe to conclude that if there really are no necessary connections, then there are no laws in nature. But Hume's arguments are chiefly epistemological: necessary connections cannot be observed and nor can they be inferred from any constant conjunctions that are observed.[21] While Hume has set up a form of scepticism that is hard to disprove, based on the acceptance of empiricist strictures on knowledge, his arguments do not constitute a disproof of necessity in nature. Indeed, if Galen Strawson (1989) is to be believed, Hume – at least the Hume of the 1748 *Enquiry* – believed that there were real but hidden causal powers in nature. Our inability to disprove Humean scepticism does not, therefore, constitute a disproof of necessity in nature, I will argue. I end Part I by looking at the treatment of laws given within the Humean metaphysic: the regularity theory and the Ramsey–Lewis theory. I argue that these tell perfectly consistent stories within the Humean world-view. But this is not adequate to persuade us of the truth of Humeanism itself. Indeed, there is no direct argument for Humean metaphysics. What is supposed to advocate it is its metaphysical economy and, in Lewis's version, the work it can do in providing all that we think the world contains. I argue that it doesn't provide enough but only after examining other views can this been seen, through comparison.

Part II is an examination of the case for nomological realism. I will look both at its general motivation and at two specific metaphysics that purport to offer an adequate account of laws: the Dretske–Tooley–Armstrong view and Brian Ellis's recent theory of scientific essentialism. I will argue that neither of these views has provided enough to establish a genuinely realist account of laws. Neither of them has adequately shown what laws are, what they do, and how they do what they do. More generally, I argue that nomological realism is weakly motivated. The argument for it, I call the nomological argument. But it is an inadequate argument, I maintain. Effectively, it challenges the claim mentioned above, that if there are no necessary connections in nature, then there are no laws, by arguing that if there are necessary connections in nature, then there are laws. But more is needed, I hold, to prove that there are laws than to show necessity in nature. There could be necessity even without laws, as a singularist about causation might hold or someone who accepts that Kripke (1972, 1980) has vindicated the category of the necessary a posteriori.[22]

In Part III, I attempt the direct metaphysical case for realist lawlessness. The argument has a negative and positive side. First, I argue for the vagueness and inadequacy of the notion of a law of nature. Natural laws are not a natural kind. Next I mount an argument against the ability of laws to do what they are supposed to do. Nomological realism, I maintain, has to be committed to the view that laws play a role in the world. If they are to be accepted as real existents, they had better do something to earn their keep in our ontology. But the nomological realists have not sufficiently shown how laws are supposed to work their influence upon the world.

How, that is, would something that stands above an inanimate world of categorical properties, have its effects on those things? A simpler way of putting this is, how does a law, understood by a nomological realist, determine its instances? In the Central Dilemma, I offer the realist two options that are exhaustive and exclusive. Both lead to insuperable difficulties. This leads me to my positive argument in favour of *de re* necessities. Properties provide the world with all the necessity we ever wanted. It doesn't matter that laws cannot do anything, therefore, because properties provide everything we thought we needed laws for in the first place. Properties are all modal, I maintain. Following Shoemaker's (1980) lead, I claim that properties are clusters of relations with other properties, these relations including causal powers to, and metaphysical connections with, other properties. Any particular entity that instantiates properties (which is every particular), is a powerful particular in virtue of that. But this is all controversial. I try to consider the most likely objections and give the most credible replies. Is this really a theory of laws by another name? Does it commit me to the relativity of properties or to Meinongianism? Couldn't there be non-powerful or epiphenomenal properties? I will try to answer these questions adequately. If I am successful, the notion of laws in philosophy will have sustained serious damage. Though I fear that others before me have seen that same hope dashed.

Part I
Humean lawlessness

2   The lawless world

2.1 Just one little thing and then another

Here is a vision of the world. There exists only a sequence of events. An event is a happening or occurrence that has a beginning, duration and end. It may be the exemplification of a property by a particular at a time (Kim 1976) or it may be a change in or to an object (Lombard 1986). This sequence of events is complex. Many events are simultaneous but many more are before and after others. Some events are at the same place but many others are at different places. These events and the complex relations in which they stand to each other – relations of before, after, simultaneity, spatial coincidence and spatial separation – are all that constitutes the spatio-temporal manifold. This spatio-temporal manifold, this complex of events, constitutes the whole world.

Human beings live within this world. Their bodies and their minds are also a part of the sequence of events. Although persons have the appearance of substances, like all other substances they are constituted by a complex series of events. But having minds, these complexes of events have a desire to understand the larger series of which they are a part. Their evolutionary success has depended, in no small part, on their attempts to predict it. For both understanding and prediction, they have attempted to extricate from the manifold some general truths about which events can be expected to follow others. Such theories are based on the events that have been observed. The predictions are rough and ready approximations but they allow people to get by, for the most part.

But while individual events have been observed and patterns in the sequence of events have been noted, nobody has ever seen a necessary connection between any two events that might be judged responsible for the occurrence of the pattern. It can be seen that one event may be followed by another in approximately the same place. It can even be seen that a certain type of event is regularly followed by another type of event. But it has never been seen that one event has made, or necessitated that, another happen. Some less-sophisticated thinkers suppose that there are such connections but they are merely projecting onto the rest of the world something that exists only in that small part of it called their minds. They have an expectation that one event will follow another. Sometimes their expectation is satisfied. But there is no valid inference to show that there is a connection in the rest of nature that corresponds to that expectation in their head.

As far as we know, the world consists of just one little thing and then another.[1] Each event – each little fact in the world – is wholly self-contained. It has its entire nature and existence within its spatio-temporal boundary. It occurs and is then gone. It is a particular whose whole being is exhausted by its happening. Significantly, it does not reach out beyond itself to any other event. It cannot be directed towards something outside itself. There is no capacity within itself to do so and nor is there any existence outside itself that makes it do so. The world is only these particular, wholly distinct, events. There are no particular necessary connections but also no general necessary connections between any of the things. Those who believe in laws in nature think there are such general necessary connections. But what would such connections be? How would they exert their influence over nature? Given that they are unobservable, what possible reason would we have for believing in them?

The problem with the notion of a real law in nature, on this view, is that it is entirely metaphysical, rather than empirical. Natural laws are a supposition. They cannot be observed. Only their alleged effects, in the order and regularity of the world, can be observed. But what valid route do we have for inferring a cause from its effect? (And what reason do we have for thinking that there are such things as causes and effects?) Without any such valid route, the scientific and reasonable thing to do is to accept as real only the events for which we have direct, empirical evidence. Our belief must be confined to our experience. Anything else is just speculative metaphysics.

2.2 A sceptical duty

Although some philosophers are in the business of constructing systems, there is also a duty of scepticism. A philosopher should believe in nothing without good reason. One of the central philosophical tasks is Socratic: to subject a doctrine to critical scrutiny and identify its weaknesses. We must, therefore, consider the sceptical questions relevant to the putative laws in nature.

We might begin, therefore, by asking what a law of nature is supposed to be. To believe there are such things, we ought to have a credible account of their nature and existence. If metaphysics can be judged as the mapping of possibilities (Lowe 1998: Ch. 1), then we must first see that laws are possible existences. To qualify as possible existences, we must be able to provide a clear and coherent account of them. To do this we must, among other things, say what laws do, what difference they make to the world, and how they do so. If reasonable answers can be given to such questions, then we can proceed to consider whether there really are such things: whether these possible existences are actual existences. This will be a move from metaphysics to an empirical study.

Such questions as these will be considered later in the book. Our Socratic scepticism further suggests another approach, however, that we can consider first. This approach starts from the view that we should try to claim as little as possible, consistent with what we know. If we are sceptical about the necessity of adding laws of nature to our ontological itinerary of the world, we ought to begin by entertaining the view that the world is lawless. By a lawless world, I mean a world that contains no real laws of nature. Humeans, as I interpret their metaphysics, claim that ours is such a world. Hume did not discuss laws directly. He did argue, however, that there is no reason to believe in necessary connections in nature. If there are no necessary connections in nature, there are certainly no laws in nature, in the metaphysically real sense of laws. There is evidence of regularities – constant conjunctions between types of events that have been so far observed – but constant conjunctions are not laws. Real laws would be things that were behind, or responsible for, such constant conjunctions. They would necessitate and explain such constant conjunctions. So if there are no necessary connections in nature, there are no such laws. Let us probe into this metaphysic a little deeper.

2.3 Humean lawlessness

Humean lawlessness is a metaphysic that follows from the Humean epistemology, as we will see in the next chapter. For now, I concentrate solely on the metaphysic.

The Hume-world consists of an enormous number of local matters of particular fact. The world is composed of discrete units, like a vast mosaic.[2] The mosaic analogy is elucidating. The world's events are like the individual tiles in the mosaic. Each tile is entirely self-contained. It has its nature entirely independently of the tiles around it. Even if the mosaic shows a recognizable pattern, such that one small tile may be a part of a larger picture, the individual tile has a nature and existence independent of that bigger picture. There is no necessary connection between an individual tile and any of its neighbours or other tiles in the mosaic. A tile will bear relations to all the other tiles, being certain distances in certain directions from every other, but these relations are matters that are external to our original tile. There is nothing about it alone, considered purely intrinsically, that in any way accounts for these relations. That tile A is one metre from tile B is not a fact about A alone, nor B alone, but about the distance between them. This relative distance is not an intrinsic or internal fact for either tile so it is an external fact for them.[3]

As there is no relation to anything else that is internal to an individual tile, there is no internal *causal* relation to anything else. Each unit of this metaphysic is intrinsically causally inert, thus incapable of 'pointing' outside itself to another such unit. Hence, there are no intrinsic causal powers of these particulars: no internal necessary connections.

There are also no external necessary connections between these units. Where a particular tile lies is accidental in that there is nothing that compels it to have one location rather than another. It could have been placed elsewhere and still have been the tile that it is. The tile's identity is not dependent on its location within the mosaic. The mosaic-maker is free to place any tile in any place as their will and desire takes them. Nothing, other than the maker's own wishes, dictates what goes where.[4]

Hence, returning briefly from the analogy, we have a world of events, which are discrete and inert units. Each event occurs and exists briefly, but there is nothing that makes it occur. There are no connections and no compulsions, whether internal or external, between any two units.

It might be wondered how our world can be analogous to a mosaic when our world is in four dimensions. A mosaic is usually two-dimensional and even if we conceived of a three-dimensional mosaic, there would still be nothing in the mosaic that corresponded to the passage of time in our world. However, we may attempt to conceive the world in its totality and regardless of any point of view on it. We would not take any temporal point of view on it, therefore. Past, present and future are not to be understood as objective and intrinsic properties of the world. They exist only relative to an observer. The events, and where they stand in relation to others, constitute the whole of the objectively real world. The mosaic of events consists of all events that ever have and ever will occur, viewed tenselessly. Some of the relations with other pieces will be spatial but, let us imagine, some will be tenselessly temporal.[5] Our mosaic contains analogues to these relations, let us imagine. Perhaps they might consist in the thickness of the tiles or some other such feature. We are asked to imagine, therefore, a mosaic that has at least four dimensions.

2.4 Necessity is in the head

While there is no necessary connection in nature, according to Humeanism, the unsophisticated among us often think that there is. Why do we think this and do we have a justification for it? The following is a statement of the Humean stance without providing full reasons in favour of that stance. Chapters 3 and 4 contain more.

It will be useful to continue the mosaic analogy. Unlike the mosaics that are made for the purpose of representation, we might imagine that the artist intends a purely abstract composition. Our mosaic has been made by the random scattering of randomly selected tiles, this method being chosen, we might claim, because the artist was keen to avoid influencing the composition subconsciously. Let us assume the method of

composition is as effective as that of a genuinely random number genera-
tor. Nevertheless, despite the random selection and arrangement, it is still
possible that we might find patterns in a randomly assembled spread of
pieces. There can be constant conjunction even if there is random genera-
tion. Thus, after studying the mosaic for a while, we might discover that
there is always a square tile next to a hexagonal tile or that a blue tile is
always next to a circular tile. Some of these constant conjunctions might
be quite complex: for instance, whenever there is a red octagonal tile,
within a distance of no more than two tiles, there is always either a blue
tile or a square tile.

Where there are such patterns, those who are philosophically
untrained might suppose that there is some reason for the constant conjunction. If a square is always next to a hexagon, it might be thought that
there is something that makes it so. From that fact that every square is
next to a hexagon, it might be thought *necessary* that every square is next
to a hexagon. But nothing about the fact of constant conjunction entails
such necessity in the world, as Hume demonstrates (see Ch. 4). Hence,
any such necessity is entirely in the head of one who considers the world.
There is no necessity in the mosaic that is responsible for any discovered
patterns. The necessity is merely believed by the observer as a result of
their habits and expectations.

According to Humeanism, we are in the same situation with regards to
constant conjunctions of events in the world as we would be with the patterns that are discovered in the randomly generated mosaic. The only
notable difference between the two cases is not significant. This difference
is one of size. The world is so complex that if to each event there corresponds a tile in a mosaic, then the mosaic will be vast beyond our imagining. There are many instances in which water has been heated to 100°C
and they have all being conjoined with water boiling.[6] However, if we
cannot infer necessity in nature from constant conjunction, the number
of instances in the constant conjunction is not relevant. Hence, whether
there are ten or ten thousand cases, necessity still cannot be validly
inferred.

Humeans pronounce, therefore, that there is no necessity in nature.
The world contains just one little thing and then another with no tie or
connection between one and the other. We may suppose there to be
necessity in nature but we are mistaken. Any such necessity is in our heads
only. This is not to suggest mere subjectivism about our views of necessity.
The world contains an objective history or pattern of events and it is this
pattern that determines our beliefs about necessity. We are not at liberty
individually to imagine necessity wherever we please. But whenever we
attribute to the world the necessity that we feel in our thoughts, we are
wrong.

2.5 Regularities and science

How might such a lawless view be thought in the least bit plausible? Is not the claim that there are no laws in nature an anti-scientific view? Could there be any science at all without the presumption of laws? And as science is so successful, might it not, therefore, be thought a very good reason why we should think there are laws?

I claim, however, as in Chapter 1, that the scientific and metaphysical approaches to laws are distinct. So different are the claims of the two disciplines, that science will be able to get along even if metaphysicians conclude that there can be no real laws in nature.

Science merely notes what it can find empirically. It attempts to stick to the phenomenal facts. It can record the constant conjunctions, perhaps after conducting further tests to find corroboration of them. But science does not posit unobserved necessitations that lie behind and perhaps cause these observable regularities. Nor does it deny them: it remains silent on the issue. There are cases where one regularity can be explained in terms of another but this is nothing like the positing of an underlying causal substructure. Instead, science might point out that one constant conjunction is an instance of a more general one: the first is a species of the second. Regularities may thus be subsumed under greater regularities. But where science has found the most general regularities, that are incapable of further explication, its task is done. Hence, science, at its terminus, describes the fundamental regularities: those that cannot be subsumed under a further genus. It might describe the probability waves associated with the subatomic particles in quantum theory (the Schrödinger equation does this). But there is no attempt to go beyond the phenomena to enter into metaphysics.[7]

Such a view fits well with the Humean metaphysic, perhaps in no small measure because of the empiricist drive of that metaphysic. Science is interested only in the phenomena and its laws are the regularities. Hence, these laws of science may be called phenomenal or phenomenological laws.[8] They provide a record of the (observed, tested and recorded) regularities of nature. Because Humeanism attempts to restrict its metaphysics to what can be either directly known or validly inferred from what is directly known, it too has no sense of laws beyond the phenomena. But even though this is sometimes known as a regularity view of laws (see Psillos 2002: 137), it is not a theory of metaphysically real laws in nature *qua* necessary connections. Rather, it is a theory of their being no such laws in nature. Such a view says that there are only the regularities. There are no laws over and above. There are no necessities that make the regularities. The laws are reduced away. Those who defend real laws in nature must counter this view: there are real, existent things in nature that are at least in part responsible for any regularities there happen to be in the world.

However, while there is a strand of Humeanism, notably logical positivism, that has no truck with metaphysics,[9] I will argue in the next two chapters that lawlessness, even Humean lawlessness, is a metaphysical claim. If *real laws in nature* is a metaphysical thesis, so is its negation. To say that the world consists of nothing but a series of discrete, inert and unconnected events, seems like a paradigmatic metaphysical claim. Furthermore, metaphysical assumptions must be behind the account of experience in the epistemology that is supposed to drive Hume's account of necessary connection.

Lawlessness is thus to be counted as a metaphysical thesis. Science, in the account given above, is agnostic about the thesis. Hume, as we will see, can be classed as supporting it. Humeanism says that there is nothing more to the world than the constant conjunctions. Specifically, there are no necessary connections, so there are no laws.

2.6 Conjunctions, connections and laws

At this point, it will be useful to say more on the geography of the debate. This may not seem of immediate relevance here but it will prove very important in what follows later in the book. Where:

CC   = there are constant conjunctions, also known as regularities
NCN = there are necessary connections in nature
L   = there are laws of nature,

we can take Hume to be arguing:

$$\neg(\text{CC} \rightarrow \text{NCN}). \tag{2.1}$$

He denies that there is any valid inference to be drawn from constant conjunctions to necessary connections (*connexions*, as he writes) in nature. Of course, Hume does allow CC, that there are constant conjunctions in nature, but he argues that their existence does not entail the existence of necessary connection. Hume also accepts:

$$\neg\text{NCN}. \tag{2.2}$$

He accepts the metaphysical picture provided by the mosaic analogy. (2.2) also gains some support from Hume's epistemology, which contains various arguments why we can have no idea of necessary connection. We have no direct empirical knowledge of necessary connections (to be considered in greater detail in Chapter 4) and inferences to them from any other thing that is directly experienced are invalid (which the claim in (2.1) instances). In this empiricist tradition, such epistemological arguments have metaphysical implications.

Hume seldom discussed laws directly. However, we can certainly take it that if there are no necessary connections in nature, then there are no real laws in nature. We can add to Hume's argument, therefore:

$$\neg NCN \rightarrow \neg L. \tag{2.3}$$

Anti-Humean metaphysicians have accepted that there are necessary connections in nature and have then moved to defend laws. But while I will side with the anti-Humeans on their first claim, I think that the move to laws is a mistake. Certainly, I will maintain, laws cannot be inferred directly from necessary connections. In practice, however, I suspect that this is what some realists about laws have done; namely, they have defended:

$$NCN \rightarrow L. \tag{2.4}$$

But it is clear that (2.4) does not follow from (2.3), so the defender of (2.4) has to base it on some other justification. I accept (2.3) but I do not accept (2.4). I take it that the existence of necessary connections in nature is a necessary condition for the existence of laws (hence (2.3)) but not a sufficient condition for laws (hence, not-(2.4)). I think this is a reasonable diagnosis because I think that laws would be a species or kind of necessary connection in nature. Not all necessary connections in nature are laws of nature or lawful connections. Causal connections are necessary connections, for instance, according to some accounts of causation; indeed, they are the exemplar necessary connections against which Hume was arguing. But even though many have argued that there is a close connection between causes and laws, they are nevertheless recognized as distinct. There are also other cases of metaphysically necessary connections in nature such as that water = H$_2$O, which, on the face of it, do not appear to be laws.[10] We are not justified, therefore, in inferring the existence of laws of nature if we have done no more than establish the existence of necessary connection.

The significance of this is that those who argue against Hume are mistaken, in my view, if they think that by refuting Hume's denial of necessary connection they are thereby establishing the existence of laws. There is still further work to establish laws even if necessary connections in nature have been exonerated. This opens up the possibility of middle ground between Humeanism and those who argue for real laws in nature. Humeanism, as I have urged in this chapter, is a lawless metaphysics. To focus on the issue of laws, we can call the position Humean lawlessness or HL. Those who argue for laws, and thus against HL, have a position we may call nomological realism or NR. The position in between, I will call realist lawlessness or RL. This third position is characterized by the acceptance of necessary connections in nature – it is a denial of Hume's (2.2), above – but also a denial of laws. This is a consistent position because (2.4), as I have argued, cannot be derived from (2.3) (which was accepted) and there is no other justification for it. Whether (2.1) is accepted or denied doesn't matter strictly to RL. However, contrary to Hume's claims, I wish to argue that we can make reasonably good sense of necessary connections in nature. Constant conjunctions, and the related order in the world, are one of the reasons why we can (§4.5). I will argue in Chapter 4, therefore, that the support for (2.1) derives purely from a radical scepticism that will grant so little that it is practically irrefutable but is also a sterile dead end.

According to realist lawlessness, therefore, we can have necessary connections in nature without having laws. RL is with NR, against HL, that there are necessary connections or modal facts in the world. But RL is with HL, against NR, in arguing that there are no laws. The differences between the three positions, in respect of propositions (2.1)–(2.4), are summarized in Table 2.1 (where Y indicates agreement with the proposition, N indicates disagreement, and – indicates no judgement on the proposition). Table 2.1 does not, however, exhaust the differences between the three positions.

Could one really accept natural necessary connections without laws? I argue that we should. Such laws in nature are an apparatus that is an essential part of a metaphysical picture that needs them. Without laws, this metaphysics is devoid of natural necessity. We have already encountered the basics of this metaphysic. It contains the inert, discrete units that Hume had in his lawless world. Those who were unconvinced thought that Hume's world required the addition of necessity. There must be, it seemed, something that grounded and was responsible for the constant conjunctions. Laws appeared to be the best candidates for the things that did this. Laws apparently made it that everything that was A was also B. But it has never convincingly been described what function laws serve that brings about a constant conjunction, nor, precisely, how they are supposed to do it. Without plausible accounts that answer these questions, we might be justified in thinking of laws as something of a stop-gap – a *deus ex machina* – that plugged the perceived hole or absence in the Humean metaphysic.

Table 2.1 The three metaphysics contrasted

	HL	*NR*	*RL*
(2.1) ¬(CC→NCN)	Y	–	–
(2.2) ¬NCN	Y	N	N
(2.3) ¬NCN→¬L	Y[a]	Y	Y
(2.4) NCN→L	–	Y[b]	N

Notes

a Some Humeans may *prima facie* deny (2.3). But this will be, I assume, where they take laws to be identical with constant conjunctions or some suitable species of constant conjunctions. This would lead them to the view that there are no necessary connections but there are laws. But such laws would not be the real laws in nature that are the current subject.

b This view is imputed to NR by me, rather than explicitly defended by proponents of NR.

In the modally realist metaphysic – the metaphysic that accepts immanent modal facts in the world – there is no such gap to be plugged.[11] Particulars are not modally or causally inert. In virtue of their properties, they are powerful. Hence, there are two stages in the attack on laws: (a) there is no credible account of their role and how they fill it; and (b) there is, in any case, no vacant role that laws would be needed to fill.

Realist lawlessness cannot be judged anti-scientific, just as we could not so judge against Humean lawlessness. Science does not consciously get involved with the metaphysics. Science requires only the phenomena, the constant conjunctions. Some anti-Humean metaphysicians are attracted by the idea of laws as a possible grounding of constant conjunctions. But I will argue that necessary connections are adequate to explain constant conjunctions and, as we saw with the rejection of (2.4), necessary connections do not entail laws.

2.7 Humean 'theories of laws'

The chief aim of this chapter has been to illustrate the sense in which Humeanism is a lawless metaphysics despite there being a so-called Humean theory of laws. That the Humean view is lawless is important for the argument of this book. The main argument is against forms of nomological realism but the chief objections to NR will not strike against Humeanism because of its lawless nature. The so-called laws of the Humean metaphysic are of a distinctly different character from those of NR. We could not expect that the same arguments will defeat laws in both these widely differing senses. Separate reasons will have to be produced, in the next two chapters, for rejecting Humean lawlessness.

It might be clearer now why the topic of this book is laws *in* nature. It is against such putative things that this book stands. Most of the arguments will be directed against an idea of laws as real entities in the world that play a role in determining the behaviour of a class of particulars. There is another tradition that treats laws as merely statements or truths about our beliefs or expectations. One would hardly want to claim that these things do not exist. But these laws are not a part of mind-independent reality. A further tradition understands laws to be some variety of constant conjunction. Again, the existence of such things cannot be denied. But where this is part of a denial of all necessity in nature, I will be opposing it.

I move, therefore, to a more detailed study of the Humean position. I examine the regularity theory and its most sophisticated variant: the Ramsey–Lewis best system theory. Following that, I look for anything compelling and conclusive in the original Humean argument that motivates the regularity and best system views. I will claim that Humean lawlessness is not an attractive metaphysic and also that there has been no compelling reason forthcoming for why we must accept it.

3 Regularities and best systems

3.1 Regularity and less-than-universal regularity

While one might believe that the whole world consists of just one little thing and then another, it is hard to deny that the sequence of events on occasion displays regularity. Humeans who think that there are no necessary connections in nature are nevertheless prepared to grant that there is regularity. They contradict, however, the sometimes held view that there are laws of nature that are responsible for such regularities. This presents us with the regularity view of laws, which says that there are only the regularities and no metaphysically real connections in nature that produce them. The regularity view of laws is thus not a theory of metaphysically real laws, as considered in §2.7. Nevertheless, the regularity view of laws is still a theory: a theory about what there is, and is not, in the world. It is just not a theory of laws *qua* necessary connections. We will see, however, that it does produce a revised, attenuated sense of law, stripped of necessary connection.

The exact nature of regularity is hard to specify but its existence is no less uncertain. We have an undoubted acquaintance with some regularities, for example, when water reaches 100°C, it boils. But there are occasions when such regularities fail. Water can reach 100°C and not boil, if it is not at standard pressure. Our regularity may then be said to hold only *ceteris paribus*, or other things being equal. But this fact does not refute the claim that there are regularities in the world. Instead, the problem is that such regularities can cut across each other. There is also a regularity that the boiling point of a liquid rises with atmospheric pressure. This takes precedence over our first regularity. Indeed, the second regularity can be an explanation of why the first can sometimes fail to hold.

We can understand what it is for different regularities to cut across each other in the following way. A regularity could be construed as a conditional of the form <when p, q>. Hence we can have different regularities (1) <when A, B>; (2) <when C, D>, and so on. When there is also a regularity (3) <when B and C, not-D>, it makes it possible that when C, there will not be D, despite (2). We could revise (2) to take account of this, so that it becomes (2*) <when C, D unless B>. This allows that (2) can have exceptions and the *ceteris paribus* clause is designed to account for all such exceptions. This is stated as (2**) <when C, D cp>. The list of possible exceptions to (2) may be open-ended or infinite, hence imposs-ible to list explicitly. How exactly the *ceteris paribus* clause catches all such circumstances is thus a difficult issue but one that need not detain us at this stage.[1]

Having acknowledged that there can be regularities that for the above reason may be less than universally regular, we may set the complication aside, though nothing that follows depends on doing so. Rather, this chapter focuses on other problems.

3.2 Irrefutable but unappealing

The regularity view of laws is thus the view that nature contains certain regular sequences and that there is nothing more to laws than such regular sequences. Psillos formulates the view simply as 'laws of nature are regularities' (2002: 137). But even more so than my formulation, this may give the suggestion, which I think is misleading, that (Humean) regularity theorists are realists about laws. Rather, we can take regularity theorists to believe neither that there are laws nor that there is causation.[2] I think that this account of the regularity theory best develops the metaphysical core around which it is built and, as will be argued below, has the best prospect of avoiding the standard objections that have been directed against the theory. I do not, however, claim complete historical accuracy for the account. I think that some regularity theorists have indeed treated their theory as a theory of laws but I also think that this was a mistake. A further source of confusion, however, is that some Humeans will sometimes allow an attenuated sense of law and causation, which will be the same as the traditional concepts but minus the necessity.

Regularity theorists will offer law statements of the form (4) $\forall x$ $(Fx \rightarrow Gx)$,[3] sometimes with the provisos discussed in §3.1, where F and G are properties of particulars. Such statements are intended to describe the empirically known or theorized regularities in nature. Given that a regu-larity may be inferred before all cases have been examined, (4) may be believed as a result of inductive inference though not necessarily so. (4) may be a corroborated, unfalsified hypothesis, as Popper (1959) describes, or key parts of a paradigm (Kuhn 1962) or research programme (Lakatos 1970).

In this chapter, I will be considering the basic form of the regularity view, known as the naïve regularity view, a more sophisticated version, and the most sophisticated version, known as the best systems view or the Mill–Ramsey–Lewis theory. All these theories have been discussed exten-sively elsewhere. I will not be offering a complete survey of the regularity and associated views, therefore.[4] A book on laws must nevertheless record a verdict on them. The verdict of this book can be summarized simply: the regularity view is irrefutable but neither compelling, appealing nor intuitive. Being unappealing, in this case, should be thought to outweigh the irrefutability of the theory. Specifically, the regularity view is only as persuasive as the metaphysical picture that underpins it. This is the metaphysics of *discreta*: the world as a mosaic of unconnected particulars. I join with others in finding this metaphysic unacceptable.[5] However, once the metaphysic is granted, the regularity view, I suggest, is a perfectly consistent account of the discrete, lawless world. It can be rejected, if at all, only by inference from the rejection of discreta. Taken on its own grounds, however, nothing can be done to reject the theory. This means that the regularity theory might seem a good account of laws to someone who has not reflected on its metaphysical basis or might not be even aware that the view has such a metaphysical basis.

What is so good about the regularity view? Presumably something about it must be. Its advantages, I surmise, are its consistency and coherence – which allow it to shrug off almost all of the standard criticisms – and an arguable compatibility with the empirical sciences.

I begin with laws in the sciences. It might be claimed that empirical science can only, and must only, record the facts of tested reliable regularities. It cannot venture into speculation about any metaphysical cause of those regularities without itself slipping into metaphysics (§§1.4 and 2.5). Any such metaphysical cause is unobservable whereas science, on this account, aims only at empirical adequacy (van Fraassen 1980). There will be some cases where laws do have a further explanation, namely where they are instances of more general or fundamental regularities, but these explanations of laws remain non-metaphysical. Hence, science employs a metaphysically agnostic sense of law of nature. Where we have a regularity that is known to be confirmed and has been preserved through a variety of tests, a scientist is disposed to ask what more one could want of a law. Philosophers who hold a regularity view believe they have an account of laws that has all the economy of the scientific concept. They will ask of a metaphysician, what more they think needs to be added to a tried and tested regularity for it to qualify as one of these laws. They say, if they follow Hume, that if necessary connection is supposed to be added, then the very idea of a law is in difficulty as the concept of a necessary connection, over and above a regularity, cannot be applied.

By a law of nature, therefore, we cannot mean anything more than the regularity itself. This leaves us with the deflated concept of a law, revised in the light of philosophical reflection, where a law is nothing more than a regularity. A Humean might also make use of a revised, deflated concept of a cause where to say that As cause Bs is to say only that there is a constant conjunction of As and Bs. These Humean revisions of causation and of laws are thus the traditional, erroneous theories, stripped of necessary connection.

Arguably, things look even better for a regularity view of laws than they do for a regularity view of causation. There is a class of regularities that appear to be non-causal. These might be a threat to the regularity view of causation but not to the regularity view of laws. For example, night regularly follows day and rain regularly follows the falling of the barometer. In neither case do we pre-theoretically think that the former type of event is caused by the latter. However, even if this is granted, it is very hard to resist the claim that it is still a law that night follows day and a law that rain follows the barometer's fall.[6] Such a reliable regularity in the world might be thought adequate for a law (though not, in these cases, fundamental laws). It seems, therefore, that there are regularities that qualify as laws but are not causal. Such cases might undermine the view of Armstrong, to be discussed in Chapter 6, that every law is instantiated in causal sequences.

So much for the compatibility of the regularity view with science. What of the claimed consistency and coherence? This claim seems easy to defend because the regularity theory is so simple. It states merely that there are regularities and that there is nothing more to a law (in the deflated sense just described) than such a regularity. If you are a Humean, and deny necessary connections in nature, the deflated account of laws is perfectly coherent. The account is irrefutable, therefore, because it is impossible to perform a *reductio* on it. Attempts to argue against the theory must take a different tack. There may be an attempt to challenge the theory through an appeal to intuitions: for instance, by appealing to an intuitive distinction between accidental and genuinely lawlike regularities. But such appeals will always be appeals to intuitions that convinced regularity theorists do not share. They are intuitively appealing only to those who already think the regularity view inadequate. Suppose instead that you follow the naïve regularity theory. If you really do not believe in necessary connections in nature, you really do not see a distinction between accidental and lawlike regularities. You will deny that there exists any extra element or property, perhaps called *lawlikeness* (following Lange 1993), that would ground the distinction. All regularities have equal ontological credentials for you and the accidental/lawlike division is a distinction without a difference.

The naïve regularity view, that has been discussed so far, is arguably more tenable than the sophisticated version because it remains on a distinctly ontological footing. Attempts to sophisticate the view have led only to a clouding of the issues. Braithwaite, for example, conceded a difference between accidental and lawlike regularities but then said that our epistemic attitude to the regularity, and this attitude alone, determined whether it was accidental or lawlike (1953: 301). Ayer endorsed this view more clearly, saying 'the difference between our two types of generalization lies not so much on the side of the facts which make them true or false, as in the attitude of those who put them forward' (1963: 230).

Whether a generalization is a law is determined by how we treat it; whether we have, for instance, a willingness to explain away exceptions, rather than treat them as showing the falsity of the generalization. The problem with these attempts at sophistication is that they introduce psychological factors into the determination of a law of nature. To say that a law is a regularity that is believed, or well confirmed, or supportive of inductive inferences, or central to one's conceptual scheme, is to say that it is what we think of a regularity, or the use to which we put it, that makes it a law. All of Ayer's criteria of being a law (ibid.: 233) invoke such psychological factors, about what we are willing to do and willing to believe. This produces an implausible account of law. As Ramsey pointed out, the more plausible view is that there can be laws that are not believed (1928: 140–1). Only if laws can exist without being thought of are they discovered rather than invented. Even if you think there is nothing more to a law than a regularity, you would surely grant, unless you are an idealist, that the regularity could exist unperceived and could have existed even if there never were minds.

Apart from this undesirable epistemic view, the mistake in such attempts to sophisticate the regularity view lies in the acceptance of the division between laws and accidents. This is only an epistemological or psychological division, not a metaphysical one, in the versions considered, but it gives ground to the intuition that there is a difference. The naïve regularity theory appears safer when it sticks to the formula *regularity = law*, without making exceptions for unconfirmed regularities, non-inductively projected regularities, and so on. If one sticks to the simple formula, and interprets it as a theory of there being no metaphysically real laws in nature, many of the standard objections to the regularity view gain no leverage. We can call this version *the pure regularity theory* of laws.

3.3 The critique of the regularity theory

The previous claim will now be illustrated by showing how regularity theorists may avoid fatal damage from the standard objections. I do not provide a comprehensive list of objections to the theory. Rather, I classify three types of attack and indicate how they are to be avoided or evaded by the kind of pure regularity theory I have outlined. Doing this will allow us to identify the key battleground. Humean lawlessness will be seen to stand or fall on the issues of necessary connection in nature, which will be the subject of Chapter 4, and the existence of discreta, which will be considered in Part III.

Accidental regularities

The idea of an accidental regularity has appeared already. This is supposed to be a regularity that, for some reason, is thought not to qualify as a law of nature. This amounts to an attack on the theory because it leads to the conclusion that laws must be regularities *plus* something else. There are some related issues that can be used as part of the same sort of attack. It has been claimed that there could be a lack of inner connection between the regularly related phenomena (Armstrong 1983: 39–40), that regularities lack necessity (ibid.: Ch. 3), that they are insufficient for laws (ibid.: 13), and that regularities cannot explain their instances (ibid.: 40–1).[7]

It can be shown that none of these types of criticism strike against the pure regularity theory that I have outlined above. The pure regularity theory recognizes no division between accidental and genuinely lawlike regularities because it recognizes nothing that could be a basis for the division.

It might be claimed by an opponent of the regularity theory, for instance, that laws manifest themselves in regularities, rather than being identical with regularities. But one who supports a pure regularity theory is at liberty simply to deny this claim. The claim assumes that there are laws that have an existence independently of the regularities, which is precisely what one denies if one adheres to the pure regularity view.

Nor must one accept that laws should explain their instances. One may accept that regularities do not explain their instances because they are constituted and entirely exhausted by those instances. To assume that laws should explain their instances is to accept, presumably, that there is something that compels those instances, or at least makes them so.[8] If the instances, however, are nothing more than the instances of a regularity, with no necessity in nature, then there exists nothing of adequate metaphysical strength that it could make the regularity. The regularity is nothing more than a set of alike particular facts. This would require, therefore, that if we settle for the attenuated sense of law, as Humean lawlessness requires, we must reassess the old realist account of the epistemic role of laws. Explanation by regularity can only say that an instance is part of the pattern of regularity. It cannot say that it is explained by the regularity, nor anything else. This is no real epistemic loss, however, as all such former explanations by laws are deemed illusory.

Likewise, the pure regularity theorist should accept that regularities lack necessity and inner connection. What is thought to be a regularity now, as a hypothesis or inductive inference, might cease to be a regularity tomorrow. A regularity cannot be counterfactually projected to new cases. One may, of course, take a purely metaphysical view on what counts as a regularity and offer a four-dimensional view.[9] This brackets the epistemological question of how we would know that we had found a regularity that holds for all time. But even a four-dimensional regularity cannot be counterfactually extended. Hence, even if everything that is A, in the whole history of our world, is also a B, we cannot say that if *c*, which is not an A, were an A, it would also be a B. Things that are A in other possible worlds might or might not be Bs because, in the metaphysics of Humean lawlessness, there is never necessity between particular matters of fact.

This view allows us to deny the general division from which we began. One regularity is no more necessary than any other. There will be, therefore, no need to try to distinguish universals of laws from universals of fact, as concerned Ramsey (1928), Goodman (1965) and Ayer (1963). This worry emerges because the standard form of a Humean law statement, (4) $\forall x\,(Fx \rightarrow Gx)$, is to be interpreted purely extensionally. Any universally quantified fact will therefore have the same form, for example, that (5) all moas die before reaching the age of fifty (Popper 1959: 427), or that (6) all coins in my pocket are silver (Goodman 1965: 20). The pure regularity theory, however, does not recognize a difference between universals of law and of fact. All statements of the form (4) are true by fact as the Humean metaphysic contains nothing but such facts. (5) and (6) are as good as universal regularities as anything else.[10]

Probabilistic laws

There appear to be laws used in some of the sciences, physics in particular, that contain an irreducibly probabilistic element. Even if there were no irreducibly probabilistic phenomena as a matter of fact, it seems that we would still want to allow the possibility that there could be laws in a probabilistic universe. But physics does seem to invoke such probabilities, for example, when stating the rate of radioactive decay of a nuclide or elementary particle. This is given in terms of a half-life, which means that there is a 50/50 chance of a particular nuclide or particle having decayed at that point. This may permit, however, that the particular might decay some time before the half-life or some time after. There is no non-probabilistic way to state the lifetime of such a particle.

The problem this presents is that a probabilistic law is consistent with any distribution of events. One can imagine that there is a law concerning the toss of a coin, or any coin like it, that gives a 50/50 chance of heads or tails. This case is not too dissimilar from the example of a particle's half-life, except the same coin can be tossed a number of times whereas a particle can decay only once. But the 50/50 chance of heads or tails is consistent with any distribution of heads or tails in a sequence of trials. We might be able to say that some distributions are more probable than others. And we might expect that the proportion of heads to tails would tend to 50:50 as the number of trials tends to infinity. But there is no reason to suppose that we could, in a finite world, get near to an infinite number of trials of anything. The upshot seems to be that we should not expect in any case that the facts of actual frequency match the corresponding facts of probability. The best we could say is that they will probably do so, but this is to encounter exactly the same problem of probability with which we began.

How might a regularity theorist account for this problem? How can they get probabilities from frequencies? We will see in §3.4 that David Lewis makes a serious attempt to tackle this issue within an authentically Humean framework. Here, however, I stick with the naïve but pure regularity theory. What can it say about probabilistic laws?

The pure regularity theorist is again at liberty to deny the extra facts that seem to be invoked in probabilistic laws, over and above the facts of actual distributions. The theory that there is a real probabilistic fact, n_1/n_2, lying behind the actual proportion $n_3:n_4$, is coherently deniable. Its acceptance, rather than rejection, seems most problematic for we may well wonder wherein lies the truthmaker of the probabilistic fact if it is not in the actual frequencies. This question raises the spectre of Meinongianism, after the metaphysics of Meinong (1904). The probabilistic facts seem to be ideal only, which means that they are non-existent. Are we to say, however, that they have some lesser-order of existence, such as subsistence? The issue of Meinongianism will be revisited in relation to realist lawlessness in §11.7, for it remains a difficulty for a number of realist positions, such as realism about causal powers. The regularity theory is at least free of the Meinongian difficulty.

If one is to deny that there are probabilistic facts, then what can the regularity theorist make of statements of probability? What do these statements mean and do they have truth values? I see no reason why a metaphysic of pure regularity cannot offer a satisfactory account of such statements, once their metaphysical assumptions are accepted. But they cannot say that there are real probabilistic laws that determine frequencies in a probabilistic way. Instead, therefore, the regularity theorist will have to say that probability statements are approximate summaries of, idealizations of, or projections of the proportions in known distributions. They may also be rational expectations of future distributions based, for instance, on Bayesian conditionalizing (see Bird 1998a: 203–13). Such accounts are of probabilistic beliefs or theories. They rest on epistemological or psychological factors. They are not fit to be laws in nature, therefore. If Humeanism is correct, however, such accounts of probability are all that we can have.[11]

There is an issue that is not too distant from the case of probabilistic laws, namely that of functional laws. Many of the laws invoked in physics have a functional nature, by which I mean that they are laws that state that one value or quality varies as a function of another value or quality. $F = ma$ is an example, as are the laws of gravitational and electromagnetic attraction. The problem such laws raise for a regularity theory is that not all the possible values might be instantiated in the actual sequence of events. To be true, however, the law must range over all actual *and* possible values. It seems, therefore, that the regularity theorist cannot provide enough facts to be truthmakers for the functional law if there are uninstantiated values.

The regularity theorist can grant the possibility of uninstantiated values without suffering serious damage to their theory. They may say that when all the actual values have been plotted as crosses on a graph, we simply draw as short but smooth a line as possible through them and the functional 'law' is provided by the line rather than the crosses. This does not provide *facts* about the uninstantiated values. Again, these exist only as projections or expectations from what is actual. In the Humean world, we can do no more, however. Humeanism really does offer no reason why, necessarily, the line should be short and smooth. There is no reason why an uninstantiated first value couldn't correspond to a completely unexpected second value, so that our line through the actual values would have to make a major detour. If there really is no necessity in nature, there is no reason this counterfactual case should fit neatly with the actual cases, only an expectation that it will.

No-case, single-case, and few-case regularities

The final class of objections to the regularity theory could also fall under the heading of accidental regularities but they also include a slightly different issue. This new element concerns how easy it might be to get the required regularity expressed in a true universally quantified conditional like (4). There could be some regularities that have very few instances. But while it might be true that (7) $\forall x\ (Ax \rightarrow Bx)$, would we really want to count it as a genuine regularity in nature if only five things were A (and all five were also B)? Where such few instances are involved, we might not even exercise our custom and habit of projecting onto other cases. Five cases just do not seem enough for an inductive inference. But suppose we also know that these five cases are all the As that there are, throughout all space and time. There is no need for an inductive inference or projection onto undiscovered cases. Does it now qualify as a regularity, as a Humean law?

This kind of concern can easily be pushed further. Can there be regularities with just one instance? There could be a property that only one particular *b* instantiates. This might be a large, conjunctive property, which we can call C. Suppose *b* now has some other property D, that is not a part of the conjunction C. This would make it true that anything (the only thing) that instantiates C, instantiates D. Such single-case uniformities seem too easily to qualify as Humean laws. In general, it seems that the fewer the instances, the more likely it is that there be a regularity. In many ways, this seems an odd finding. We would ordinarily feel more confident that we have a genuine regularity when more instances are involved. From a single instance, one would have thought a regularity theorist would be reluctant to infer a law because a single instance does not seem to qualify as a regularity.

The no-case regularity seems the closest to an absurd consequence of the theory. As Molnar noted, if it is a fact that no S is P, it is a regularity, hence Humean law, that all S is non-P, by equivalence (1969: 81). But this means that all that is not the case becomes, according to the theory, contrary to law.

There are two ways the Humean might go in response. The first is to try to rule out no-case and few-case regularities by making a more sophisticated regularity theory. Psillos thinks this option must be taken (2002: 139–41). Again, however, I think that the brave Humean can simply deny the problem. The world as they describe it contains nothing more than a spread of unconnected events. A few-case regularity is no less a regularity. It may be a regularity that is less well confirmed, but no matter how well a regularity has been confirmed, it can never become necessary. The idea that something metaphysical is missing from a few-case regularity is mistaken and misleading. Only if one believes in such necessities, and is trying to discover them from their instances, might one have a concern with enumerating those instances. If not, not.

It should now be apparent that there is a form of the regularity theory that is radical enough to remain untouched by the standard objections. It is clear, however, that this rests on the metaphysical stance that denies necessary connections in nature. The issue of necessary connection has thus become the key battleground in an assessment of Humean lawlessness. It is further arguable that it is one of the key battles in contemporary metaphysics.

I will be arguing, in Chapter 4, that Hume's argument against necessary connection in nature is inadequate. This will be followed with an argument in favour of necessity in nature, and this will occupy much of Part III.

We have not yet fully explored all that Humean metaphysics has to offer, however. Though irrefutable, I said that the naïve regularity view was unappealing. Perhaps there is a more compelling version of Humeanism. I will now proceed to two aspects of Humeanism that have been explored by David Lewis, namely the best systems approach to laws and the general issue of Humean supervenience.

3.4 The best systems theory

One of the leading philosophical outlooks on laws is the Ramsey–Lewis theory, or Mill–Ramsey–Lewis theory. Psillos also calls it the web of laws theory (2002: 148–54). This phrase emphasizes one of the key features of the theory. Whether something is a law is not a purely intrinsic feature of it. Rather, something is a law when it is part of a systematic account of the world. Laws must cohere. One could not have a single, detached law that dangled alone, unrelated to the rest of the laws. The theory is thus consistent with the systematicity that is found in science. The account nevertheless remains a Humean and lawless one, in the sense already established.

Laws are not some special, separate class of nomological necessity. Lewis's metaphysics contains the same sequence of unconnected events that the regularity theory has. The Ramsey–Lewis theory is the view that the laws should be understood in terms of having a certain place within a system, rather than being merely a free-standing regularity. Not any old system will do, however. The laws will be a part of the best systematization of the world's history; hence this can be called the best systems theory.

The basic commitment of the Ramsey–Lewis theory is that the laws of nature are the theorems or axioms of the best possible systematization of the omnitemporal history of the world, where the criterion of being the best such systematization is that it is the one that offers the best combination of simplicity and strength. Here is how Lewis first spelled out the claim:

> a contingent generalization is a *law of nature* if and only if it appears as a theorem (or axiom) in each of the true deductive systems that achieves a best combination of simplicity and strength.[12] A generalization is a law at a world *i*, likewise, if and only if it appears as a theorem in each of the best deductive systems true at *i*.
>
> (Lewis 1973: 73)

The idea of a systematization of nature did not appear first in Lewis. Mill hinted at the idea in 1843, saying:

> What are the fewest and simplest assumptions, which being granted, the whole existing order of nature would result? Another mode of stating it would be: What are the fewest general propositions from which all the uniformities which exist in the universe might be deductively inferred?
>
> (Mill 1843: Bk III, Ch IV, Sec 1, p. 207)

Mill goes on to mention Newton. He could have got the idea from Newton's *Principia* (1687) because he would have found there that another term Newton used for law of nature was *axiom*. Further, the three axioms of motion indeed had the look of the three simplest and strongest truths that God needed to impose on the world to thereby impose all its motions. I will not speculate further on whether Newton had a Ramsey–Lewis theory of laws, nor whether any of its adherents were deliberately following Newton. There will be, however, further consideration of Newton's *Principia* in Chapter 9.

Instead, we can note that the theory was revived some time later, though very briefly, when Ramsey said that: 'even if we knew everything, we should still want to systematize our knowledge as a deductive system, and the general axioms in that system would be the fundamental laws of nature' (Ramsey 1928: 143). At this point, Ramsey was attempting to distinguish the fundamental laws of nature from derived laws and perhaps gave a better summary later: 'causal laws were consequences of those propositions which we should take as axioms if we knew everything and organized it as simply as possible in a deductive system' (Ramsey 1929: 150). But Ramsey had already rejected the theory by this stage, on the flimsy ground that 'it is impossible to know everything and organize it in a deductive system' (ibid.). While Ramsey's assertion is no doubt true, it does not rule out the theory as an account of what we should think the laws to be, considered purely metaphysically. What we can know about the laws does not determine what the laws are. The theory was in need of a more rigorously metaphysical development, therefore, which David Lewis provided.

The best systems theory adds a number of new elements. Laws are not seen as regularities but, rather, as those things from which regularities – rather, the whole world history including the regularities and everything else – can be derived. Laws must also cohere in a systematic way with each other to qualify as laws. But they must also be a part, the axioms or theorems, of the *best* systematization of the world. The best system has the right balance between having as few axioms as possible but from which enough of the world's history can be derived. These are the requirements of simplicity and strength respectively.

Why would one want to hold a theory that introduced all these novel elements to the concept of a law? Lewis claimed he was adopting this version of the theory because it had six advantages (Lewis 1973: 74). I will argue in §3.6 that there was a more fundamental commitment that better explained why Lewis was attracted to the theory. First, I will mention the six claimed advantages that Lewis explicitly avowed. But I will also provide some possible responses and comments. The advantages are, paraphrasing:

(1) *The theory explains why lawhood is not just a matter of the generality of a single sentence. The sentence must also fit with other truths to make a best possible system.*

(R1) Lewis is right to note that some general statements might not be laws; for example 'all gold cubes are smaller than one cubic mile'. What, then, is the difference between a general statement that is a law and one that is not? Lewis's answer is that the laws are those general statements that fit in such a way as to make a best system. This has more than a look of coherence about it: to be laws, these systems must cohere in the right way, as specified by the requirements of a best system. Would we be comfortable with this? Many find a coherence theory of truth unattractive.[13] Would they accept a coherence theory of laws? One might think, instead, that such coherence is neither necessary nor sufficient to determine the world's laws. The world need not have a very neat nomological structure. Perhaps it is being too optimistic to expect this kind of tidy coherence.

However, the best systems theorist might argue that there are significant differences between the cases of truth and laws, such that it is unfair to draw the parallel. If so, a proponent of the theory should spell out such differences.

(2) *It explains why lawhood is a contingent property. Some worlds have other truths that make a generalization part of a best system.*

(R2) Other explanations of the apparent contingency of laws are available and, one could argue, they are simpler than Lewis's. If one were a realist about laws, for instance, one could still allow, if one wished, that laws differ in different worlds but, in contrast to Lewis's theory, whether a statement was a law-statement at any particular world would not depend upon what other statements were law-statements in that world. Again, such a set of statements attains the property of lawhood, for Lewis, by being part of a consistent and strong systematization, rather than by corresponding to a real necessity in the world. This may lead us to wonder what the property of lawhood is. Arguably, a key feature of it might be *truth about necessitation*, where such truth is something more than coherence.

(3) *It explains how we can know, by exhausting the instances, that a generalization is true while not yet know whether it is a law.*

(R3) Anyone who rejects the pure Humean equation of laws with true generalizations will accept Lewis's point that we can know all instances of a generalization to be true without knowing it to be a law. But this leaves many options open. Some have thought that a law was a Humean regularity *plus* some extra factor. Some say the extra must be of an epistemic nature, some say metaphysical. Out of the options on offer, we may want to resist Lewis's preference. He says a law must have combinability with other generalizations into a best system. But is combinability with other true generalizations into a best system really sufficient for lawhood? The pure regularity theory, as we saw above, would not accept (3) at all.

(4) *It allows laws of which we have no inkling. Being a law is not the same as being regarded as a law or even being regarded as a law and being true together.*

(R4) Any realist will allow that there can be laws of which we have no inkling. Indeed, even a Humean account that equated laws with regularities, rather than known statements about observed regularities, could allow laws which were unknown. Ability to account for this is not, therefore, a unique virtue of the Ramsey–Lewis account. The way in which the Ramsey–Lewis theory does account for this feature is revealing, however. For the acceptance of unknown laws means that the best system, or at least part of the best system, may be unknown. But then, we may wonder, what are we to understand by a systematization of the history of the world that is unknown? What status does such a systematization have and what onto-logical commitments follow from that status? Is it to be regarded as having almost a transcendent, Platonic existence? If so, that is a point of contro-versy for the Ramsey–Lewis view. Or is it to be regarded as having an immanent existence in the events themselves that constitute the world? This may be a more plausible account of what the systematization is but from where would the feature of 'best-ness' come? Could the events them-selves be seen as favouring any particular systematization and, if so, why would they favour the systematization which best combines the features of simplicity and strength, which look conspicuously epistemological rather than metaphysical matters? Furthermore, if the world really does have its own nomological structure, that the systematization merely describes, why are the laws not to be equated with the nomological structure itself rather than with the system that describes it?[14]

>   (5)   *It explains why we should take the theorems of well-established theories provisionally to be laws. Our actual scientific theorizing is an attempt to approximate the best deductive systems that combine simplicity and strength.*

(R5) As in the case of the regularity theory, it can be conceded that the Ramsey–Lewis theory coheres with the practice of science. But does that make the theory satisfying metaphysically? I argued in §1.4 that the scient-ific and metaphysical accounts of laws have different aims and ambitions. Science restricts itself to the phenomena, or that which could become phenomena. Humeanism is a sparse metaphysics that attempts to adhere to similar strictures. Does that mean that there is nothing behind the phe-nomena that is responsible for the world's events or its regularities? That is what we hope to find out. The approach that science takes cannot, however, be taken as a wholly dependable guide to the metaphysical truth about laws.

>   (6)   *It explains why lawhood is a rather vague and difficult concept: simplicity and strength, and the right balance between them, are only roughly fixed standards.*

(R6) It is a strange advantage of one's theory of laws to claim that it is equally as vague and difficult as laws themselves. Is Lewis suggesting that the true account of laws must be vague and difficult because the concept of lawhood which it analyzes is equally so? What if we found a philosophi-cal theory without vagueness and difficulty? Would it be false on those grounds alone? I think not. However, in Chapter 8 I will argue that the concept of a law is indeed vague, so I think that Lewis has a point here. I think this shows the unimportance for science of the idea of a law of nature. Perhaps Lewis would agree with me in some sense. This might be because, ultimately, we both have what I would classify as lawless metaphysics: we are both standing against nomological realism.

While none of Lewis's six points seem conclusive, in favour of his theory, individually one might nevertheless think that the theory does a good job overall of meeting our desiderata of a theory of laws. The theory does not answer all our concerns but perhaps the theory might be better placed than any other theory of laws. Nothing else might account for these six points better. However, I am now going to consider some of the perceived major disadvantages of the theory.

3.5 Problems for best systems

A major point of controversy for Lewis's version of the theory, and arguably for Ramsey's and Mill's, is the issue of Humean supervenience. This is the thesis that the world's history is a patchwork of unconnected events and everything else, including the laws, supervenes on that history. This issue, taken as a philosophical thesis in its own right, will be discussed in the next section. Here, I concentrate on two other issues that objectors to the Ramsey–Lewis theory have raised.

Simplicity and strength

Armstrong and others have raised the issue of the standards of simplicity and strength that determine the best systematization of the world's history. Armstrong thought that this introduced an element of subjectivism into the laws (1983: 67) because the best system seemed to be determined by what we took to be simple and strong in a system. As well as making the determination of a world's laws mind-dependent, Armstrong noted that we might not even agree as to the standards. A rationalist might think that simplicity should have greater weight, for example, while an empiricist might give greater weight to strength.

Further, Armstrong objected (1983: 70) that because this is essentially a coherence theory, the possibility could not be ruled out that a number of different systematizations of the same history might be tied for first place as equally best. These systems might have different sets of laws, so what shall we say are the laws in that instance?

The theory seems able to provide answers to these objections, even though it appears to be by a series of *ad hoc* moves. Indeed, Lewis has varied his responses over time. Nevertheless, it seems possible to provide senses of simplicity and strength that avoid these standard objections.

Lewis used to think that the standards of simplicity and strength were our actual and present standards (1973: 74), and if we considered laws in other worlds, that had other thinkers, we rigidified those standards regardless of the standards adopted by the inhabitants of that world (1986c: 123). But Lewis came to reject this view and said: 'The real answer lies elsewhere: if nature is kind to us, the problem needn't arise' (1994: 232). If fortune favours us, the best system will come out best under any reasonable standards of simplicity and strength. This response does not deny a possible psychological element in the account of laws, therefore. Instead, it claims that it shouldn't be necessary for it to come into play. The world is such, we trust, that even if we disagree over the exact standards of simplicity and strength, we are likely to agree on what is the best system because no other system will come near it. It will be, in this sense, *robustly* best. Nevertheless, Lewis admits:

> that *if* nature were unkind, and *if* disagreeing rival systems were running neck-and-neck, then lawhood might be a psychological matter, and that would be very peculiar ... But I would blame the trouble on unkind nature, not on the analysis.
>
> (Lewis 1994: 233)[15]

We will see that this is not Lewis's only 'we had better hope not' response. It remains, however, a concession of a psychologistic element in the account. What is the best possible systematization of nature is not, therefore, an entirely objective matter. Would this be acceptable to us?

The imagined problem also raises the issue of tied best systems. Originally Lewis's solution was to allow that there might be a tie for best and to take as the laws only those axioms or theorems that appeared in *all* the best systematizations. This is evident in Lewis's original statement (1973: 73), where the axiom must be 'in each of the true deductive systems that achieves a best combination of simplicity and strength'. Later Lewis put this in terms of choosing between the intersection of the axioms of the tied best systems or the union (1986c: 124). He chose the intersection: L is a law if it is an axiom in *all* the tied systems. But this response has the troubling consequence that there may be few or no axioms in the intersection. If there are tied best systematizations of a world's history, therefore, that world may have no laws. Lewis later admitted that this could leave us with next to no laws and he offered a slightly different answer. In such a case, there are 'no very good deservers of the name of laws' (1994: 233). He went on, 'But what of it? We haven't the slightest reason to think the case really arises.'

I think Lewis is able to get away with these responses, which in most philosophical contexts would be considered unsatisfactory, because of his essentially Humean starting point with respect to laws. The responses betray an anti-realist attitude to metaphysically real laws. If laws really have no existence other than as parts of systematizations, then it hardly seems problematic to say that there may be no best systematization, therefore no laws. If one thought, however, that there were real laws in nature, or nomological structures, that the systematization was an attempt to describe, they would have to be completely untouched by our standards of simplicity and strength and our attempts at best sytematization. That Lewis does not feel troubled by the issue confirms the classification that I think best fits. The best systems theory is not a theory of metaphysically real laws but, rather, a theory of there being no such laws.

Chance

The same goes for Lewis's take on chance. Chance is relevant to our subject because of the already mentioned probabilistic laws, which seem to be an important class of laws for physics. It was noted that Humean accounts begin by attempting to get chances – single-case objective probabilities – from frequencies. Lewis concedes, however, that this strategy is plausible only when there are 'enourmous classes of exact copies' (1994: 229). The few-case problem in Humeanism reappears:

> Tritium atoms are abundant; not so for atoms of unobtainium[346]. It's hard to make the stuff, in fact in all of space and time, past present and future, there only ever exist two Un^{346} atoms: one with a lifetime of 4.8 microseconds, as chance would have it; the other with a lifetime of 6.1 microseconds. So exactly half of all Un^{346} atoms decay in 4.8 microseconds. What does this frequency make true concerning the half-life of Un^{346}, in other words concerning the chance that an atom of it will decay in a given time? Next to nothing, I should think.
>
> (Lewis 1994: 229–30)

How do we read the probabilistic laws of radioactive decay from the history of events when that history contains only two instances of the atom in question? Naïve frequentism says that the law is determined simply by the frequency of events so the half-life of Un^{346} can depend on no fact other than the average of the lives of its two instances. Lewis acknowledges the failure of this approach where the number of instances is low. The case of his unobtainium[349] is even worse: there are no samples in the entire history of the world. It is a no-case frequency. Again, there is no fact of chance about its decay.

The feeling that there is more to probability than the frequency of events is a threat to Humean supervenience. It must find some way to get from the world's history, an omnitemporal history of unconnected events, to chance. Lewis offers a solution that he hopes will explain away the inconclusive Un^{346} and Un^{349} cases:

> single-case chances follow from general probabilistic laws of nature . . . There are general laws of radioactive decay that apply to all atoms.

These laws yield the chance of decay in a given time, and hence the half-life, as a function of the nuclear structure of the atom in question … Unobtainium atoms have their chances of decay not in virtue of decay frequencies for unobtainium but rather in virtue of these general laws.

(Lewis 1994: 230–1)

This seems a sensible strategy. The main difficulty, however, is that the few-case problem of Un^{346} could reappear at a more, or the most, basic level. It is assumed that these more general laws of radioactive decay involve enough instances that their probability assignments can be reliably determined by the actual history of events.[16] (Exactly how many instances are enough, and the basis on which this number will be determined, is left unclear.) In our world, it is plausibly the case that there are many atoms, each of which decays. What of the world, however, that contains just two atoms, which decay after different durations? What, then, can we say is the general rule for radioactive decay? Lewis would be obliged to follow the same reasoning as the Un^{346} case, which is to conclude next to nothing about half-life. This world has, therefore, no laws for radioactive half-life even though it contains atoms just like our atoms and which decay.[17]

The response we might expect would again be that we had better hope nature has been kind to us and that our world is not such a world. Indeed, there is every reason to believe that our world is not such a world. When it comes to the testing of metaphysical theories, however, what just happens to be the case, contingently (on Lewis's own criterion), is not strong enough. A theory of laws should suffice for any world, even the one containing just two atoms. Hence I am not placated by the response that we had better hope our world is not such a world. Lewis has not shown convincingly that frequencies – more precisely, the pattern of events in the world – make *all* the chances. The thought may remain, therefore, that – on the contrary – chances make the pattern of events in the world, albeit in a chancy way. Humean supervenience, on this issue at least, remains in difficulty.

3.6 Humean supervenience

According to Humean supervenience, as described and developed by Lewis, the history of a world's events is *all there is* to that world. The world 'is a vast mosaic of local matters of particular fact, just one little thing and then another' (Lewis 1986b: ix). Everything else, including laws and chances, to be real must supervene upon this history. It is no good invoking unrealized probabilities or metaphysically real laws determining the history of the world. These things cut no mustard with the Humean.

There seems no way to find a direct refutation of Humean supervenience, as is true also of the pure regularity theory. Lewis has consistently followed the consequences of his premises. The counterexamples we might invoke carry weight only if one begins with anti-Humean intuitions. They will not persuade an opponent. But are the premises convincing? Are there really no necessary connections in nature but only a mosaic of unconnected matters of fact?

There is a strong intuitive appeal in the view of Humean supervenience because we are inclined to agree that all that exists is actual: all and only that which is actual is real. To exist, laws must have some kind of Being but what can this be? For Humeans, the world is a world primarily of events. The laws are given no independent existence in their own right. They must, therefore, if they are to have any Being at all, have an existence supervenient upon what is. According to Humeanism, this must be supervenience upon the history of events. But is it plausible that the world is atomistic: built out of units that are unconnected and exist independently of each other? And does Humeanism have too restricted a sense of actual? *Actual* must mean actual *events*: the contingencies of what happens to be the case.

Let us suppose that we can allow more things actuality. If we allow, for instance, propensities to count as actual, over and above the frequencies of events that emerge from them, then we have in sight a possible account of probabilistic laws that is not subject to the Un^{346} difficulty. Not just two but also the solitary atom can have a half-life if this is understood as a propensity for decay within a certain time with a certain chance. The facts of chance will not then be at the mercy of numbers of instantiations and frequencies of events, which are contingent matters. They can depend, instead, on propensities of kinds of object. Whether there would be a fact of radioactive decay in a world where there were no atoms can be treated as a different case. Could there be a law that ravens are black if there are never any ravens? Arguably not, because there is nothing that instantiates such a 'law'.

Powers may be taken as actual, which could then play a role in determining any regularities there happen to be in the world. Powers are *connected* with a class of events, however: their manifestations. They are, in virtue of this, un-Humean entities. But if a world of connected particulars is a more plausible metaphysic than one of unconnected particulars, that looks so much the worse for the restrictions of Humean supervenience. I will be developing these themes in Part III.

The regularity and best systems theories rest upon, I conclude, a certain metaphysical picture. Once the picture is accepted, the theories follow. Lewis has given good reasons for preferring his more sophisticated version of Humeanism but I have argued that there are no conclusive reasons why even a naïve, pure regularity theory cannot consistently be held. The metaphysical picture depicts a world of unconnected particulars with no intrinsic causal powers and no real laws. Is there a good argument for that picture? I will next consider this question, specifically by looking at Hume's argument.

4   Hume's argument

4.1 The Humean view of necessity and laws

Hume has many arguments but most of them will be ignored in this chapter as it is not intended to be a comprehensive survey of his philosophy. I aim to be selective and focus on the issues that are of particular relevance to our present subject. The claims in Hume that are of particular interest in respect of laws and necessity in nature are set out below. This recapitulates but slightly revises §2.6. Where:

CC = there are constant conjunctions, in other words, regularities
NCN = there are necessary connections in nature
NR = there are laws of nature = nomological realism,

Hume accepts:

$$CC. \tag{4.1}$$

But one of his most famous arguments is that:

$$\neg(CC \rightarrow NCN), \tag{4.2}$$

that is, while there are constant conjunctions, or regularities, Hume thinks this does not imply that there is any necessity in nature, a tie between the conjoined events, an ultimate spring or principle, or any such related thing.

Hume has further arguments against necessity in nature. It is not just that necessity cannot be inferred from constant conjunction but also that we have no direct, non-inferential experience of it either. The outcome of these arguments, added to his empiricist principles, is that Hume believes he has established:

$$\neg NCN. \tag{4.3}$$

There is little direct discussion of laws of nature in Hume.[1] However, it is relatively safe to attribute to Humeanism the view that:

$$\neg NCN \rightarrow \neg NR. \tag{4.4}$$

The claim that the so-called regularity view of laws is not a theory of real laws in nature is also pertinent here. A regularity view does not qualify as what I call a nomological realist theory. Laws are something more than regularities according to nomological realism. In the nomological realist view, a law is some kind of Principle of Order that makes the world regular in some respect.[2] Hume's arguments, in the *Treatise*, T: I and III, and *Enquiry*, E: VII, seem designed precisely to resist the inference to such a Principle from the world's regularity. Hence, NR is committed to some kind and degree of necessity in nature, as this is a natural way of thinking of such laws. NCN is thus a necessary condition of NR, in this sense of NR where laws are something over and above the regularities that they determine. Humeans and nomological realists alike should accept (4.4), therefore.

Despite developing a position that is neither Humean nor nomological realist, I too accept (4.4). I also accept (4.1), which cannot profitably be denied.[3] (4.2) and (4.3), and Hume's arguments for them, are far more revealing and controversial. I turn now to the details of Hume's argument for them.

4.2 The arguments of the *Treatise* and *Enquiry*

The starting point of Hume's argument is his theory of ideas. We can note the general commitment of his epistemology, namely, that all legitimate ideas concerning matters of fact have their origin in impressions. As Hume puts it: 'all our ideas are nothing but copies of our impressions, or, in other words, that it is impossible for us to *think* of any thing, which we have not antecedently felt, either by our external or internal senses' (E: 62). This produces a test of legitimacy that our ideas must meet. If they are legitimate, we should be able to say what the experiences or impressions are from which they derive. Hence, 'By what invention can we throw light upon these ideas, and render them altogether precise and determinate to our intellectual view? Produce the impressions or original sentiments, from which the ideas are copied' (E: 62). There are two kinds of reasoning that Hume deems acceptable. Reasoning concerning relations of ideas is known a priori; reasoning concerning matters of fact is known a posteriori. Anything that does not fall within these two categories is to be committed to the flames, 'for it can contain nothing but sophistry and illusion' (E: 165). This is, of course, a version of the standard empiricist epistemology, according to which nothing can be known to be real unless it is revealed in experience or can be inferred validly from what is revealed in experience.

This general commitment dictates the structure of Hume's argument against causes, powers, and necessary connections in nature. Hume argues:

1   that necessity in nature cannot be known a priori;
2   that necessity cannot be known through observation of any object;
3   that necessity cannot be known through observation of many objects and the relations between them.

Hume takes it that 2 and 3 are adequate to establish:

4   that necessity in nature cannot be known a posteriori.

Hume's 'fork' dictates more than the conclusion just that necessity in nature cannot be known. Necessity in nature is unavailable as a legitimate idea. We can form no positive conception of it so we cannot meaningfully talk of it. The very concept of a power, real cause, or any other variety of necessity in nature, cannot be applied.[4] I treat all these cases of necessity in nature as alike. Hume thought so too, as he said '*efficacy, agency, power, force, energy, necessity, connexion,* and *productive quality,* are all near synonyms' (T: 157). Necessary connection in nature I take to be the more general term to capture the whole of this family of concepts.

Here I will evaluate Hume's case for 1 to 4. In §4.4, I will consider the general conclusion he draws from 1 to 4, namely that there are no necessary connections in nature.

1   *Necessity in nature cannot be known a priori.*

Hume makes this claim, in a number of places, in the context of his discussion of whether causes can be known. For example:

> there are no objects, which by mere survey, without consulting experience, we can determine to be the causes of any other; and no objects, which we can certainly determine in the same manner not to be causes. Any thing may produce any thing. Creation, annihilation, motion, reason, volition; all these may arise from any other object we can imagine.
>
> (T: 173)

and

> I shall venture to affirm, as a general proposition, which admits of no exception, that the knowledge of this relation is not, in any instance, attained by reasonings a priori; but arises entirely from experience, when we find that any particular objects are constantly conjoined with each other.
>
> (E: 27)

These are instances of the more general empiricist view that 'reason alone can never give rise to any original idea' (T: 157). A priori reasoning concerns only the relations between the ideas. It cannot, on its own, generate new ideas but show only how they stand to each other.

I follow Molnar (2003: 117) in judging Hume to be right in this respect. There are, however, some cases where a priori reasoning may appear to bring new knowledge. This involves making inferences to things that may not have been self-evident prior to reasoning. However, there seems to be no obvious way of knowing specifically the causal powers of things a priori. If there is necessity in nature, then the best explanation seems to be that it is discovered a posteriori.[5] There is no longer any motivation for the realist to avoid this position as Kripke (1980) and Putnam (1975) have shown that something need not be knowable a priori just because it is necessary. The necessity in nature that is under consideration is to be dissociated, therefore, from logical and analytic necessity (see Ellis 2001: 11). While logically and analytically necessary truths do seem to be knowable a priori, one of the things that might distinguish necessity in nature is that it is not a priori knowable.

Hume has a related argument, however, that should be viewed with greater suspicion. It invokes a conceivability criterion of possibility, the adequacy of which has now come into question (Gendler and Hawthorne 2002).[6] Hume invokes it at T: 173, above, in terms of imagination, and in the following argument in terms of conceivability:

> There is no object, which implies the existence of any other if we consider these objects in themselves, and never look beyond the ideas which we form of them. Such an inference wou'd amount to knowledge, and wou'd imply the absolute contradiction and impossibility of conceiving any thing different. But as all distinct ideas are separable, 'tis evident there can be no impossibility of that kind.
>
> (T: 86–7)[7]

This complex passage contains at least three important and contentious claims, paraphrased in H1–H3:

> H1 No object implies another.
> H2 If an object implied another, it would be impossible to conceive them apart.
> H3 All distinct ideas are separable.

H1–H3 are contentious in the following ways. First, H1 may be true if the subject really is nothing more than objects, that is, substances as traditionally conceived. No substance, or particular, seems in an obvious way to imply another, distinct one. But Hume is commonly understood as standing against the traditional concept of a substance.[8] When Hume uses the term *object*, he often seems to be suggesting something much broader, where it means any thing or entity, including an event.[9] It is far from clear, with this broader sense of *object*, that no object implies another. In Chapter 10, I will be arguing that some *properties* imply others. By this, I do not mean entailment in the (solely) logico-linguistic sense. Rather, this implication is a *natural entailment*, or necessity, immanent in the world itself: between the properties rather than between the predicates we use to denote those properties.

Second, H2, whether true or not, is at least controversial as it is an epistemic and psychologistic criterion of possibility. The passage from T: 86–7 may be difficult to interpret with confidence, because of its mention of an 'absolute contradiction'. But it is clear that Hume accepts an important connection between conceivability and possibility, as illustrated by his assertion: '*whatever the mind clearly conceives includes the idea of possible existence,* or in other words, *that nothing we imagine is absolutely impossible*' (T: 32). But Molnar (2003: 181–5), Ellis (2001: 231–4) and others have argued that our own psychologies are not good indicators of what is really possible or impossible. What is really possible, impossible or necessary, must be independent of what we believe to be so. Our theory of modality must allow that we can have mistaken beliefs about what the modal facts are.

Third, H3 can be challenged because it involves what is controversial in H1 and H2. Being separable could be understood as an opposite of necessitating. What goes for H1, goes for H3 also, therefore, for it could be interpreted as a claim about immanent possibility just as H1 could be a claim about immanent necessity. It is not clear that all distinct ideas really are separable. But, also, Hume uses H3 as an intended support for H2. It seems to be an example of the conceivability test of possibility in practice: all distinct ideas are separable so they indicate objects that are genuinely, metaphysically, separate. What goes for H2 must, therefore, also go for H3.

While I do not take issue with Hume's view that the causal powers of a thing cannot be known a priori, therefore, I find his general account of modal knowledge to be less than satisfactory.

2   *Necessity cannot be known through observation of any object.*

Immediately following his dismissal of knowing an object's causal powers a priori, Hume argues that we cannot know an object's causal powers from an a posteriori examination. The following is a fine illustration of this view:

> Let an object by presented to a man of ever so strong natural reason and abilities; if that object be entirely new to him, he will not be able, by the most accurate examination of its sensible qualities, to discover any of its causes and effects. Adam, though his rational faculties be supposed, at the very first, entirely perfect, could not have inferred

from the fluidity and transparency of water that it would suffocate him, or from the light and warmth of fire that it would consume him. No object ever discovers, by the qualities which appear to the senses, either the causes which produced it, or the effects which will arise from it.

(E: 27)

The more general point is discussed later:

From the first appearance of an object, we never can conjecture what effect will result in it ... In reality, there is no part of matter, that does ever, by its sensible qualities, discover any power or energy, or give us ground to imagine, that it could produce any thing, or be followed by any other object, which we could denominate its effect. Solidity, extension, motion; these qualities are all complete in themselves, and never point out any other event which may result from them.

(E: 63)

Is Hume's view defensible? In one sense it is; namely, in the outlandish instance Hume asks us to imagine. Adam is perfectly capable of thinking, and he is rational, and yet he has never encountered water or flame. Can he discover their possible effects just from inspecting their qualities? Perhaps he could if he had seen similar substances that had similar effects but to allow that he had such other experiences would be to alter the spirit of Hume's argument. Rather, we are to suppose that, though perfectly rational, Adam has had no experiences at all to draw upon. Could he then, just from inspecting a substance, know what effects it can have? I agree with Hume that he could not. But I am concerned about the real possibility of the example. To Hume, though, the case seems conceivable and we have seen that this is enough for him to conclude that it is possible.

In practice, our reasoning seems to mature as we experience the world (which is not to say that our reasoning is made by experience). And in practice, it seems that there are cases where we can discover the possible effects of something by inspecting its qualities. To see that something has a sharp, rigid point is to see that it could cause pain, to see that something flows is to know that it will spread out if it is not contained, and so on. Certainly, this knowledge is based on previous experience of the world and Hume does not deny – indeed, he affirms – that we can discover from our experience what is constantly conjoined with what.

What is really at stake in 2 is whether the idea of necessity in nature, or necessary connection, can be discovered a posteriori through the inspection of a single object and consideration of no other matter of fact. Hume thinks that there is nothing in a single object that explains the origin of the idea of necessity. There is nothing in experience that explains the origin of the idea, which eventually is attributed to our own minds (T: 165–6: 'some internal impression'). This idea arises, Hume thinks, only when we move to consider many objects and the relations between them. While this explains where the idea originates, Hume does not think that the idea is evidentially licensed.

> 3   *Necessity cannot be known through observation of many objects and the relations between them.*

This is the point in Hume's argument where (4.2), above, comes into play: constant conjunction does not imply necessary connection in nature. This is stated clearly by Hume on a number of occasions:

> From the mere repetition of any past impression, even to infinity, there never will arise any new original idea, such as that of a necessary connexion; and the number of impressions has in this case no more effect than if we confin'd ourselves to one only.
>
> (T: 88)

This is repeated at (T: 163), then followed by a further argument:

> t'will readily be allow'd, that the several instances we have of the conjunction of resembling causes and effects are in themselves entirely independent, and that the communication of motion, which I see result at present from the shock of two billiard-balls, is totally distinct from that which I saw result from such an impulse a twelve-month ago. These impulses have no influence on each other. They are entirely divided by time and place; and the one might have existed and communicated motion, tho' the other never had been in being.
>
> (T: 164)

Hume sums up his commitment to ii at (E: 74), in such an clear and eloquent way that it might stand as representative of his whole metaphysic:

> upon the whole, there appears not, throughout all nature, any one instance of connexion which is conceivable by us. All events seem entirely loose and separate. One event follows another; but we never can observe any tie between them. They seem *conjoined*, but never *connected*. And as we can have no idea of any thing which never appeared to our outward sense or inward sentiment, the necessary conclusion *seems* to be that we have no idea of connexion or power at all, and that these words are absolutely without any meaning, when employed either in philosophical reasonings or common life.
>
> (E: 74)

This is a powerful and tempting line of argument. It has a special empiricist flavour. It allows that while I can observe the occurrence of X, Y or Z, I can never observe that X, Y or Z are necessary. Such modal facts are simply unobservable. *Necessarily-X* has no extra empirical content more than does simply X alone. As a matter of psychological fact, Hume thinks that constant conjunction is the explanation of why we have an idea of necessary connection in nature. Hence, if X and Y are constantly conjoined, we think them to be necessarily connected. But there is no evidential licence to move from X and Y being constantly conjoined to them being necessarily connected.

An upshot of this position is that it leaves us with a problem of inductive scepticism, as Hume acknowledged (T: 89–90). If X and Y were necessarily connected, there would be a reason to expect the next X to be a Y. But they are not connected so there is no reason why future Xs should be like past Xs, in being accompanied by Ys.

This concludes the initial presentation of the arguments of the *Treatise* and the *Enquiry* regarding necessity in nature. Bearing in mind that I have consented to proposition (4.4), that if there are no necessary connections in nature, there are no laws, a response to these arguments has an important place in the present book. But first I will divert into a different issue, namely, whether the above account entirely misconceives Hume and whether he did believe in necessity in nature after all. If he did, his position, which I have called Humean lawlessness, might not be so different from the realist lawless position that I will argue for in Part III.

4.3 Was Hume a sceptical realist?

Galen Strawson (1989) argues that Hume was not a denier of necessary connections in nature. Strawson is not alone in supporting a reappraisal of Hume as Wright (1983) and Craig (1987) have argued along similar lines. This flies in the face of the traditional interpretation of Hume but might be supported by appeal to occasional passages such as at (E: 66) where Hume says: 'And experience only teaches us how one event constantly follows another; without instructing us in the secret connexion, which binds them together, and renders them inseparable' (E: 66). Strawson argues that Hume was a realist about causal powers but that he thought such powers were always concealed from us by nature. The latter is only an epistemological claim, says Strawson, and Hume 'never seriously doubts that these powers and principles *exist*' (1989: 14).

Strawson's reappraisal of Hume has provoked vigorous debate (see Blackburn 1990; and Craig's 2000 and 2002 compromise). Most Humeans take Hume to be arguing against the reality of necessary connections in nature, not just to be arguing against their epistemic accessibility. When I speak of Humeanism, I will be referring to this traditional interpretation. Sceptical realism will be the name for the position of Strawson's Hume.

Even if Strawson's interpretation were right, a distinction can still be drawn between Hume and Humeanism, however. Hence, I think Strawson is wrong to accuse O'Hear of expressing the view that 'Hume held a regularity theory of causation' (1989: vii). Certainly it is not supported by the quoted passage, from O'Hear, that: 'Humeans hold that there is not "any more to causality than 'regularity of succession'" '(O'Hear 1985: 60). This remains, on the whole, true of Humeans even if Hume himself was a sceptical realist.

However, I think that David Lewis's interpretation of Hume was the right one, which is most borne out from readings of the *Treatise* and *Enquiry*. Lewis's interpretation is traditional and simple, namely that Hume was the great denier of necessary connections:[10] 'all there is to the world is a vast mosaic of local matters of particular fact, just one little thing and then another' (1986b: ix). Does Strawson mount an effective argument against this traditional interpretation? I claim not.

First, Strawson quotes extensively from the *Treatise* and the *Enquiry* in particular. The *Enquiry* seems most to support the idea of causal powers being real but hidden. But even the quotations that Strawson uses in support of the sceptical realist interpretation are not always obviously so. He prefaces his book with three quotations, for instance, which it is plausible to suppose he selected because they indicate Hume's alleged sceptical realism. But it is not clear that they do so. For example, '[W]e are ignorant of those powers and forces, on which [the] regular course and succession of objects totally depends' (E: 55). The claim 'we know of no X' does not obviously, or naturally, support the interpretation that 'there is an unknown X', which seems to be the interpretation Strawson would have us support. And for an empiricist, 'we know of no X' is an even more important claim than for others, as empiricists are committed, as we have already seen above, to the view that knowledge concerning what exists can only originate in experience.

I can see that there is at least some ambiguity in the selected quotation, which the sceptical realist may seek to exploit. While 'we know of no X' clearly does not entail 'there is an unknown X', might Hume's subsequent characterization of the X – that the regular course and succession of objects totally depend on it – indicate that he thought the X did exist? Much would depend on whether we could attribute to Hume the view that regularity and succession do depend on something or whether he thinks they just occur. The latter is the more common understanding of Hume. It is far from clear, in any case, that 'we know of no X that φs' entails 'there is an unknown X that φs'. If the sceptical realist's textual evidence is at best ambiguous, it does not provide strong support for their interpretation.

I will pick up these points again, presently, but first I wish to continue the question of the text. Strawson tells us that there are many occasions that Hume employs terms such as power, force, ultimate cause, tie and ultimate springs or principles. Strawson questions why we have not taken these uses at face value, as 'apparently referring uses of these expressions' (1989: 177). The traditional attitude has been to dismiss these uses as ironic. In the previous quote from the *Enquiry*, for example (E: 55), Hume is traditionally understood to be using irony against those who believe in such things as powers and forces. But Strawson thinks it improper to systematically read irony throughout such a series of apparently referring expressions.

Is Strawson's non-ironic interpretation more plausible? There are cases where Strawson helps himself to certain 'natural interpretations' of Hume's referring expressions and these seem questionable. For example, Strawson offers the following interpretations of Hume (where REF = referring expression, EP = epistemological point, and NI = natural interpretation):

> On [E] p. 42, Hume says that [REF]
>   *'the particular powers, by which all natural operations are performed,*
> [EP] never appear to the senses' (p. 42)
> And yet [NI] they certainly exist. He goes on to say that experience can [EP] never give any idea or knowledge of
>   *'the secret power,* by which the one object produces the other.'
> And yet of course it exists.
>
>   (1989: 184)

But is it really the natural interpretation of 'X never appears to the senses' to say that 'X certainly exists'? Compare 'a square circle never appears to the senses'. We would be reluctant to infer from it that, nevertheless, 'a square circle certainly exists'.

In helping himself to a putative natural, referring interpretation of Hume, Strawson makes what could be called the Meinongian inference. Meinong (1904) is sometimes associated with the view that we could only make sense of statements if all their terms referred (though see §11.7). If true, 'a square circle never appears to the senses' makes sense only if, in some way, there is a square circle that is referred to in the statement. We cannot even deny the statement if it fails to refer, on this view, as it would make no sense, hence have no truth-value. Russell's (1905) theory of descriptions shows what we should do to resist this kind of Meinongian-inference.[11] This would provide some reason, in answer to Strawson (1989: 178), not to take Hume's use of the words *power* and *tie* at face value and not obviously to be referring expressions. It is possible that something might exist that never appears to the senses, but there is no entailment from never appearing to the senses to existing.

Strawson appears to make the same Meinongian move when he says:

> to say that X is unintelligible or inconceivable or incomprehensible is simply to say that although X surely exists (or at the very least may

exist) it is something to whose nature we can form no positively con-
tentful conception on the terms of the theory of ideas.

(1989: 179)

To say that X is unintelligible is not obviously to say that X exists. Was this
really Hume's intention at (E: 74), when he said 'we have no idea of connexion or power at all, and that these words are absolutely without any
meaning, when employed either in philosophical reasonings or common
life'? Perhaps what is most important in this argument, however, is that it
leads us to the apparent inconsistency between causal realism and empiricism. While it is plausible to maintain that something exists of which we
have no conception, can an *empiricist* say, as Strawson urges, that X (a
power) exists even though X is unintelligible? If X is unintelligible, an
empiricist will assert, the words 'X exists' say nothing. If X is unintelligible, so is 'X exists'.

This makes it very implausible to say that Hume could have been a
sceptical realist *and* a traditional empiricist. Strawson favours the realism
about powers and acknowledges the inadequacy of the empiricist epistemology (1989: Chs 10 and 12). However, he still does not think that
Hume made a mistake because Hume did not hold the standard empiricist epistemology we usually attribute to him. Hence, we are not just mistaken if we think Hume was against powers, we are also mistaken in
thinking him a traditionally conceived empiricist. Instead, Strawson thinks
we can grant that Hume allowed that 'words can be supposed to *reach out
referentially beyond our experience*' (1989: 124). There may be a 'meaning
tension' (ibid.: 121) but no inconsistency in Hume because, says Strawson:

> Causation terms may manage to *refer* to something which we can intel-
> ligibly *suppose* to exist, and which Hume firmly believes to exist, even if
> we can form no positive *conception* of the nature of this something on
> the terms of the theory of ideas. Certainly this can be said to give rise
> to a 'Meaning Tension'; for Hume claims that Causation terms are
> 'unintelligible' or 'meaningless', as applied to objects, and yet he uses
> them.

(ibid.: 179)

If there is a tension between attributing both causal realism and empiricism to Hume, Strawson chooses to jettison the empiricism. To other
readers, this might make Strawson's case even less persuasive. If causal
realism is incompatible with empiricism, Hume could not have been a
causal realist, we might prefer to say.

Here is a further interpretation, which might be called a Molnar-inter-
pretation of Hume. Molnar spoke of a case where there was a triumph of
Hume's good sense over his ideological commitments (2003: 123). This
suggests the hypothesis that Hume might have been inconsistent. His

empiricist strictures rule against having any idea of the secret connection but he might yet have believed in such a thing. Hume scholars have tried to provide a single, consistent position for him. But even a great philosopher is capable of inconsistency. Indeed, inconsistency seems a priori a more plausible interpretation than any that attributes perfect consistency throughout a body of work.

Nevertheless, in this at times inconsistent way, there seems insufficient evidence to support Strawson's sceptical realist interpretation as being the intended meaning of Hume's stance. Humean lawlessness, on this analysis, is not therefore the same as the realist lawlessness that I will develop in Part III. Strawson's own preferred metaphysic will be closer to the realist view that I support. I have taken Strawson to task only for his view that Hume held our position.

I am nevertheless with Strawson in rejecting the standard empiricist epistemology, certainly in its pre-Kantian form. This empiricism generates a semantic argument against powers. It cannot cash out talk of powers in experiential terms, so declares talk of powers meaningless. I am not yet, however, offering an alternative epistemology, of the kind Strawson ventures above. I am rejecting the limitations imposed on concept acquisition by empiricism.[12] But I have not yet a positive epistemology, of the same comprehensiveness as Hume's, to offer in its place.

Having justified, to some extent, my support for the traditional interpretation of Hume as a denier of necessary connections, I return to the assessment of the worth of that position.

4.4 Humean scepticism

If the world really were a patchwork of unconnected events, would we be able to find so much regularity in it? Is the world far too ordered and predictable for us to believe that there are no necessary connections? Are all the patterns to be found in the world mere coincidences or are they indicative of real connections that result in reliable and testable sequences of events?

There are some reasons for supposing there to be a ground of the world's order, I hold, but these reasons do not amount to deductive certainty. Further, I will explicitly reject a move straight from regularity to laws. Such an inference will come under attack in Chapter 5. Those who think there is some necessity in nature must acknowledge the sceptical concerns about their position. Nevertheless, it seems that there is also a responsibility for anyone who adopts a lawless position to say something about the regularity and predictability of the world. They might argue, for instance, that it is plausible to hold that the world's regularity is coincidental or uncaused. My own position is that this is not the most plausible account of regularity. This will be a lawless position but one in which there will be some form of necessity in nature. Such necessity can provide a grounding for the regularity. But Humean lawlessness has necessary connections of no kind. The realist view will not convince the committed sceptic, of course. But I will argue that the arguments for realism are more persuasive than scepticism.

A (traditional) Humean sceptic will be at liberty to point out that Hume's position was precisely that nothing more than the constant conjunctions can be known. Hence, anything that is supposedly behind the conjunctions, necessitating and thereby explaining them, is nothing more than a posit. But why are we not entitled to say that we know, through their effects, that there are some necessities in nature? Nature is so well ordered, we might try to say, that we can judge there to be a Principle of Order responsible for regularity. According to Strawson (1989: 190), this was indeed the position of the sceptical realist Hume.[13] It seems the reason why this inference has been resisted by Humeans is that it is not deductively valid to infer necessary connections from constant conjunctions. Hume's (4.2) rests on his scepticism in cases where there is no deductively valid proof. But such scepticism gains leverage, I argue, by setting too high a standard of proof on the anti-sceptical realist. Should we really believe only that for which there is a deductively conclusive proof? What should count as a conclusive proof? And can we realistically aspire to conclusive proof concerning empirical matters, as the nature of the world to an extent is?[14] If not, then what better empirical evidence could there be for necessity in nature than the order and regularity of nature? But this is evidence that Hume is at pains to rule out, saying always that he can see the constant conjunction but can never see the necessity.

Strong scepticism is very hard to refute. Only when it lapses into self-contradiction, such as by asserting the knowledge that nothing is known, can we reject it with assurance. Though practically irrefutable, it yet remains unattractive. It is a sterile philosophy that unjustly prizes the ill-defined 'experience' as the (sole) source of knowledge (see Bealer 1992). It permits only the inferences from such experience that are deductively valid.[15] But as Molnar (2003: 123) argues, there are many other forms of reasoning: extrapolation, interpolation, and other arguments from analogy, that are useful but deductively invalid. Hume himself has occasion to use such arguments and yet rejects those of his opponents.[16] If we accept only those arguments that are deductively valid, then not only do we become sceptical about necessity in nature, we must also be sceptical about the existence of objects, other minds and the past (Molnar 2003: 123–4). If we combine empiricism and deductivism, we come up against a dead end. The acceptability of Hume's argument for (4.2), $\neg(CC \rightarrow NCN)$, depends on the acceptability of the scepticism that empiricism and deductivism generates. If we find the scepticism unattractive, there might yet be instances where CC is accepted as good but non-deductive evidence of NCN.

Perhaps, though, Hume was not committed to deductivism. Stroud

(1977: Ch. 3) rejects the deductivist interpretation of Hume. In this case, I will not enter the debate on the correct interpretation of Hume. Instead, I will note that were there not to be a constraint of deductivism, the argument against inferring necessities from regularities will have been weakened. We might, instead, be permitted non-deductive grounds for the acceptance of necessities. The less that Hume is a deductivist, therefore, the less force his argument against powers has.

Does anything other than scepticism recommend the lawless view? I believe so. If we cannot give a plausible account of what laws of nature are and what they are supposed to do, we might yet return to a lawless metaphysic. If one discards scepticism, therefore, one has not automatically accepted laws in nature. As yet, one has only accepted necessary connections in nature. We could, therefore, reject the sceptical argument against necessary connections in nature and also reject laws. This would be a return to a pre-Newtonian way of thinking, which Rom Harré (Harré 2001; Harré and Madden 1973, 1975), and others, have sought to revive. If necessity resides in the propertied particulars in nature, there will be no need for laws. Particulars are powerful in virtue of their properties. They are not powerless discrete units so do not require laws to make them act. Immanent necessity in nature might then become a good reason why there are not laws of nature.

4.5 Conjunction as evidence of necessity

Some anti-Humean metaphysicians have accepted necessary connections in nature but have then moved to defend laws (for example, Armstrong 1983). It seems that there is meant to be an evident connection between necessity and laws so the inference is drawn from NCN to nomological realism. This provides for us a further proposition to consider, namely:

$$NCN \rightarrow NR \qquad\qquad (4.5)$$

(4.5), I argue, is neither deductively valid nor, on reflection, non-deductively persuasive.

The reason to reject (4.5), as stated in §2.6, is that necessary connection in nature is a necessary condition for nomological realism but not a sufficient condition. Laws are a species of necessary connection and not all necessary connections are laws. One might, for instance, have a singularist view of causation in which a cause necessitates its effect but causal necessity is not the same as nomological necessity (cause and effect need not be subsumed under a law). One might also think that identities, such as the identity between the evening star and the morning star, are metaphysically necessary without being laws of nature.

If one accepts that the existence of necessary connections is insufficient for nomological realism, then the possibility of the third position between

Humeanism and nomological realism becomes apparent. This position is characterized precisely by the acceptance of necessary connections and rejection of laws, hence it is modally realist but lawless. Such a position involves the rejection of Hume's (4.3) and, for the reasons just given, the anti-Humean (4.5). (4.4) is accepted as is, of course, (4.1).

(4.2) has proved to be more complicated than it seemed. If it is intended to mean that NCN cannot be deductively inferred from CC, then it is not being challenged. But I have argued that it is unnecessarily strict and sterile to impose a deductivist constraint on (4.2). Does CC instead give good empirical evidence for NCN, without logically entailing NCN? I say it can, even though there remains the possibility of a constant conjunction that is accidental only. We can deliberately try to eliminate such possibilities. In designing experiments, we are looking for ways to test such conjunctions severely. As Popper said:

> [a scientist] will, with respect to any non-refuted theory, try to think of cases or situations in which it is likely to fail, if it is false. Thus he will try to construct *severe* tests, and *crucial* test situations.
>
> (Popper 1971: 14)

Our tests should be about seeking out the accidental conjunctions and thereby seeking out, through a process of elimination, those that indicate necessary connections. The better the tests, the greater will become our confidence that we have identified such a connection. But we never attain deductive certainty and nor should we expect to because CC is never more than symptomatic of NCN.

In cases where such appropriate measures have been taken, therefore, CC→NCN might be thought of as an acceptable inference. When understood as this kind of inference, and with a relaxation on empiricist strictures on what can be known, there might be reasonable cases where we can non-deductively infer NCN from CC. In Part III, I will offer a theory of what such necessity in nature might be, and in what way something could be regarded as a necessary connection without being a law.

Part II

Nomological realism

5 The nomological argument

5.1 What is nomological realism?

To be an anti-Humean means to accept that there are necessary connections in nature. Some anti-Humeans call these necessary connections laws of nature. Such laws must be, if this is an anti-Humean account, something more than a regularity of events or invariances or patterns. Rather, opponents of Hume think that there is something that makes there be a regularity, invariance or pattern in the world: there are necessary connections in nature. The subject of this second Part of the book is the theory that these necessary connections are the laws of nature. This view is to be called nomological realism: realism about laws. The Humean theories of laws that have been considered so far do not count as instances of nomological realism as they take a broadly deflationary approach.

What is essential for a theory to be nomological realist is that laws are understood as an addition of being. They must be something more than the regularities or patterns that are to be found in the world. If these anti-Humeans are right, and the necessary connections in nature are laws, then such an account has good credentials for being a theory of laws: a theory of nomological realism. Laws are seen as an addition of being that, it might be maintained, play some role in determining their instances rather than being entirely constituted by and exhausted by their instances.

The importance of stating this distinction – between genuine theories of laws and deflationary theories – is that many of the arguments to follow strike only against theories that are genuinely nomological realist. In Part III, the Central Dilemma will be raised against nomological realism. This dilemma is a problem for accounts that hold that laws are additions of being that are supposed to determine their instances. The dilemma challenges the plausibility of such an account of the world. But the dilemma will not strike at all against Humean deflationary accounts that take laws to be no addition of being. The Central Dilemma is only a problem for nomological realism, not for Humeanism.

Furthermore, the arguments for the existence of laws, evaluated in this Part, must be arguments for something more than regularities or patterns.

Nomological realism is a metaphysically stronger claim than Humeanism. It claims that there is something in the world that Humeanism denies. The aim of this Part is to discover how good the arguments are for that view. Is the addition of being, that nomological realism requires, warranted?

5.2 Do we need a nomological argument?

Before considering the arguments for nomological realism, I wish to consider whether there must be an argument at all. For some, it might be thought so obvious that there are laws of nature that it is a claim that does not require justification. The existence of laws might be thought undeniable. Nevertheless, as a matter of fact, I think that there is an argument for the existence of laws. I call this the nomological argument. Some philosophers have presented various forms of this argument.

The question addressed first is whether we need a nomological argument. If we do not need a nomological argument, little hangs on its success. If we do need an argument for the existence of laws, then the effectiveness of the nomological argument is an important matter.

Do we ever have a right to assume that something exists, without any further argument? Rarely, I judge. An argument for the existence of something can always be desired in metaphysics. There might be, however, different degrees in which the existence of something might be doubted. In some cases, the existence of some categories of things can be argued very quickly. There are some self-evident arguments that seem to demonstrate easily that some categories are non-empty. 'Something happens' is a self-evident and self-confirming argument that demonstrates that there are *events*. Certainly, the stating or considering of the argument is an event, so to understand the argument is to know that it is sound. The same consideration shows that 'there is something' is true.

But what about universals, substances, minds or sense data? The existence of these things seems less certain and more argument is needed to establish them. Self-evident arguments are harder to find for these categories.[1] In the case of laws and causes – indeed, any modal phenomena – a whole host of new complications are introduced that make their existence far easier to dispute. We saw in Part I that empiricists have a problem with allowing that something has a (non-trivial) modal-value in addition to its truth-value. This is based on a theory of what can be known: I can know P to be true or false but not that it be necessary in addition to being true, or possible in addition to being false.[2] According to this empiricist view, therefore, real causes and laws, if they are to be understood as involving modal commitments above and beyond regularities, are unobservable and we should doubt their existence pending a good reason not to.

Furthermore, it might be argued that the idea of a law of nature came into being relatively recently. As Ruby (1986) shows, laws were not a part of ordinary or intellectual parlance until Descartes (1644). This itself is not a good argument against the existence of something, as electrons and radiation were not conceived until even more recently yet we have little doubt that they exist. There is, however, strong theoretical and observable evidence for the existence of electrons and radiation. Is there equally compelling evidence for the existence of causes and laws? If not, then we might question whether the introduction of the idea of a law was warranted or was, as some think, erroneous.

I claim that we do need an argument for nomological realism, therefore. Primarily, this is because nomological realism is a theory that something exists which is not obviously an observable event and can coherently be doubted. Historically, many philosophers have doubted the truth of nomological realism. There will be more on what it might mean to say that there are no laws in Part III, as I will argue that Humeanism is not the only option if one rejects the idea of a law in nature. But now I move on to consider what the argument is for the existence of laws.

5.3 The argument

The nomological argument that is presented here is an idealized and regimented form of various arguments that have been offered more informally by those who have favoured versions of nomological realism and have taken the time to offer arguments in its favour. When I speak of the general sort of argument that has been advanced for laws, I will speak of the nomological argument. When I speak of the specific regimented form I have distilled from this collection of arguments, I will speak of argument NA. Though idealized, argument NA is intended as an honest depiction of some of the main things that have been said in favour of nomological realism. NA is the positive case for nomological realism. It offers more than reasons for disliking the regularity view of laws, though accounts of nomological realism may justifiably begin by illustrating the inadequacies of their opponent's position (see Armstrong 1983: Chs 2–5). The sort of argument that is typically presented is this:

[NA]:
      A There is a set *S* of features in the world.
      B There is *S* because there are laws of nature.

The characterization of the set *S* in NA is not an easy matter. This is partly because NA synthesizes what different philosophers have said at different times and places but also because there appears to be uncertainty and vagueness about what the features are in the world that laws are supposed to ground (see Chapter 8). I will leave the exact nature of *S* unstated, as it need not be resolved in order for us to proceed. But it might reasonably be thought to be something, in part or in total, like this:

$S = \{$Regularity (invariance, statistical regularity), order, universality, centrality, objectivity, explanation and prediction, necessity or counterfactuality$\}$

The argument is, therefore, that there are various things or phenomena in the world, such as regularity, necessity and predictability, and there are these things because there are laws of nature.

Note the ontological nature of NA. It might have an epistemological sibling, namely the claim that laws *explain* the existence of S but the ontological NA is taken to be primary. Laws are taken to be the ontological grounds of regularity, necessity and predictability. Laws explain such things because, and only because, they are the putative grounds of them.[3]

On what basis are the members of S selected? Regularity or order is the phenomenon in nature to which appeal is most frequently made, as the examples in the following sections will illustrate. The intended meaning is an association of events or properties; roughly, whenever A is instantiated, B is instantiated, where A and B are types of property or event. But this feature has come under detailed scrutiny of late, partly because of Nancy Cartwright's challenge. She has noted that pure regularities are not nearly as common as might have been thought. Such regularities are usually to be found only in simplified or idealized conditions. The pure, exception-less regularities are produced artificially, she suggests (1999: Ch. 3) by the carefully controlled experimental set-ups that she calls nomological machines. But this is not the only strategy for explaining the exceptions to regularities. Another is to accept the some regularities hold only given *ceteris paribus* qualification (see Schiffer 1991; Lipton 1999; Lange 2000: Ch. 6).

Two special cases should be noted: statistical regularities and invariances. Some associations are less than 100 per cent but are nevertheless significant and important for science. It may be noted, for example, that when one kind of event A occurs, another kind of event B occurs in 20 per cent of the instances. If this proportion remains constant, it may be deemed a regularity of sorts, namely, the regularity of a statistical proportion. While there is not a constant conjunction of As with Bs, one in five As are conjoined with Bs. Hence, we might prefer to say that there is a one in five conjunction of As and Bs. Such a statistical regularity might well be a part of the phenomena in S that we think real laws in nature might ground and explain. The exact relation between actual statistical frequencies and any statistical laws that are supposed to ground them, is difficult to outline. The nature of any real statistical law, certainly on a propensity interpretation (see Popper 1957; Mellor 1971), allows that the actual frequency of an occurrence of Bs in a sample may differ from the proportion in the law that is supposed to ground the frequency.

The idea of invariance originates with Haavelmo, when he spoke of 'invariance with respect to certain hypothetical changes' (1944: 29). The idea of invariance is useful in expressing what is regular or constant in the functional laws that must be expressed in equations (see Woodward 1992, 1997; 2000). Hence, for the case of gravitational attraction, we are able to find many particular degrees of attraction for objects of different masses and distances apart. But regularity can be found in these different degrees. What remains regular, or invariant, is the function $F = GM_1M_2/d^2$, through all the different values of M_1, M_2 and d.

The idea of order is intended to be more general than regularity, though regularities, in the kinds just described, would all be instances of order. Order might include things other than mere regularities or associations of events or properties, such as the neat patterns that we are able to find in nature. The periodic table shows how well ordered all the chemical elements are, for instance, with a rich structure and ordered similarities.

Universality is meant to convey the unchanging, stable nature of the world's order and similarity. The relations that held in the periodic table yesterday, hold also today and, we believe, for the whole of time. $F = GM_1M_2/d^2$ is true at every place and every time. There are many instances of this universality phenomenon and we might wonder why it is so. According to the nomological argument, it is because there are universal laws of nature that make it so. In contrast, many truths are less than universal. My front door is blue but my neighbour's is brown and others on the road come in a variety of colours. There is no universality to be explained here hence, we might suppose, no law of nature determining house door colours.

Centrality is a feature emphasized by Carroll (1994: Ch. 1). His thought is that our concepts (and the world to which we apply them) are nomically pervaded. Our way of cognizing the world depends upon the assumption of nomic phenomena. For instance, to say that something can be perceived is to say that it can cause a perception. But for one thing to cause another is for it to fall under a law, some believe. Hence, if there are no laws, there are no perceptions (1994: 10), and likewise for many other things. Carroll's argument will be considered in more detail below (§5.5) but the idea that there is some central feature of the world, holding together and pervading the rest, is a tempting one. What better explanation for this than that there are laws?

All these features in *S* are intended to be objective. Explanation and prediction have a look of anthropocentrism but are nevertheless intended to be mind-independent features. Hence, while human beings can give explanations and make predictions, there is also a sense in which the world is objectively explicable and predictable, in a non-psychologistic way. Hence, what makes something, P, a true and good prediction is not solely a subjective matter. What makes something, E, a true and good explanation is not solely a subjective matter. That the world can be explained and predicted, in these senses of explanation and prediction, is not a subjective matter and nor are the facts that the world is regular and ordered by something that is universal and central. Regularity is intended to be more than expectation and whether something is a good explanation or prediction is intended to be more than a matter of us thinking it so.

Necessity and counterfactuality are two of the most controversial features I include in *S* and are two of the most difficult to outline definitively and neutrally. There is, nevertheless, a widely held view that there are such things in the world. Humeanism is criticized for failing to accept these things (see Part I). We are urged to recognize that statements such as:

    i   no sphere of uranium 235 has a diameter over 100 yards
   ii   no sphere of gold has a diameter of over 100 yards

differ not in their logical form, nor in their truth, but in their modal value. i is thought to be true necessarily while ii is not (Armstrong 1997: 223).[4] Because i is necessary it can be said that it would support a counterfactual such as 'if *a* was a sphere of uranium 235, it would be less than 100 yards in diameter' while ii would support no similar counterfactual. If there is a division in reality between what is necessary and what is 'merely accidental', there had better be some reason for the difference. According to NA, the difference is that i results from a law of nature while ii does not. Laws are intended to explain, therefore, nature's *de re* modal division.

It was admitted at the outset that the argument presented in this section is idealized. Has anyone actually advanced an argument for laws of nature that resembles argument NA? In the next three sections, I provide some examples where things very close to NA have been said.

5.4 Without laws, there would be no order

I accept that the world is regular or, as I prefer to say more generally, ordered. It displays a discernible and distinctive array of patterns that, as Stevens says, 'bring harmony and beauty to the natural world' (1974: 3).

I take the central instance of the nomological argument to be the inference from regularity or order to the existence of real laws of nature as their explanation and ground. Here is a fine exemplar:

> Coconuts fall from trees and bounce when they hit the ground, puddles evaporate in the heat of the sun, running water erodes river banks, lightning strikes trees, pulsars radiate and so on. I . . . take it for granted that the explanation of such natural effects, and our capacity to purposefully and actively intervene in them, assume that they are in some way governed by laws.
>
> (Chalmers 1999: 5)

Sometimes we get a circular version of the argument, for example, 'although not logically conclusive, the lawful behaviour of the universe is the best evidence there is for nomic necessities (or probabilifications)' (Armstrong 1978b: 161). Armstrong may have meant merely that the world behaves as if there are laws. More usually, we get some ordered or regular feature of the world that is accounted for in terms of a law. This is apparent in the following argument, which reveals also a number of other things. It exemplifies a contrapositive version of the nomological argument before going on to offer a more standard version. Instead of arguing 'order, because there are laws', the contrapositive variety is the argument that 'without laws, chaos':

> The range of phenomena and objects in the universe is huge, from stars thirty times as massive as the Sun to microorganisms invisible to the naked eye. These objects and their interactions make up what we call the physical world. In principle, each object could behave according to its own set of laws, totally unrelated to the laws that govern all other objects. Such a universe would be chaotic and difficult to understand, but it is logically possible. That we do not live in such a chaotic universe is, to a large extent, the result of the existence of natural laws ... It is the role of natural laws to order and arrange things, to connect the seemingly unconnected, to provide a simple framework that ties together the universe.
>
> (Trefil 2002: xxi)

Trefil's view depicts the possibility of a world without general laws but then argues that such a world would be very unlike ours. In principle, he claims, there could have been a world without laws. Members of the same kind might not then have had the same kinds of behaviour. Each particular could be a law unto itself. The fact that it is not, is supposed to be evidence that there are general laws that control the range of qualities and possible interactions of a member of a kind. Without general laws of nature, we would then think it a mystery why all kind members have the same behaviour.

I will be arguing in Part III that this view of the world just like ours (containing the same kinds of thing) but without laws is wholly incredible, metaphysically unappealing and, contrary to Trefil's claim, is not a possibility at all – not even in principle. But if it is not a possibility, then does the argument that our world *looks as if* it is regulated by laws, carry any force?

The final class of arguments that fall under this category is the modally strengthened regularity arguments. These are the anti-Humean arguments that recognize that regularity or constant conjunction are not enough for us to infer laws of nature. A division between accidental and genuinely *lawlike* regularities is accepted and the inference then drawn from modally strengthened regularities to laws. This argument appears, as seen above, in Armstrong (1997: 223) and also in Carroll (1994: 2–3). The argument is roughly that there must be laws because there is something that is stronger than an accidental conjunction. Ellis (2001: 207) also accepts that laws must be more than accidents: 'Most philosophers would agree that laws are not just de facto or accidental regularities'. Laws are thus to contrast with accidents.

5.5 Without laws, there would be nothing

There is a radical form of the nomological argument, which says that without laws there would be nothing at all, or nearly nothing. If it can be shown that the existence of almost everything depends on there being laws of nature, then that would be a very compelling argument for there being such laws.

The argument has been advanced by Alexander Bird and, at greater length, by John Carroll. Carroll states bluntly: '*if there were no laws, there would be little else*' (1994: 3) – because laws are 'conceptually entwined at least' (ibid.: 4) with many other things, such as counterfactual conditionals, causality, generality and necessity, indeed 'nearly all our ordinary concepts are' (ibid.: 10). At greater length, he argues:

> these considerations greatly support *the centrality of the nomic*. It has become clear that if there were no laws of nature, then there would be very little else. If there were no laws, then there would be no causation, there would be no dispositions, there would be no true (nontrivial) counterfactual conditionals. By the same token, if there were no laws of nature, there would be no perception, no actions, no persistence. There wouldn't be any tables, no red things, no things of value, not even any physical objects.
>
> (ibid.: 10)

The argument is that all these things have nomic commitment: for them to be, there must also be laws. Without laws, the world would contain very little of significance. It would be an extremely emaciated world because 'The class of concepts without nomic commitments is just much too barren' (ibid.: 11).[5]

In Bird, this sort of argument follows after a more familiar version of the nomological argument:

> laws are important, a fact which can be seen by considering that if there were no laws at all the world would be an intrinsically chaotic and random place in which science would be impossible. (That is assuming that a world without laws could exist – which I am inclined to think doubtful, since to be any sort of thing is to be subject to some laws.)
>
> (Bird 1998a: 26)

According to this version, to be a thing is to be subject to laws. Given, as was earlier allowed, that 'something exists' is a certainty, then 'laws exist' is equally certain if, as Bird claims, the existence of any thing entails the existence of a law.

How plausible is this kind of argument and what is its force? I begin with Carroll's version. The first thing to note is that it is about lawhood being *conceptually* entwined with other concepts: 'concepts that all have a massive role to play in our habitual ways of thinking and speaking ... these other concepts infiltrate nearly all our ordinary notions' (Carroll 1994: 3). So this is a conceptual point. It does not seem to warrant the claim that without laws, there would be little else. At most, it shows that without the concept of a law there would be few other concepts. One cannot take the lack of a concept to show the lack of a non-conceptual thing in the world. It is plausible to assume that there yet remain things in the world that have not been conceived of. So none of this shows that if there are no nomic concepts, there is no world or that any remaining world would be a barren place.

Second, is it really not possible to have a consistent and coherent conceptual scheme that is free of laws? Might there not be mindful aliens that have conceptual schemes without nomic or any other modal concepts? Might there even have been humans who have had such conceptual schemes? Hume professed to have no idea of necessary connection (see Chapter 4). He may have accidentally allowed himself some modal concepts but Lewis achieved a greater consistency and outlined a view of our world that appeared to be entirely free of (intra-world) modal, hence nomic, concepts (see Chapter 3).[6] While Carroll does not appear to have ruled out a way of conceptualizing the world without laws, he might have succeeded in showing that nomic and modal concepts are central to *our current* conceptual scheme. But, as noted in the first point, this does not appear to prove the ontological claim that there are laws because a conceptual scheme does not prove the existence of its terms, just as the concept of phlogiston did not entail the existence of such a substance.

Later, Carroll does become more ontological, for example, when he says 'If there is any causation at all, then there is at least one law of nature.' (1994: 6). The same inference is also claimed if there is at least one disposition, perception and if there is persistence. The reason is that a cause must instantiate a law, according to Carroll, and all the things listed require there to be causes. In addition to this, Bird's version of the argument is also ontological rather than conceptual. Does the ontological version of the radical argument succeed? Again, I claim not. Whereas the conceptual version failed to prove that if there are no nomic concepts, there is no world, the ontological version fails to show that if there are no laws, there is no world (or no things, which we can grant amounts to the same). What I think the ontological arguments show, if they succeed, is that the world must contain some modal facts, some necessity in nature. But we have seen (§4.5) that we are not entitled to the inference NCN→NR. The things Carroll cites, such as perceptions and persistence require there to be causation. But it is controversial that causation entails laws as singularists deny this (Anscombe 1971; Armstrong 1999, 2004d). They give priority to the intuition that if *a* and *b* are particulars (events or facts), and *a* causes *b*, then nothing other than *a* and *b* – nothing extrinsic to them – grounds the fact that *a* causes *b*. What Carroll establishes seems to be, I propose, the *centrality of the modal*. Unless there is a further argument for equating the modal with the nomic, without assuming the falsity of singularism, he cannot claim to have proved the centrality of the nomic. Similar things can be said in response to Bird's view that to be a thing is to be subject to laws. What might motivate such a claim is that things are involved in a modal net: things in the world are interconnected. But the precise nature of these interconnections would have to be considered. They might not be laws. Chapter 10 offers an account of interconnections that are not laws. As long as some necessity holds the world together, it need not specifically be laws.

5.6 Without laws, there would be no science

Bird's argument also contained the claim that without laws, science would be impossible. This is an instance of a further version of the nomological argument, which has also been put forward by Chalmers and Lange.

Lange argues that much of science would not make sense without the assumption of laws. He takes his lead from actual scientific practice, saying: 'I am making my philosophical theory fit the facts of scientific practice rather than construing those facts to fit my theory' (2000: 6). He presents a specific argument from science to laws:

> I elaborate various intuitions suggesting that our beliefs about the laws make a difference to our beliefs about certain other matters ... I argue that scientific practice includes phenomena that the concept of a natural law should be used to save. This is the best way I know to argue against scepticism regarding natural law.
>
> (Ibid.: 4)

I take this to be an argument that can be summarized thus: there must be laws for there to be science. And, as there is science, there are laws.

Chalmers says something similar, with an emphasis on the scientific manipulation of the world: 'I ... take it for granted that the explanation of such natural effects, and our capacity to purposefully and actively intervene in them, assumes that they are in some way governed by laws' (1999: 5). Further: 'The facility with which physicists strive to manipulate unobservable entities in the laboratory, fully acknowledged by Cartwright, is difficult to reconcile with a position [hers] that denies that the behaviour of those entities is governed by fundamental laws' (ibid.: 9).[7]

Does this argument carry weight in favour of the existence of real laws in nature? I don't think the weight is ample. There are two reasons why it is insufficient. First, it is not clear why scientific practice should be taken as a reliable guide to philosophical, specifically metaphysical, truth. Even if science presupposed laws, it is not obvious that it would entail that there are real laws in nature. In Chapter 1, I tried to show why we cannot expect science to solve distinctly philosophical problems. We are still able to ask, therefore, whether science's presupposition of laws is valid.

This can be accompanied with a second point, however. Even if science requires, for it to make sense, that there are certain features of the world – predictability, counterfactuality and so on, it has not yet been demonstrated that science has any further metaphysical commitment to something that makes for these features, as NA would require. In particular, it is far from clear that there is a commitment to real laws in nature that provide these features. Indeed, Giere (1999) thinks that science has no such commitment.

This second point is a particular version of the general objection I would have against the arguments for laws that resemble NA, the idealized form of the nomological argument. These arguments do not show that laws, and only laws, are that which deliver the features of the set *S*. Nagel said, in his classic survey of science, that: 'Laws of nature are in fact commonly used to justify subjunctive and contrary-to-fact conditionals, and such use is characteristic of all nomological universals' (1961: 51). But could something else justify or make true subjunctive and contrary-to-fact conditionals and all the other features in *S*?

5.7 How compelling is the nomological argument?

I argue that the idealized form, NA, of the argument is not compelling and nor are the particular examples and variants of the argument that have been examined. The main vulnerability of the argument, in all these forms, is the failure to consider the alternatives to laws that might be responsible for the set *S* of features in the world. The world may very well contain *S* but it has not been shown that nothing other than laws could deliver *S* to the world. Indeed, in Part III, I advance a positive argument that things other than laws explain these features and I couple this with problems for real laws in nature delivering *S*.

If one is to claim that NA is flawed, in failing to consider the alternatives to laws, one approach has to be ruled inappropriate as an interpretation of the argument. It might be said that what NA is really about is defining law of nature as a theoretical term. If this is so, then it becomes an analytic truth – true by definition – that laws of nature are whatever ground the set of worldly phenomena listed in *S*.[8] It is not open to an opponent of laws, therefore, to claim that there are no laws because something other than laws grounds S. What one would be doing is merely providing a different theory of laws: an account of what it is in the world that constitutes a law. NA cannot, therefore, be criticized as an argument for failing to consider the alternatives to laws, as possible grounds of S, because it is analytic that laws are precisely that which ground S.

How worthy is this as a defence of NA? Ultimately, I think, it has to be rejected. The key issue is whether it is correct to treat S as supplying the content of a Ramsey sentence for laws and for which a theoretical identification is to follow in the form of one's preferred theory of laws. This approach could proceed as follows, loosely following the strategy of Lewis (1972). First, we say that there is something that grounds S:

R]: $\exists x \, (x \, \text{grounds} \, S)$.

We can then decide that x, whatever it is, will be called the set of laws of nature:

D]: $x = $ the laws of nature.[9]

A third stage would follow, of supplying the theoretical identification of x. This provides the positive, non-definitional content of x, of what it is in the world that delivers S. This will be provided by a theory T_L.

I]: $x = T_L$.

Finally, by transitivity of identity, we can conclude that:

C]: $T_L = $ the laws of nature,

which means that T_L is the theory of what instantiates the laws. If T_L correctly describes what it is that grounds S, then it tells us what, as a matter of fact, occupies the same role that *laws of nature* occupy as a matter of definition. Any two things that occupy the same role are to be identified.

The reason why I think this strategy is inappropriate in the case of NA is that I do not think the premise D can be upheld. It is not convincing that D is true by definition. Indeed, even if it were true by definition, it would provide an unconvincing version of nomological realism as it would then rest crucially upon a definitional *fiat*. The reason why we should not define the laws as that which grounds S is that the notion of a law is not sufficiently established as a functional term. Lewis invoked his strategy in the case of mental terms which, under functionalist theories of the mind, are defined in terms of what they do, or what causal role they occupy (1972: 248). Now although laws are, within some theories, said to perform certain roles in the world, this claim remains theoretical and one which it is logically possible to dispute. There has yet to be the kind of convergence of opinion that would make it true by definition that laws occupied this role (the role alluded to in R).[10] What this suggests is that the claim that laws occupy the role x is more akin to the theoretical identification at stage I of the Ramsey-analysis, where stage I, as we have seen, is not a purported definitional truth but is synthetic and a posteriori. If this is the case, then it is all that we need to respond to this particular defence of argument NA. It means that it is not true by definition that laws are that which ground S and it allows the possibility that there are other things that could ground S. What, if anything, grounds S can be decided only after the evaluation of the competing theories.

My main objection to NA is, therefore, that the alternatives to laws, that might ground S, must be considered. An alternative account might explain S just as well, or even better than laws do (Chapter 10). Indeed, I claim that one alternative account explains S much better than the laws of nature account. The reason for this is that it has never been adequately shown how laws could ground S. How could something be correctly identified as a law and yet deliver these features to the world? I argue (Chapters 6, 7 and 9) that it has not been shown that laws can do the job that has been asked of them. This would be a strong case against NA.

In summary, I think it can be shown that (a) other things can do the job we intended laws for; and (b) laws cannot do the job they were intended for. If successful, these arguments will make things look very bad for laws.

Before proceeding, however, I will consider briefly the view that S could be granted – the world has all these features – but that no further explanation of them is required. If this challenge is just, it might show that NA has a further flaw.

5.8 Cosmic coincidence

Swartz (1985, postscript) is sceptical about the idea of a law of nature. Laws, he thinks, come from the idea that the world *has to be* a certain way, rather than it just *being* that way. Swartz's own view comes from a denial of necessity in nature ($\neg NCN \rightarrow \neg NR$). He supports a regularity view, 'regularism', and offers the following diagnosis of the origin of the concept of a physical law: 'Having abandoned God, the next best thing to do is to invoke a depersonalized necessity' (1985: 204). Those of us who believe in necessity in nature, therefore, are unable to let go of an idea that someone or something makes the world the way it is.

Instead, Swartz proposes that the state of the world can be accurately described as a cosmic coincidence. It is just the way it is, for no reason at all. He accepts that it could be pure coincidence that 10^{60} things in the universe – electrons – could have all the same properties (ibid.: 203–4).

Some, however, have asked why these 10^{60} things have all the same properties. They have treated the fact, E, as an explanandum:

E: 10^{60} things have the same properties.

A putative explanans to this explanandum has been offered:

L$_1$: It is a law of nature that these 10^{60} things have the same properties.

Swartz's view is that E is not an explanandum, in the first place, so it does not need an explanation and certainly not an explanation in terms of laws. L$_1$ suggests that these 10^{60} things *have to* have the same properties, instead of it just *being the case* that they have them.

This position allows that there might be the features *S* in nature, or at least a number of them (minus necessity), yet we cannot infer a metaphysical ground of these features. If there is no ground to *S*, then there are no laws to be identified with that ground. There could just be regularities, including statistical regularities and invariances, and an objective order that permitted explanation and prediction, but nothing that gave the features *S* to the world. According to Humeanism, this is indeed the case.

What does this mean for NA? To show the way in which Swartz would reject it, we need to outline a slightly more elaborate version of NA, called NA*:

[NA*]:
    A   There is a set *S* of features in the world.
    B1 *S* has a ground.
    B2 The ground of *S* = laws in nature.

Swartz's view would mean that B1 is false, so we need not even consider B2 as one of its terms would have no reference. Laws are to be equated with the regularities in the world. They are exhausted by their instances, and this illustrates the difference mentioned in §5.1 between genuine nomological realisms and deflationary theories of law.

What are we to make of Swartz's claim that E is nothing more than a cosmic coincidence: a fact about how the world is but not about how it has to be? E has been selected, no doubt, because it appears to be one of the biggest coincidences of all. There is a vast number of objects in the world that are all the same. Such is the size of the number, it is highly suggestive that there is a reason for this fact. So is Swartz right to maintain that there is no such reason? I think, in one sense he is, and, in another sense, he is not. It depends what you think counts as an explanation.

Whether or not E needs an explanation, I do not think that L$_1$ would be a good one. I agree with Swartz that such a law has all the appearance of a *deus ex machina*, though perhaps without the God. However, I think that something illuminating can be said about E. In a sense this explains E, or at least explains why E is not a mystery or cosmic coincidence. This is the natural kind explanation of E:

K$_1$: these things have the same properties because they are members of the same natural kind.

But in a sense, K$_1$ also tells us that there is nothing at all to explain about E. This is because it tells us that there is no cosmic coincidence to explain. There is no mystery that all electrons have the same properties because any particular thing would not be an electron if it did not have exactly these properties.[11] We do not need laws to explain E but nor is E, as Swartz says, a cosmic coincidence. We could never have had $10^{60}-1$ electrons sharing all their properties while one recalcitrant electron, e^*, had different properties. If e^* does not have the same properties as the rest of the electron kind, it is not an electron.

What this shows is that if there is something wrong with the idea of a law of nature, because it is a depersonalized necessity, there is arguably also something wrong with the cosmic coincidence view. I explain this in terms of Figure 1.1 p. 15. Laws were a solution to a misconceived problem. The Humean view was a demodalized view of the world. Anti-Humeans then gave the world laws in an attempt to reintroduce the necessity they thought the Humean picture lacked. If the Humeans then take back the laws, they are still left with a demodalized view and, what Swartz refers to as, the cosmic coincidence view of regularities. Instead, I suggest, that we accept a world that has necessity inherently and intrinsically. If we accept this world, then we do not need laws to add the necessity that would otherwise be lacking and nor is the world's order a cosmic coincidence. Laws solved a spurious problem. Swartz spurned the solution but retained the problem. I seek to replace both the problem and its solution.

5.9 Patterns without laws

Stevens (1974) knows well and understands nature's patterns. But he doesn't invoke laws. There is nothing that needs to be added to nature to produce its patterns because nature has no alternative:

nature has no choice ... Her productions are ... encumbered by the constraints of three-dimensional space, the necessary relations among the sizes of things, and an eccentric sense of frugality. In the space at nature's command, five regular polyhedrons can be produced, but no more. Seven systems of crystals can be employed, but never an eighth. Absolute size decrees that the lion will never fly nor the robin roar. Every part of every action must abide by the rules.

(ibid.: 4)

Stevens explains away a number of mysteries where formerly laws of nature may have appeared. The structures of snowflakes and growth patterns of leaves, for instance, can be explained away in terms of the necessity to fill space or to save material. There could not be snowflakes with a pentagonal structure. The supposed contingently false law of nature, that snowflakes are pentagonal, was never a possibility. While space can be filled by an arrangement of triangles, squares or hexagons, it cannot be filled by pentagons (ibid.: 14–15).

This provides a model of how real necessity in nature could replace the old metaphysic of laws in nature. It shows how at least some part of *S* could be explained or explained away by something that does not look at all like a law of nature. Such geometrical explanations are not intended to explain the whole of *S*, however. Stevens uses them specifically for nature's patterns only. In Part III, I will outline some of the other relations that hold in nature, some of which are necessary. They are intended to show that laws are not needed.

5.10 A less direct argument for laws?

The nomological argument, as outlined in this chapter, is judged unpersuasive. Arguments of this ilk appear to be the best direct arguments that have been given for the existence of real laws in nature.

However, although there is no sound, direct argument for the existence of laws, might there not be, nevertheless, good reasons to believe in them? Often, things are not wholly clear-cut. We ought, therefore, to look at some of the best theories of laws of nature. They might offer us a persuasive metaphysical package that, overall and on balance, we think is acceptable. In the next two chapters, I consider two of the leading recent theories of laws. These are theories that seem correctly describable as instances of nomological realism. I will be trying to discover whether they are sufficiently compelling that we should accept either of them and thereby be supporters of realism about laws.

6 Natural necessitation relations

6.1 Real laws and their role

The theory of laws developed independently but simultaneously by David Armstrong, Fred Dretske and Michael Tooley has proved enduring and popular since it appeared in the late 1970s. Such popularity could be attributed to two main virtues. First, the theory, certainly as developed by Armstrong, has a neatness, simplicity, and yet systematicity that makes it very attractive for its own sake. Second, the theory contains a compelling critique of Humean approaches to laws. It professes to contrast sharply with regularity theories and what it offers in their place explains why such theories are irredeemable.

Because the theory is so neat, it has an almost aesthetic appeal. If true, it would offer a unified account of the relationships between laws, universals and causation. Unfortunately, aesthetics is no infallible guide to truth in metaphysics. For a reliable evaluation of the theory, we will have to weigh its metaphysical strengths and weaknesses. I will conclude that the weaknesses outweigh the advantages. Nevertheless, the advantages, were the theory correct, would be considerable. The theory succeeds in showing why universal quantification over particulars would not produce laws of the required necessity. Instead, laws are understood as connecting universals directly and their instances in particulars only derivatively. If you are going to accept that there are laws, this account is greatly superior to those that try to make laws from aggregates of particular associations. The latter account contains no reason why the next, or a counterfactual instance, should be like former instances. This weakness generates the problem of induction and has laws so devoid of necessity that they are at best only surrogate or deflated laws. In Part I, I considered such accounts and said that such metaphysics should properly be classed as lawless.

Armstrong's theory is realist about laws but, I will argue, it does not contain a sufficient justification for the claim that there are laws. Its nomological argument, like the others that were considered in Chapter 5, is insufficient. This need not be fatal to the theory as a future justification of laws might be forthcoming. However, I argue that the theory faces a more critical problem. This will be presented as a part of what I call the Central Dilemma.

Armstrong's realist theory is caught on the first horn of the dilemma. His laws are external to the things they govern. An account would be required of how such laws can govern properties from which they are apart. To deserve the status of real laws in nature, the role they play in relation to their instances must have some serious metaphysical power: the laws must do something. Their role, which is sometimes called a governing role, cannot be purely metaphorical or attenuated, for even the Humean might be prepared to say that regularities govern in a (completely) attenuated sense. Nomological realism – the theory of the reality of laws – is committed, therefore, to laws having a specific, ineliminable role of their own. The Central Dilemma presses the issue of what this role is and how it operates.

The first horn of the Central Dilemma suggests further that if a response can be given to this first issue, in terms of laws that are external to what they govern, the resulting position would imply quidditism. The undesirability of this implication will be explained in some detail. The core idea, however, is that the theory implies that we could have a world with entirely different laws that nevertheless contained the very same properties as our world. I argue, with others, that this is implausible. The reason why can only be seen after consideration of the theory of properties. Can the theory avoid its quidditist implication? I argue not. If any theory has laws that are external to the properties they govern, it is logically possible that they could vary independently of them. Indeed, Armstrong exploits this very point in his argument for the contingency of laws. Were someone to deny this aspect of the theory, perhaps in an attempt to avoid quidditism, they would owe us an account of how laws and properties were distinct existences yet were connected in such as way as to forbid independent variation. Further, this would have to be an account that was not prey to the second horn of the Central Dilemma. The danger of the second horn will be illustrated in Chapter 7, while the dilemma as a whole will be the subject of Chapter 9.

I have started with this broad overview in order to make clear the place of the theory in the book's argument as a whole. Much of the rest of this chapter will be concerned with detailed arguments but we must not lose sight of what is ultimately at stake. Has the theory justified the category of laws of nature and has it produced a credible account of what such laws are? I answer both questions in the negative after, I hope, a fair assessment of the detail of the theory.

Finally, by way of introduction, there is a point of nomenclature. I will henceforth refer to the subject of this chapter, following Armstrong, as the DTA theory of laws (or just DTA), named after its co-discoverers, Dretske, Tooley and Armstrong.[1] As there will be many references to the works of the co-discoverers, they will be denoted simply as D, T and A in this chapter.

6.2 The basic DTA theory

In this section, I will set out enough of the core of the DTA theory to allow
the argument to proceed. There is some slight variation in the details of
the theories of Dretske, Tooley and Armstrong, but I will describe those
later, in §6.4. Here I am concerned with the common core of DTA. More
specifically than that, I am concerned with the common core that is useful
for my own purpose, which is to show that such a theory cannot be satisfactory and thereby to motivate my own lawless position. It is inevitable
that I make most reference to the theory as provided by Armstrong
(1983), however, as his is the most detailed presentation of the theory we
have.

The basic core idea is that we have a law of nature when we have a relation of natural necessitation that holds between other universals. Relations
are more commonly thought of as holding between particulars, such as *a*
being to the left of *b*. We represent such as relation with the form R(*a,b*),
where R is the relation involved and the particulars are taken as an
ordered pair. But this is not the only possible case of a relation. It is a first-
order universal (a relation) between first-order particulars. There is no
reason, however, why there cannot be a second-order relation between
second-order particulars (A 1983: 88). A second-order particular is a first-
order universal. Hence we could have the relation R between two universals F and G, which would be represented R(F,G). According to DTA, laws
of nature are such cases of relations between universals. There is a law
when the relation between universals is the nomic necessitation relation
N, hence laws have the form N(F,G).[2] There is room for some variation in
this necessitation relation, however. Some laws may be probabilistic only,
in which case the relation would best be described as one of nomic proba-
bilification (A 1978b: 158–9). Some laws might not concern necessitation
between universals but, instead, nomic exclusion. And some might relate
more than two universals. The central case remains the basic necessitation
relation N, however.

An ontology that permits real universals is a pre-requisite for this theory
of laws. N, F and G must be taken as universals, so this theory is not available to the nominalist (A 1983: 81–5; D 1977: 267; T 1977: 667). That the
law concerns a relation between universals explains the universality of its
instances. It adds the necessity missing from the regularity theory. Regularity theory took the form of a law to be a universal quantification over
particulars, $\forall x\,(Fx \rightarrow Gx)$. But this will not suffice to represent a law. Laws
do not relate particulars, directly. Rather, they relate the universals that
those particulars instantiate. The main innovation of DTA was the claim
that laws were about the relations between universals or properties and
only indirectly did they concern the particulars that instantiate those
properties. Hence, the fact that *a* was an F and a G, *b* was an F and a G, *c*
was an F and a G, and so on for any finite number of particulars, could

never entail that the next, or a counterfactual, particular was that an F would be a G. There is no necessity at all in the purely extensional $\forall x$ $(Fx \rightarrow Gx)$. Some attempts were made to patch up this formulation, but none were successful, for the reasons given in Part I. Instead of trying to revise this kind of approach, we need to accept that laws relate universals. If there is a necessity from F to G, this explains why everything that is F will be a G, for anything that is, was, will and might be F. N(F,G) is therefore said to entail $\forall x$ $(Fx \rightarrow Gx)$ but, because of the inadequacies just explained, $\forall x$ $(Fx \rightarrow Gx)$ does not entail N(F,G).

The nomic necessitation relation N must relate distinct universals (A 1983: 138). This means that the theoretical identities, such as water = H_2O, are not laws of nature. Where it is true that water = H_2O, we do not have two, distinct properties to relate. Armstrong has an a posteriori realism about properties where they are not simply predicates or the meanings of predicates. Water = H_2O would tell us that being water and being H_2O were the same property. They would not be genuinely distinct properties that are fit to be related nomically. It is wrong, therefore, to speak of composition laws (Pap 1962: 363), bridge laws (Fodor 1974) or any theoretical identity being a law (Mellor 1980: 148).[3] Later, I consider further what does and does not qualify as a law (Chapter 8).

There is an instant problem with the necessitation relation N. It seems to be a mere posit. While this may be true of Dretske's and Tooley's more brief presentations of the theory, Armstrong has tried to mitigate the appeal to N (1978b: 164–6). This also explains how causes and universals are related to laws, in Armstrong's systematic position. Armstrong has a broadly Aristotelian view of universals in which they exist in their instances, immanently, instead of transcendentally. This means that, to be real, a universal must have at least one instance, at some place and time. But laws, as conceived by Armstrong, are universals. They are relations between properties, so higher-order universals.[4] To be real, therefore, laws must have instances. What would the instances of laws be? Armstrong says that particular causal sequences are the instances of laws. This accounts for the tempting intuition that we are prepared to say that *a* causes *b* only when *a* and *b* fall under a general law. The relationship between laws and causes is very neatly explained by Armstrong's version of DTA, therefore. But this also provides a way for Armstrong to say that N is something more than a mere posit, in his theory of laws. N can be known, like all universals, through its instances. Hence, we know of the nomic relation through knowing causes. Whether causings can be experiences is a contentious matter, but Armstrong, for one, believes that we can have direct, non-inferential knowledge of causes (1978b: 165), in contradiction to Hume. In the cases of our own bodies, where forces are applied to it or exerted by it, for instance, we experience causation. We have direct experience of instances of N, thereby, so N is arguably something more than a mere posit.

6.3 Key virtues over the regularity theory

The regularity theory has been faced with a number of problems, some of which were outlined in Part I. The DTA theory does considerably better, if you accept that these are genuine problems. Committed and consistent Humeans might deny that there were serious problems in their lawless metaphysics and claim that the features the regularity theory supposedly omits are not there to begin with (see §3.3).

Let us take stock of the things the DTA theory claims to provide that the regularity theory allegedly cannot. I will break these claimed advantages down into individual items though they are connected – indeed, the DTA theory explains how they are connected.

First, the DTA theory is able to distinguish between accidental and genuinely nomic regularities in a way that the regularity theory could not (A 1983: 99). We have seen, in the previous section, that everything that is F also being a G does not entail that there is a law that N(F,G). While a law entails a regularity, then, not every regularity – where we have a constant conjunction of universals – will be the result of a law. Those that are not are merely accidental and involve universals that are not nomically related.

Second, the modal character of laws is explained. Where we have a law relating F and G, we do not say that this F just happens to be a G, or that every F just also happens to be G. Rather, we think that something which is F *must* also be a G (D 1977: 263–4). The DTA theory thus can allow that there are modal features within nature and that laws are more than accidents because they have such modal force.

Third, and closely related, DTA laws support counterfactuals (A 1978b: 149 and 1983: 103; D 1977: 255, 264–5). Where we have a law connecting F and G, we think that if this x, that is not an F, were F, it would also be G. $\forall x \, (Fx \rightarrow Gx)$ would not support this inference as it says nothing about things that are not F. But N(F,G) entails that anything that was F, even something that is actually not F, would be G if it were F. The DTA theory claims a major victory over the regularity theory, here, as the concept of a law seems to include the support of counterfactuals (see §5.3).

Fourth, 'grue-some laws' are ruled out (A 1983: 99). These would be laws based on 'pseudo-uniformities' that involve predicates like grue (green before tomorrow, blue after). Science will show (Armstrong is confident) that this predicate is not a natural one; that is, it is not a predicate to which a real universal corresponds, on the a posteriori realist view of universals. Laws can connect only the genuine universals, which are things that exist in the world rather than just in language, so will never connect the spurious grue-some cases.

Fifth, a reason is given why laws cannot be spatiotemporally limited, certainly in Armstrong's version of DTA (A 1983: 100). Laws, as universals, have an identity in all their instances. Every instance of a particular universal F is the same. This applies for every time and place. Where there is a relation between universals, therefore, it also holds omnitemporally and omnispatially, claims Armstrong (A 1983: 79).

Sixth, as has already been stated, the account explains the link between laws and causation better than any other theory (A 1978b: 149; Heathcote and Armstrong 1991). Contrary to the claim of singularism, every case of causation does fall under a law. But the theory also explains the appeal of singularism. Only the particular events, α and β, and their properties, F and G, are involved in α causing β. Causation thus remains intrinsic to α and β even though it is in virtue of the properties F and G, and their nomic relation, that there is a causal relation between α and β. Properties are wholly present in their instances and so, too, are the relations between those properties, hence we can accept the singularist insight that nothing extrinsic to α and β is involved in the causation of β by α.

Seventh, regularities do not explain their instances but relations between universals do (A 1983: 102). The Humean account of laws states only that there is a regularity. It cannot, therefore, explain *why* there is a regularity. The regularity theory only summarizes its instances (D 1977: 267) while DTA laws relate universals so there must be identity in all their instances (A 1983: 87–90). N(F,G) thus explains why $\forall x\ (Fx \rightarrow Gx)$.

Eighth, universal regularities cannot be confirmed (D 1977: 256) but DTA laws can be (D 1977: 267 and T 1977: 687–93 using Bayes' theorem). There is a potential infinity of instances of a law and on the pure regularity theory there is no reason at all why the next instance should be like the last. No matter how many instances have been observed, therefore, we cannot confirm that a regularity is genuinely universal, therefore genuinely a law. If laws are nothing more than universal regularities, therefore, they will remain unconfirmed. But DTA laws are not merely about regularities. They are about the nomic relations between properties. Investigation of a property, and its nomic relations, would thereby be sufficient to know what would happen in unobserved instances and would, thereby, constitute confirmation of the law.

Ninth, regularity theory permits, perhaps invites, inductive scepticism. For reasons that should by now be apparent, the DTA theory claims that it does not (A 1983: 103–6).

Tenth, the basic account can be extended to account for functional laws, probabilistic laws, and qualified laws, Armstrong claims (A 1983: 101). The regularity theory struggles to find accounts of these cases, which might, after all, be the most common cases. Laws might rarely involve natural necessitation, for instance, but instead might involve just the probability of a second property, given a first property. David Lewis has conceded how difficult it is to find a plausible Humean theory of chance (1986c). The problem is that Humeans try to get chances out of frequencies of actual events. But real chances or probabilities do not entail any actual frequency so there is no reason why the frequency of Gs, in a sample, should be proportionate to the probability of G (§3.3). I will detail at the end of the next section how Armstrong extends his basic account to cover probabilistic, functional, and qualified laws.

Finally, there is a more general advantage that perhaps unites what is common to a number of the particular claimed advantages. DTA laws *govern* particular states of affairs (A 1983: 256), which they cannot possibly do in the regularity theory. Humean accounts tell us that the laws supervene on particular states of affairs – the vast mosaic that makes up the whole manifold. But this means that their metaphysic lacks any modal features. If there are no modal features, there is very little metaphysical backing for our epistemology to build on. Hence, Humean resources struggle to provide accounts of induction, confirmation and explanation. The DTA theory does not, of course, prove that there are modal features in nature and nor does it prove that induction, confirmation and explanation are rational. But if we are already attracted by the rationality of these things, and the need for some *de re* modal truths, DTA wins easily over the regularity theory because it is consistent with their rationality. The most difficult Humean response to counter, we have already seen, is the one that simply denies necessity and the rationality of any belief in it or from it. The notion of governance, in the DTA theory of laws, brings much with it, therefore, and is a key mark that distinguishes such a nomological realism from Humean lawlessness.

6.4 Variants on the DTA theory

The core of the DTA theory, we have seen, is the idea that laws are the holding of relations between universals, which can be represented as N(F,G). There are, however, some points of detail on which the three main proponents of the theory take different attitudes. Some of these differences entail further differences within the theory. There are also some points that are developed in one version of the theory but not others.

One important difference is between Armstrong and Tooley over the issue of uninstantiated laws. Tooley allows that there could be some laws that are without instances (T 1977: 671), whereas Armstrong explicitly rules out uninstantiated laws (A 1983: Ch. 8). The cause of this disagreement is that Tooley accepts Platonic realism about universals or at least accepts that it is not incoherent (T 1977: 686). We have seen, already, that Armstrong favours an Aristotelian immanent realism, a central commitment of which is that every property must have at least one instantiation at some time or place. This can be called the *instantiation requirement*. Armstrong accepts a general assumption of four-dimensionalism, which means for the instantiation requirement that an instance is required only at some place and time in the total world history. Armstrong came upon his theory of laws from developing a theory of universals (A 1978a, 1978b) but Tooley came across it by thinking directly about laws. Tooley uses the case of an uninstantiated law to motivate the core theory. If there are laws that are instantiated in no particulars, then this would seem to favour the theory that laws connect universals rather than particulars. Tooley also cites another case, to motivate the theory, which is the emergent property case. Tooley thinks that emergent properties are possible (T 1977: 683). Like other properties, it would be natural to think that they could be involved in laws. But if an emergent property just happens never to be instantiated, because of the accidents of the world's history, then the laws which govern that property would also never be instantiated.

Armstrong is sceptical about these cases (A 1983: 123–6). He does not think that an uninstantiated property is even possible because he supports a combinatorial theory of possibility in which all possibilities are recombinations of existing elements (A 1989).[5] Tooley would not be free, therefore, to avail himself of untutored intuitions about the possibility of uninstantiated laws and properties.

I will not judge on the issue of uninstantiated laws as I aim to develop a lawless metaphysic in which there are no laws at all, neither uninstantiated nor instantiated.[6] But I will have something to say on uninstantiated properties and combinatorialism in Chapter 10.

This issue relates to two further differences between Tooley and Armstrong. First, Tooley allows that logically equivalent sentences must express the same law (T 1977: 695–7). But Armstrong identifies constraints on what equivalences there are for laws, which follow from his instantiation requirement and theory of universals. N(F,G) may be a law but the apparently equivalent N(¬G,¬F) is not. For there to be a law that N(¬G,¬F), ¬G and ¬F would have to be instantiated, which they cannot be because they are not real properties. Armstrong rules, in principle, that there are no negative properties (A 1978a: Ch. 14). N(¬G,¬F) cannot be a law, therefore, because we have a law only when we have a relation between universals, which ¬G and ¬F are not. Therefore, laws do not contrapose. It would nevertheless be true that $\forall x \ (\neg Gx \rightarrow \neg Fx)$ whenever N(F,G) because N(F,G) entails $\forall x \ (Fx \rightarrow Gx)$, which does contrapose to $\forall x$ $(\neg Gx \rightarrow \neg Fx)$. But the key feature of the DTA theory is that for there to be a law, more than the truth of a universally quantified conditional is required: namely, there must be a relation between universals. Without these constraints of instantiation on universals, Tooley explicitly permits contraposing for laws (T 1977: 697).

A second difference concerning the issue of instantiation is that Tooley permits *exclusion laws*, where having one universal excludes, rather than necessitates, the having of another. Armstrong initially endorsed the possibility of exclusion laws (A 1978b: Ch. 24), which would have the form N(F,¬G). But for the reasons given above, about the instantiation of negative universals, he then worried about how an exclusion law could be instantiated. In (1983: 143–6), Armstrong considered various ways to avoid uninstantiated (underived) exclusion laws,[7] such us permitting higher-order 'totality facts' (1983: 145). If we have the positive laws plus the totality fact that these are all the laws, then we would not need additionally specific exclusion laws to account for exclusions. Armstrong, at one point, even countenanced the acceptance of negative universals (1983: 146) as a way to allow that such exclusion laws have instantiations. When he revisited the topic (A 1997: 233–4), his discussion was again inconclusive. Because Tooley has no instantiation principle, he has no problem with exclusion laws (T 1977: 676, 679).

As I believe Armstrong's Aristotelian realism is a more plausible theory of universals than a Platonic realism, and because Armstrong's version of DTA has been developed in greater detail, I will henceforth be discussing Armstrong's version with its instantiation requirement for laws. We have seen, above, that this makes it harder to account for some cases of putative laws. However, while I argue mainly against what I take to be the best form of the DTA theory, I think also that Tooley's more liberal attitude to universals generates its own problems. Armstrong's theory, I will argue, has a problem explaining how laws could govern their instances. But if Tooley prefers, instead, a Platonic view of law governing, I suspect it will fare little better.

A further difference between Tooley and Armstrong, which is independent of the issue of instantiation, is that Tooley allows, or at least takes very seriously, the possibility of spatiotemporally limited laws. We have seen already, above, Armstrong's reason for not permitting these. An example Tooley discusses, throughout his paper, is a law that seems to apply only to fruit in Smith's garden. They are all apples (T 1977: 668). Any fruit tree planted in Smith's garden grows apples, whether or not it was an apple tree that was planted. Any fruit brought to Smith's garden either turn into apples upon entry or are barred from entering by some unseen force. Can we say there is a law that applies only to Smith's garden? Given that acceptance of the DTA theory, it would seem not, but Tooley considers the possibility that there be some property that figures in a law but which can only apply to one kind of thing, such as fruit in Smith's garden. The problem with spatiotemporally limited laws, however, is that they lack the universality that is supposed for laws. This is one of the key features of the world that laws were supposed to ground; hence they are part of S in the nomological argument NA (§5.3). It is doubtful that we could relax the requirement of universality and still be talking about laws.

I move now to the version of the theory developed by Dretske and how it differs from Armstrong's. Two points are worthy of note. The first is the analogy Dretske makes with legal laws, which does not occur in Armstrong or Tooley. Dretske notes (1977: 264) that 'The legal code lays down a set of relationships between the various *offices* of government'. Laws are about the power of the presidency, for example, and thereby, but only indirectly, they are about the particulars that occupy (or instantiate) the presidency.

The analogy has not been taken up by others.[8] Largely, metaphysicians have tried to keep apart the notions of legal and moral laws from natural laws though, I think, it is sometimes a struggle to do so (see Chapter 12).

A more obvious difference between Dretske and Armstrong is that Dretske leaves open the possibility of many different nomic relations (1977: 253, n. 7) while Armstrong takes it that the same, or one of just a few, nomic relation(s) is involved in each case. Dretske uses a single connective '→' for all laws, reading it as 'yields', but says that it is merely a dummy connective and the precise meaning can differ in different laws. Armstrong uses the same N relation for all laws but allows some variety. Probabilistic laws can be allowed (A 1983: Ch. 9) by saying that they are probabilities of necessitation (A 1983: 131), instantiated only when the probability is realized. Functional laws can be admitted as higher-order laws having instances in the particular laws relating specific values (A 1983: Ch. 7). Finally, 'oaken' or qualified laws can be permitted (A 1983: 147–50), which are cases where N(F,G) *unless* H. This is an attempt to deal with the *ceteris paribus* problem for laws. Armstrong admits that such qualifications may be of infinite length (A 1983: 149).

6.5 Some perceived weaknesses of DTA

Just as I did not attempt a comprehensive survey of all the past criticism of the regularity theory of laws, in the case of the DTA theory, I will not attempt to be complete. I will ignore most of the vast wealth of literature that the theory has generated and, instead, concentrate on the aspects and weaknesses of the theory that are relevant to the lawless stance that I will advocate in Part III. I begin with a list of some of the relevant perceived weaknesses of the theory. I will not offer too much detail until later in the chapter but I will say, at the end of this section, how the perceived weaknesses relate to the lawless metaphysics I want to support. I consider seven perceived weaknesses of the DTA theory. They are addressed most directly to the version of the theory expounded by Armstrong (1983), but the Dretske and Tooley versions of DTA are either subject to the same problems or other problems in their place.

First, the theory contains a limited form of Humean supervenience. It tells us that there is a law if and only if there is an instance of a law in a particular causal sequence. But whether there is such an instance depends upon which properties happen to be instantiated. Hence, H, which would be a basic determinate property, may not be instantiated. In other words, there is no (instantiated) property H. There can be, therefore, no law that N(H,I). To a degree, therefore, what laws there are depends or supervenes upon what particular events, with their properties, happen. Note that there cannot be a law that makes H be instantiated. Because it is uninstantiated, it can figure in no law.[9]

Second, the relation between laws as universals and their instantiations is unclear. The first perceived weakness, above, means that the instances to an extent determine the laws, rather than vice versa, and this is a surprising situation for a supposedly realist account of laws. It might be wondered, therefore, whether laws explain their instances as the singular causal transactions appear primary. Is it the case, therefore, that the instances instead explain the laws? If laws do not explain their instances, in what sense is the DTA theory a theory of nomological realism?

Third, the relation of natural necessitation invoked in the theory appears *sui generis* and *ad hoc*. We might well be concerned, therefore, whether there is any such thing and whether it has merely been created just for the purpose of filling in a huge gap in the immanent realist metaphysic. The situation might be even worse than this. Armstrong speculates that the nomic necessitation relation N, might be the *only* second-order relation (A 1983: 84). The relation would then face the *sui generis* charge *qua* specific relation that it is (nomic necessitation) and *qua* second-order relation. Is there any independent reason to think that there could be second-order relations? Can no other plausible case be found? Is Armstrong's view that we can have direct awareness of the instances of nomic necessitation compelling evidence of their existence? If not, what do we really know about the nomic necessitation relation?

Fourth, the natural necessitation relation is required to be at once contingent and necessary.[10] There appears to be no other example of something that combines these different modal values. Armstrong's view was that when there is a relation between universals, any instance of those universals, in our world, must also instance the relation between those universals. This follows from his view of instantiation and his four-dimensionalism. But there are other worlds where those same universals stand in a different relation to their actual-world relation (A 1983: Ch. 11). Hence, F and G might be nomically related in our world and thereby everything that is F, in our world, must (nomically) be a G. But in another world, F and G might not be nomically related and there could be things that are F but not-G. Similarly, there might by nomically unrelated universals in our world that in other worlds are nomically related.[11]

Fifth, it is contestable that laws of nature are universals rather than particulars (or as well as being particulars). Armstrong at first thought that a law must be a particular because of a principle he called the *victory of particularity* (1978a: 115, n. 1). This principle ruled that a particular *a* plus a universal F made a further particular, hence the principle might be expressed in the formula $<P + U = P>$. *Fa* is a particular because it is incapable of repetition, hence it is the sort of thing he later called a fact or state of affairs (A 1997). The same consideration would also apply to relations and rule, where *a* and *b* are particulars and *R* a relation, that $R(a,b)$ is a particular. But Armstrong then extended the treatment of relations to higher-order relations. A higher-order relation, such as R(F,G), even though it involves only universals, is also a particular because, he thought, it is incapable of repetition. It is an obtaining of a relation, where an *obtaining* is particular. In (1983: 88–93), Armstrong reverses this decision and says that laws are capable of repetition. As we have seen, he came to think that laws have instances in causal relations between particulars. It is hugely advantageous to Armstrong's metaphysic that he has found something – causation – that can count as the instantiation of law. But this advantage is real only if, first, Armstrong was right to change his mind to the view that laws are universals and, second, if causes can correctly be viewed as instantiations of laws.

Sixth, why should nomological relations be external to their relata? This question raises a potentially serious problem for the DTA theory.[12] It is the problem that, I argue, leads us towards the eventual downfall of the theory. It can be put another way. Why do we need the relation N, in addition to F and G, to get the entailment that $\forall x\ (Fx \rightarrow Gx)$? The question is simple but opens up a Pandora's box of metaphysical issues. Might it be argued that F alone makes it that anything that is F will also be G? This is controversial, though I will be arguing for it in Chapter 10 within the context of a causal or relational theory of properties. If F is intrinsically or internally related to G, then we do not need to add an extra relation N (which might be contingent, *ad hoc* and *sui generis*) to F, in order to get G.

But Armstrong could not say that it is F alone that necessitates G. There are two reasons why not. First, Armstrong wished to allow that there could be other worlds that contained F but in which being F does not necessitate being G. This can only be maintained if it is claimed that there is something extra, added to F, that makes it nomically necessary that G. This something extra, N, must be a distinct existence from F and capable of independent variation from it. For laws to be contingent, therefore, there must be something outside the relata that relates them nomologically. This kind of relation is known as an external relation: a relation external to its relata.

This may appear to be no big worry as there is a view, important in the development of analytic philosophy, that external relations are the only relations we should permit. Russell's (1911) view was that the most important step in overcoming British Hegelianism was the rejection of its doctrine of internal relation. But the rejection of *all* internal relations is now being thought by some as an over-reaction on Russell's part.[13] In trying to escape Hegelianism, Russell has committed himself to a doctrine that has a thoroughly Humean basis. Relations are taken to be external, it might be thought, precisely because there are no necessary connections in nature and any particular thing might therefore be combined or related with any other thing. This may not seem a concern to Russell, nor so much to the 1983 Armstrong. But those of us who reject Hume, as I have done in Part I, may be suspicious of it. If we want to revive internal relations,[14] a place to start could be properties and laws. If F has an internal relation to G, a relation contained entirely within the natures of F and G, then there is no need to invoke a separate and external nomic necessitation.

The second reason why Armstrong must add N to F, in order to get G, is that he thinks that all properties are categorical (A 2004a). There are no irreducible dispositional properties or powers, in Armstrong's metaphysics, so F alone could never have the power to create a G. Only if a law N is added to a categorical property F, will something else G be necessitated.

Seventh, if the nomic relation is an external relation, the DTA theory of laws appears to entail quidditism about properties. As we have seen, the theory permits that different universals might be nomically related in other worlds to those that are actually nomically related in our world. But this would mean that a property, F, might be the very same property even if it featured in different laws to those it actually features in. This entails, on Armstrong's version of DTA in which causes are instances of laws, that the instances of properties could have different causal roles. The objection to such a view is that there is no adequate reason for saying that it is this very same property F that has a different causal role in the situation where there are different laws. It might be thought that its causal role exhausts a property in that there is nothing at all more to it than what it does, or its relations with other properties (see Chapter 10). Change those relations and one thereby changes the property. If this is true, then a property's identity is connected necessarily with its causal role. How could one avoid this conclusion? One might try to claim that a property has some individual essence, some quidditas, that would make it the same property in the two different situations with different laws (Black 2000). But this is not offered as a serious way out of the difficulty. Rather, it is usually suggested in the spirit that it would be such a desperate move that one should instead reject the commitment that prompted the difficulty: the doctrine of external relations.

This completes the seven perceived weaknesses of the DTA theory. I have already indicated that my reasons for rejecting the theory are that it does not have a sufficient justification for why there should be laws and that, as I will go on to argue, it is caught on the first horn of the Central Dilemma. But before moving on to that, I will explain what will become of the seven perceived weaknesses. In Chapter 10 I will explain away some of them. Specifically, I will argue that the idea of a relation that is both contingent and necessary is ultimately acceptable. This will mean that the third, fourth and fifth perceived weaknesses are not fatal in this respect. I will not be following the DTA theory exactly, but I will show that some claims similar to these are sensible. The second, sixth and seventh perceived weaknesses are weaknesses indeed. These are that DTA laws do not determine their instances, that they are external to their relata, and that they dissociate a property from its causal role.

These weaknesses arise from the general problem the theory has of how laws can govern or play any role that would be appropriate for real laws in nature. This will be the first horn of the Central Dilemma. How can laws govern their instances if they are external to them? What role do they have in determining events? I answer that they can have no such role.

Finally, whether the first perceived weakness really is a problem depends on your attitude to Humean supervenience. I have tried to make the case against it in Part I. Given that Armstrong is generally against the Humean approach, it might be thought that he is vulnerable to some of his own attacks against Hume. Ellis's (2001) diagnosis of Armstrong's view is that he has only rejected some but not all of Hume. His external relations, for instance, are Humean and remain. Ellis claims that the problems besetting Armstrong's position originate in its attempt to marry the irreconcilable Humean and realist positions. Humean supervenience seems a case in point as it raises the awkward question of how laws can govern the things upon which they supervene.

6.6 Armstrong's nomological argument

I have already outlined the general structure and worth of the nomological argument in Chapter 5. Here, I will examine the merits of Armstrong's own nomological argument. This will serve a number of purposes. It will serve as a case study of the argument as deployed by a leading theory of nomological realism. It will show, also, how well motivated is the DTA theory of laws. In the wider context of this book's argument as a whole, it will serve to show that no sufficient and philosophically satisfactory justification is given for realism about laws.

Some general words of warning, already mentioned in Chapter 5, apply to this specific case. The argument that can be found for laws, in Armstrong's version of DTA, probably is not intended as a conclusive proof of the existence of laws. Like many other philosophers, Armstrong, I suspect, thinks that the existence of laws is so obvious that it does not stand in need of proof. A few things are said in support of the assumption but they may not have been said consciously as an explicit attempt at proof. My concern, therefore, is whether anything said by Armstrong might be useful in the construction of an explicit proof.

The basic structure of the idealized metaphysical version of the nomological argument (NA) was suggested as:

A. There is a set *S* of features in the world.
B. There is *S* because there are laws of nature.

An epistemological version was also suggested, where *B* says instead that the laws explain *S*. The metaphysical version was taken to be primary as the best justification of explanation, in this case, is metaphysical. I will be attempting to answer three questions. Does Armstrong say anything that resembles NA? If so, what does Armstrong take the set of putative nomological features *S* to be? Finally, does he offer an adequate justification of the move from the premise *A* to the conclusion *B* of NA?

Armstrong does make some claims in support of the view that there are laws. We have already seen, in Chapter 5, the argument where he says: 'although not logically conclusive, the lawful behaviour of the universe is the best evidence there is for nomic necessities (or probabilifications)' (A 1978b: 161). Under a literal interpretation, this argument would indeed be conclusive, though in a trivial, hence unconvincing, way. There is lawful behaviour only if there are laws. Further, this would indeed be the best evidence for there being laws, as it would *entail* that there are laws. But if you do not accept that there are laws, you will not accept that there is lawful behaviour, in this sense, so you will not accept the argument as compelling. I have little doubt, however, that Armstrong did not intend such a trivial interpretation of this argument, though it may be indicative of him holding a view that the existence of lawful behaviour – behaviour governed by laws – needed little justification.

Is there a non-trivial interpretation of Armstrong's argument? It could be intended to mean that there is behaviour in the universe that is in accord with laws, or as if there were laws. But could we specify this more precisely in a way that avoids any reference to laws? Elsewhere, Armstrong makes claims that might do the job. He argues from regularities to laws in a later work (A 1997: 220–3). The regularity theory had attempted to build laws entirely from regularities without appeal to anything further. Armstrong accepts that there are objective regularities – regularities in nature – but argues that such objective regularities could be delivered only by appeal to universals, as in the DTA theory. Nominalism cannot deliver the right kind of regularities. Nominalists who have realized this have had, therefore, to deny that there are laws (van Fraassen 1989). We have seen that the Humean metaphysics has to be an essentially lawless one. Humeans may have things that they call laws, but these are surrogate laws such as the axioms of systematizations, useful tools in prediction, and so on. There are, however, no laws *in* nature. The realist view, in contrast, says that there is something that grounds and explains the world's regularities. Moreover, according to the DTA theory, the right kind of regularities can be grounded only by higher-order relations between real universals, in the way that has been described.

Before evaluating Armstrong's nomological argument, it should be noted that this is not the only thing he says in support of there being laws. He notes, for instance, that it is one of the tasks of science 'to state the laws which things in space and time obey. Or ... to state the laws which link sort of thing with sort of thing, and property with property' (A 1983: 3). A little more detail is added later: 'The scientist trying to establish the geography and history of the unobserved portion of the universe must depend upon what he takes to be the laws of the universe. Otherwise he is helpless' (A 1983: 4). It is one of the central assumptions of science, therefore, that there are laws to be found, investigated and used in prediction (§5.6). What is more, there is no rational inference to unobserved cases unless there are laws: 'on the supposition that there are no laws, the inferences would not be rational' (1983: 4). Armstrong admits, however, that these are purely epistemological concerns though they might lead us to enquire into the ontology of laws. These points cannot be taken as a persuasive justification of the existence of laws. They show only that the laws of nature are assumed or that there are epistemological questions to be answered if they are not assumed. They do not seem to fit the metaphysical version of NA.

Is Armstrong's version of NA, as described above, and with a non-trivial interpretation, persuasive? I think not. Armstrong seems to acknowledge the vulnerability of the argument when he says: 'The causal connection between state-of-affairs types remains a postulate, of course. But who ever thought that laws were not postulated, were not an inference from the regularities in the world?' (A 1997: 229). This is suggestive, contrary to NA, not that there are regularities because there are laws, but that there are laws because there are regularities. To demonstrate that there are laws in nature, according to NA, is to show that there is some feature in reality that could not be there if there were no laws. Laws, and laws alone, would have to be the only things that could ground these features. There would be objective regularities because, and only because, there are laws. But the quotation above suggests, instead, that laws are merely inferred from those regularities. There must be laws because there are objective regularities. But how safe would this inference be? Not very, I maintain. It may be that there are regularities but there is some other reason for them or, as Humeans think, no reason at all.

There is some consideration of the possibility of regularities without laws. In one place (A 1983: 5), it is dismissed as 'truly eccentric'. Elsewhere, Armstrong is more conciliatory. He is prepared to consider the *powers* view, which says that it is powers, rather than laws that deliver the world's regularities. This is similar to a claim that will be developed in Part III of this book so it is necessary to consider whether Armstrong lands an early, fatal blow against the view. Surprisingly, he thinks that the powers view might bestow an evolutionary, psychological advantage on its holder (A 1997: 254). If we treat the things around us as intrinsically powerful, it might help us in planning how to interact with the world. But this practice is metaphysically mistaken and a Humean diagnosis of 'projection' is offered. Armstrong thinks that the laws view has a distinct advantage of unifying phenomena (A 1997: 235–6). DTA laws posit a single (nomological) fact that explains by uniting all the particular phenomena. The alternatives – regularities and powers – lack this unification as they refer only to many, dispersed facts about particular associations between events or of many particular powers.

However, there has been recent work on alternatives to laws that suggest the unification problem is not insurmountable. The question, 'why is it that everything that is F is a G?', is seen as misconceived, by the powers view. If it were a genuine problem, it would indeed be possible to answer that every F is a G because there is a law to that effect. But those who prefer powers to laws are prepared to say, in some cases, that if something is not G, it is for that reason not F.[15] The property, F-ness, may have an internal relation to the nevertheless distinct property, G-ness. If so, then there is no genuine problem of unification. The phenomena unify themselves, in virtue of their properties, so do not need laws to do it for them. Armstrong's claim of simplicity may count against his theory, therefore. The powers view does not invoke lots of extra nomological facts, in addition to properties. The view just invokes the properties alone and it is Armstrong's ontology that is seen as over-inflated because it requires, additionally, laws *qua* external relations between universals.

Armstrong has other concerns about the ontology of powers (A 2004a) but these will not be considered and countered until later, in Chapter 10.

We can now answer the three questions about Armstrong's version of NA. It has been shown, first, that Armstrong does indeed say something that resembles NA. Second, we have seen that he has identified certain features of the world that could be taken to constitute S in his version of NA. But, third, we have seen that he has not adequately justified the inference from premise A to conclusion B. An argument has been advanced that could be seen as an attempt to infer laws, rather than anything other than laws, from S, but we saw that this was not conclusive. Perhaps Armstrong considers a view of objective regularities without laws 'truly eccentric' only because such a view has yet to be sufficiently developed and vindicated. This shows that we have a task ahead of us.

6.7 The nomic relation

The conclusion of the last section was that it had not yet been proved that laws were the only things that could deliver to the world the so-called nomological features of S in the nomological argument. If something other than laws can ground and thereby explain things such as objective regularities, then the argument is not a proof. The existence of laws would not have been justified.

But the situation might be even worse than that, as far as nomological realism goes. It might be possible to show that although other things could deliver the desired features in S, real laws of the kind nomological realism advocates cannot. If this can be demonstrated, things look very bad for nomological realism and the nomological argument. From here until the end of this chapter, I will develop the claim that the DTA view struggles to find a credible explanation of how laws would generate the required regularities and other features of laws. The argument is that it is implausible that the world contains such a special relation (this section) that is at once supposed to govern the world's events (§6.9) while, to an extent, it appears supervenient on them (§6.8). But even if there were such a thing, it would almost certainly entail quidditism, which is a bad consequence (§6.10).

What, then, is the nomic relation? We have already seen that it is to be understood as a higher-order relation, that is, a relation whose relata are also universals. It is an external relation that Armstrong characterizes (A 1983: 155–7) as irreflexive and non-symmetrical. Armstrong also thinks the relation is non-transitive and does not contrapose. Tooley (1977: 697) thinks the relation does contrapose and that it is transitive.[16] They both say that the relation is contingent (A 1983: Ch. 11; T 1977: 673; see also D 1977: 264). Dretske and Tooley tell us in addition that the relation is non-extensional in that one cannot replace its relata with extensional equivalents and be certain still to have a law (D 1977: 250; T 1977: 697).

These bare logical properties still do not seem to tell us what the nomic relation is. They do not tell us what the relation does, what indispensable role it has and how it is able to satisfy that role. Our best idea of the relation seems to be provided entirely by its name: it is nomic necessitation. But this has only raised the concern that such relations are '*ad hoc* because there is nothing more to them than what they are defined to do' (Mellor 1991: 168). What they are defined to do, their *only* role, is to entail the associated regularity. Hence the claim that $N(F,G)$ entails $\forall x\ (Fx \rightarrow Gx)$ is allegedly all we know of the nomic necessitation relation and the only apparent reason for its name. Tooley says that a law *logically* entails the universally quantified conditional (T 1977: 672), but how? Just being called nomic necessitation is insufficient to make it so, as Lewis has wryly observed (Lewis 1983: 40).[17]

Armstrong has attempted to rise to this challenge and add an explanation of how and why $N(F,G)$ necessitates $\forall x\ (Fx \rightarrow Gx)$ and thereby deserves its name. While the attempt is commendable, however, the detail he provides may just succeed in highlighting further potential problems.

Armstrong's explanation depends upon his commitment to an immanent realist general theory of universals. This is the theory that universals (properties and relations) exist only immanently; that is, they exist only in their instances. The same is then true of laws, *qua* universals. Put in terms of states of affairs, the nomic relation is described (A 1997: 225–6) simply as a causal relation that holds between state of affairs *types* (universals) instead of particulars. But because the law $N(F,G)$ is itself a universal (a state of affairs *type*), it must be identical in its instances (its *tokens*). Identity of instances is what is supposed thereby to ensure that $\forall x\ (Fx \rightarrow Gx)$ whenever $N(F,G)$.

This seems to be the only serious attempt within the DTA theory to explain the required entailment. But it generates its own problem by having a universal so closely connected with its instances. Universals as transcendent forms, existing apart from and independently of their instances, are rejected. How, then, can the universal, the law, govern its instances when it is existentially dependent upon them, or nothing more than them?

6.8 Instantiation and supervenience

Although Armstrong presents his theory of laws as an alternative to Humean accounts, there is within it, nevertheless, a limited form of the Humean supervenience claim. The law, as a universal, has no existence without its instantiation in particular causal sequences. But which such particular events are instantiated in the world's history cannot be upheld as anything more than an accident. Which (underived or atomic) events occur cannot be bound by or determined by laws because laws have no existence outside such events. This makes it hard to understand how Armstrong can maintain the claim that the nomic connection 'is a "direct" connection between these state-of-affairs types, that is, between universals. It does not hold between universals via their instances' (A 1997: 226).

The supervenience claim of Armstrong's DTA theory can be illustrated as follows.[18] For it to be a law that N(F,G), there must be at least one instantiation. Suppose that F and G are basic atomic universals so that N(F,G) is an underived law. Suppose, also, that the law has only a single instance in the whole of our space–time. Hence, there is just one instance of F, in a particular a, and a's being F causes a's being G. The theory permits this possibility. Next consider the possible world that is just like our first but in which there is not this single instance of F, nor any other instance of it in the whole of this world's space–time. There is no instance, therefore, of something's being F causing the same thing to be G. Even Armstrong's combinatorialism allows that where P is a property (pleonastically, an *instantiated* property), it is possible that it be not instantiated so it is possible that it be not a property.[19] N(F,G) is not a law in this world, therefore, as it has no instance. It is a world in which there is no F. Thus, it is a world in which there is no Fx causing Gx. Thus, it is a world in which there is no law N(F,G).

Can there be anything that makes F be instantiated in the first case but not in the second? Not according to the theory. The instantiation of F is that in virtue of which the law exists: the universal exists only in its instances. So the law cannot determine that F is instantiated because unless F *is* instantiated, there is no such law.[20] Nor, does it appear, that anything else in Armstrong's metaphysic could determine that F is instantiated.

The possibility produces at least two findings, therefore. First, the theory of laws as universals, coupled with an Aristotelian, immanent account of universals, makes laws metaphysically dependent, or supervenient, on their instances. For example, on a's being F causing a's being G. As their instances are causal sequences between instantiated properties, laws are also thereby dependent on the instantiation of these universals: in particular, on the instantiation of F. Second, the instantiation of F, where F is an atomic, underived universal, is dependent on nothing. Whether or not it is instantiated, in this sense, is an accident of the world's history. A law may supervene upon such an accident, therefore.

The case presented is not, then, too dissimilar from the Humean supervenience that we encountered in §3.6. There, laws supervened on the vast mosaic of unconnected events that made up the total history of the world. Nothing determined what those events were; their occurrence was entirely contingent. Laws did not govern their instances, as they were supervenient upon them. Armstrong's theory allows real causal connections, so is anti-Humean in that respect. But we have seen that his instantiation requirement for laws means that laws supervene upon the instantiation of their component universals. There are at least some cases, the underived laws, where nothing determines the instantiation of those component universals. Their occurrence can be entirely contingent. We can question, therefore, to what extent Armstrong's laws can be said to govern their instances.

6.9 How can Armstrong's laws govern?

If the DTA theory is to be a genuinely realist theory of laws, and a genuine alternative to the Humean conception of laws as supervenient upon an essentially lawless natural history, laws must play some specific, ineliminable role in that history. But what role are DTA laws supposed to play and can the proponent of the DTA theory provide a credible explanation of how their laws play that role? If they cannot answer these questions, the credentials of the DTA theory as a viable realist, anti-Humean, theory of laws will look suspect.

Is there a strong sense in which laws govern the world's events? If this is supposed to mean that laws are outside nature but nevertheless sending down their orders to nature, as Plato once described (*Phaedo*, 1961a: 102–7), then such governance is a 'profoundly mysterious doctrine' that Armstrong cannot advocate (A 1997: 226).[21] Is there a weaker, more naturalistic sense of laws playing a governing role? Armstrong offers a story of metaphysical ascent that is supposed to explain such a sense of governance (A 1997: 227). There is nothing to a law other than instantiations in causal sequences. But we can make a 'scientifically minded', 'likely supposition' that 'every singular causal sequence is in fact governed by law'. Once we have made this ascent, we can throw away the ladder that has got us there and accept that 'The fundamental causal relation is the nomic one, holding between state-of-affairs types, between universals.'[22]

Apart from the admission that DTA laws are a supposition, we can well wonder what the sense is in which they govern their instances. To adapt Lewis's point, just calling laws *governing* does not make them so. The only relation between laws and causal sequences that has been adequately described, and which seems reasonable if laws are higher-order universals as the theory says, is the instantiation relation. Causal sequences are the instances of laws. But, as we have seen, this makes laws existentially dependent on their instances, under the most credible account of universals. They are supervenient in the sense that a universal is nothing in addition to its instances and depends on its instances in a way illustrated in the previous section. It is highly implausible to suppose that laws could govern something upon which they are supervenient. The scientifically minded supposition that laws govern their instances looks *nothing more* than an assumption, therefore – one might say prejudice. It is an assumption, further, that does not square particularly well with the details of the DTA theory.

Reflection on this finding supports the view that it is very damaging, perhaps fatal, to the theory. This was a theory that was supposed to be an alternative to the Humean lawless metaphysics. But if laws exist, they must do something. Ideally, they would play some role in determining the behaviour of natural events. But is there any naturalistic explanation of how this could be? I claim that Armstrong has not succeeded in providing this. The laws seem to depend entirely on their instances and have no existence apart from them. To ascend to governing laws, and throwing the ladder away that got you there, as Armstrong suggests, seems to require an ability on the part of laws to stay aloft unsuspended. Only the *supposition* of governing laws is keeping them there.

6.10 Quidditism

Perhaps the attack on Armstrong's most developed version of the DTA theory does not prove what I have claimed. Perhaps sense can be made of DTA laws governing or perhaps some other role can be found for laws that justifies taking a realist as opposed to Humean view of them. There could be some flaw or oversight in my argument about which I am ignorant. Suppose that at least one of the above is true and the DTA theory is unaffected by everything I have argued so far. Would this mean that the DTA theory was the solution of the metaphysical problem of laws? I think not. Even if the DTA theory is a coherent theory of laws it has, I will argue, an incoherent implication, or at least an implausible one.

The key features of DTA laws, for this criticism, are their contingency and their externality to the properties they 'govern'. We have a law when we have a contingent, external relation of natural necessitation, as described in detail in earlier sections. The incoherent implication of laws having these features is, I argue, that properties can have different causal roles to the causal roles they actually have.

Laws could be other than they actually are. Instead of N(F,G), it might not be N(F,G). Instead of N(G,H) not being a law, it might be a law. But if these laws were actual, instead of counterfactual, the properties involved would have different causal roles. The criticism challenges the implication that the causal role of a property can vary. It challenges the view that these would be the same properties, F, G, H if their causal roles were different. What would there be about F, other than its causal role, that would permit us to say that we were still speaking of it in the world where its causal role were different? Would we not have to say that F had a property essence, a quiddity, in addition to or underlying its causal role, that enabled counter-nomic identification (Black 2000)? But isn't it implausible that there are such quiddities underlying the causal roles of properties (Shoemaker 1980)? Would that be rather like supporting the idea of an unknowable substratum of substances?

This issue will be considered in more detail in §9.5, as a part of the Central Dilemma. But a very simple example will illustrate what is at stake. The property of having a certain mass m_1 plays a causal role in that having m_1 determines some of the things an object can and cannot do. One of the things that could be done by such an object, in virtue of its mass m_1, is to gravitationally attract another object with a certain force, as described by the inverse square law. But now let us make a counter-nomic supposition, permitted by the theory. The laws that govern the causal roles of massive things now differ. Assume, what Armstrong's combinatorialism permits, that no laws other than those involving mass differ. The theory would seem to allow that the value of m_1 might now bear no relation to the object's degree of gravitational attraction, and yet still be a value of mass. Or it might allow the attraction produced by mass m_1 was now produced by mass m_2 and vice versa, and yet m_1 is still m_1 (and m_2 is still m_2).

The telling question these cases produce is how, if the causal role of a property is altered, are we still talking of the same property? If something has the causal role of F, why are we not now talking of F? And if F now has the causal role that G had, why is F not G? The only available answer seems to be: if the property had a quiddity over and above its causal role. But this allows that F and G could swap their entire causal roles and yet still be the same properties they were.

This apparent absurdity shows the general weakness of the *categorical properties-plus-laws* view. This view, professed recently by Armstrong (2004a), suggests that properties have no internal causal relations. They are intrinsically static and passive. Only because there are laws governing their behaviour do properties have causal roles and, because laws are contingent, their causal roles are not essential to them.

I said at the start of this chapter that the Dretske–Tooley–Armstrong theory of laws has proved popular and enduring since its inception. The theory was simple and neat and united the categories of law, property and cause. But I also said that such aesthetic appeal was sadly no reliable guide to truth in metaphysics. The criticisms I have developed of the theory are, if correct, highly damaging to it. We are motivated, therefore, to look for a better metaphysic. But whatever this new metaphysics will look like, we will be lucky if it is nearly as beautiful as Armstrong's.

7 Necessitarian essentialism

7.1 The New Essentialism

Brian Ellis has presented a novel theory of laws of nature that rests on the acceptance of natural kinds and their essential properties. His theory has the notable consequence that the laws of nature are necessary. This challenges the received view, which has largely been the orthodoxy, that the laws of nature are contingent. Contingency was a cherished, central feature of laws, perhaps because it was thought originally that God had the power to impose any laws on the world he wished. But we have also seen that contingency has a highly problematic consequence: a property's identity is independent of its causal or nomological role (§6.10). This might lead us to quidditism. If the laws of nature are necessary, at least one major problem will have been overcome.

The New Essentialism is presented by Ellis as a very general metaphysical stance. In one book (Ellis 2002), he has shown that it has wide-ranging implications, both inside and outside philosophy. It has consequences for physics, biology and social theory as well as for the philosophy of science, mind and logic. However, it is the specific theory of laws produced by the essentialist metaphysic that I will examine. While it is a very powerful theory, as I will show, it contains two very serious difficulties. First, I will argue, it is built on a form of essentialism that is far from proved. While I will not rule out the possible truth of this essentialism, nor a possible demonstration of it at a future date, I will argue that it contains at its core a notion of essence that remains obscure. Second, I will show that even if Ellis's essentialism is granted, his theory of laws would still contain a serious problem. The Central Dilemma for laws, which I raised in Chapter 6, also strikes at Ellis's theory. The easiest reading of Ellis's theory is what I will call an internal view of laws. Laws are not external to the things that they govern. They do not exist independently of them. But, if so, then it is unclear how they are to play the appropriate 'governing' role, or any other role, to which nomological realism is committed. Ellis's theory is caught on the second horn of the dilemma. If we are to say that laws are internal to the things they govern, which avoids the problem of quidditism because laws and their instances are not independent existences, how can laws nevertheless play an appropriate role that qualifies them as real laws in nature?

I will begin the serious business of this chapter by laying out the important features of Ellis's account of laws. I will show that the central posits of the theory are natural kinds and essential properties. This will lead to closer inspections of those two notions. I will argue that while the case for the existence of natural kinds is a compelling one, the case for essential properties is less so. Ellis needs both of these for his theory of laws. He appears to assume that the two come together. I will argue that they do not. Is there, then, a case for essences apart from the case for natural kinds? I will argue that no adequate case has yet been made. There is no demonstrable path from reference to essence, as Nathan Salmon (1982) has already argued in detail. There is also no path from science to essence, as such a justification would be instrumentalist 'only'. Essences remain, therefore, nothing more than a posit. Metaphysics may often proceed in this way but, when it does so, it falls short of proof. A more secure path to essence may be found at some future time, however, so an undiscovered proof of the theory cannot be ruled out. I continue, therefore, to look at the status of Ellis's theory as if essentialism were true. I argue that it still contains a problem as a theory of laws, even if we accept essentialism, and this is exposed by the Central Dilemma.

The upshot of this is that Ellis has not shown adequately that we specifically ought to accept laws. Nevertheless, he has a view of the world with which I have a degree of sympathy. His critique of the old metaphysics is devastating and accepts the modal properties that I would want in a metaphysics instead of laws (Chapter 10). What I see as the shortcoming of the theory, therefore, might be nothing more than Ellis's failure to draw the inference that is staring us in the face: the world does not need laws. Laws are a metaphysically misleading metaphor (§12.3). The metaphor suggests that there is something that the world needs in order to become ordered and dynamic. The Central Dilemma suggests that there can be no adequate account of how laws are able to deliver these features to the world. Further, Ellis argues that the world in intrinsically ordered and animated. Effectively, he has shown the redundancy of laws of nature. I think he has no need, therefore, to persist with the metaphor.

7.2 The essentialist theory of laws

The essentialist theory of laws, at its core, is relatively simple. Ellis presents a number of short and clear statements of it; for example, 'essentialists claim that the laws of nature spell out the essential properties of the natural kinds' (2002: 101). Giving slightly more detail, he says elsewhere:

> all the laws of nature, from the most general (for example, the conservation laws and the global structural principles) to the more specific

(for example, laws defining the structures of molecules of various kinds, or specific laws of chemical interaction) derive from the essential properties of the object and events that constitute it, and must hold in any world of the same natural kind as ours.

(Ellis 2001: 4)

Superficially, the theory is simple, therefore, yet it invokes a deeper structure of metaphysical claims about the sorts of things that exist. We should start by taking stock of them.

There are natural kinds in nature that are what they are irrespective of our thoughts about them. Nature has joints, real cleavages, that science discovers rather than invents. This is a rejection of the basic nominalistic position that allows that we divide up the world using our mind-derived concepts and there can be no claim of any correspondence between our conceptual schemes and non-conceptual reality. Apart from the claimed cleavages in nature, there are more philosophical reasons for accepting kinds into our ontology. Because nominalism is rejected, there is no permitted reduction of kinds to particulars. Nor are kinds reducible to classical universals (properties) either. There is, thus, a rich ontology in the background of Ellis's theory. It would be an ontology that accepted, at least, particulars, properties and kinds. E. J. Lowe (2002b) has discussed and defended such an ontology explicitly, though his is a four-category ontology that also divides particulars into individual substances (objects) and individual property instances (tropes or modes).

Ellis's theory is noteworthy for its extension of the notion of a natural kind beyond its traditional main use. As classically conceived, natural kinds were always natural kinds of *object*, but this is not the only kind of natural kind. The traditional concept is of natural *substantive kinds* but nature contains also, and science deals in the investigation of, natural *dynamic kinds* (events and processes) and natural *property kinds* (see Ellis, 2001: 74, table).

There is an all-pervading *natural kind structure* to the world, according to Ellis's 'Basic Structural Hypothesis' (2001: 22). Nature is hierarchically ordered with the more general kinds towards the top of the hierarchy. The most general kind is the world kind. Even our world could be understood as a member of a natural kind: perhaps the only actual member of its kind and perhaps the only world-kind that has an actual member (see Bigelow *et al.* 1992; Ellis 2001: 249–53). There are certain properties and processes that characterize this kind. These are features of the world as a whole, rather than some part or parts of the world. Hence, we can characterize our kind of world as being an expanding four-dimensional space–time, which displays symmetry principles, is physical and conservative (of energy, momentum, and so on). Lower down the hierarchy are the more specific kinds, species of the general kinds, and so on throughout nature. This hierarchical structure runs through kinds under all three categories in the broad conception of kind: substantive, dynamic and property.

Kind members have some of their properties essentially and some only accidentally. A property (or cluster of properties) P is essential where a particular could not be a member of a kind K if it failed to have P. If P is a unique cluster of properties, any particular that has P is thereby a member of K. P constitutes, in this case, the kind essence. It is necessary that all members of K have P, therefore. In contrast, there can be properties that members of K possess only accidentally. Such a property, Q, is not a part of what it is to be a member of K and some members of K may have Q and some not.

An important part of Ellis's metaphysics is the insight that some of the essential properties of things could be dispositional properties. This is the core insight of the position called *dispositional essentialism* (see Ellis and Lierse 1994). It will prove to be a crucial claim for Ellis's theory as his account of causal laws depends on it. Dispositional properties must be permitted as real, therefore, and at times basic and irreducible (Ellis 2001: 114, 2002: 74–5). This permission is controversial and filled with difficulties but I will not be discussing it in great detail here as, in Chapter 10, I will argue that it is ultimately acceptable.

Once this rich metaphysical backdrop is granted, laws are accounted for quite easily. There is a law of nature wherever there is an essential property of a natural kind. Laws are just the havings of essential properties by natural kinds. Given the all-pervading natural kind structure of the world – the Basic Structural Hypothesis – this can account for laws of a very general nature down to laws of a very specific nature. A basic division in the hierarchy of laws is presented (2001: 205–6). The most general laws are *global laws*, such as conservation laws, that apply to all events and processes in a world of our kind. Next are the *general structural principles* that define the space–time or energy structures of our world and are also global in scope. Then we get to laws about the *essential natures of specific kinds*; for example, that electrons have negative unit charge. Finally, we get to the *causal or statistical laws* that are about the natural dispositional properties of specific kinds: 'causal laws just describe the natural kinds of process involved in [a causal power's] display' (ibid.: 4).

The necessity of laws of nature is an immediate consequence of identifying laws with the essential properties of natural kinds. It was noted above that the essential properties of things are necessary for kind membership. If laws simply are about what is essential for kind membership, then they are necessary. Hence, it is a law that electrons have negative unit charge, because this property is essential for being an electron, and it could not have been otherwise. Anything that did not have negative unit charge would not be an electron. Hence, there is no possible world in which there are electrons that lack negative unit charge, which is what is needed for this law to be necessary. One might think that one can *imagine* a world where electrons are positively charged or have a different negative charge to their actual charge (ignoring the complication that this different charge might be adopted as the new unit). But this would not be indicative of a real possibility. To think it was, would be to invoke the imaginability test of possibility, but this is an unreliable test of real possibility (see Ellis 2001: 231–4, Molnar 2003: 181–2 and §4.2 in this book). Whatever it is that one imagines that is lacking negative unit charge in these other worlds, it is not electrons.

Because essentialism is adopted as a strong metaphysical thesis, the necessity of laws is *de re*, in the nature of things. Ellis accepts only one kind of necessity but there are different ways something can be necessary. These ways are differentiated by the nature of their grounding (2001: 11). Logical necessities are grounded in logical form, rather than content. Analytic necessities are grounded in the meaning of words. Metaphysical or real necessity is grounded in the nature of things; they are the *de re* necessities. Laws are metaphysically necessary: necessities whose grounding is metaphysical.

Despite the initial intuition that the laws could have been otherwise, which is dealt with by Ellis, such a straightforward notion of necessity for laws is refreshing. It avoids the problem we explored, in the last chapter, of the natural necessitation theory of laws in Dretske, Tooley and Armstrong. That, we saw, was an attempt to combine necessity with contingency in a single relation that appeared *ad hoc* and *sui generis* if not a *deus ex machina*. Ellis insists that contingency and necessity cannot be combined. We must opt for only one of the two. Essentialism shows why we should be attracted to necessity. Quidditism – part of the first horn of the Central Dilemma – shows why we should be repulsed by contingency. Ellis's theory is therefore clearly distinguished from Armstrong's. It is also set apart drastically from the Humean view. One of the chief perceived deficiencies of Humeanism is the failure to distinguish accidental from genuinely lawful regularities (see §3.3). If true, essentialism solves this problem (among many others). Only where we have an essential property of a natural kind, on this view, do we have a law. Only where we have a causal power displaying a natural kind of process do we have a causal law. An accidental regularity would be neither of these, according to the theory. I shall, however, be suggesting below that this recalcitrant problem resurfaces and threatens the whole essentialist programme.

Enough has been said on the New Essentialism for a critique to begin. There is a further wealth of ideas to be found in Ellis's work. But as the present book is not solely an examination of that philosophy, we must move on. In the next two sections, I will examine the key essentialist categories of natural kind and essential property, which, contrary to the way some philosophers have argued, may be treated as distinct subjects.

7.3 Natural kinds

Empiricists want to play down the significance of natural kinds or, in the case of 'porridge' nominalists, deny their existence altogether. A 'porridge' nominalist thinks that there are no objective divisions in reality and that concepts or words can be used by a community of thinkers to divide the world up in any way that suits their (social, evolutionary, etc.) purposes. The world itself is an undifferentiated porridge. Concepts cannot carve the world at its joints as the world has no joints. Further, empiricists dislike the association between natural kinds and essential properties. A property being essential suggests some necessity in nature and we have seen in Hume's empiricism that one of the defining features of this metaphysics is a denial of necessary connection. If there are essential properties, it suggests that a kind is connected necessarily with a certain property.

However, we are to put aside the subject of essential properties until the next section and try to consider natural kinds, as much as possible, without them. There are, in any case, empiricists who think that there are kinds without essences. They think that the properties of kinds of thing are to be discovered empircally and that none of the properties of a thing or kind are more special than any other of their properties.

What is the argument for there being kinds? Two arguments are to be found in Ellis and two more in Lowe. These arguments can be called the empirical, the philosophical, the linguistic and the pragmatic. I will consider each.

The *empirical argument* is presented by Ellis, very briefly, early on (2001: 3). It is the claim that science has discovered real divisions in nature, so there is no continuum (we might also call this the *no continuum argument*). If as a matter of fact there is no continuum, there is no porridge on which the nominalists can work their unconstrained divisions. Hence, Ellis argues thus:

> There is no continuum of elementary chemical variety which we must arbitrarily divide somehow into chemical elements. The distinctions between the elements are there for us to discover, and are guaranteed by the limited variety of quantum mechanically possible atomic nuclei. Many of the distinctions between kinds of physical and chemical processes are also real and absolute.
>
> (ibid.: 3)

Though non-philosophical, this argument is nevertheless attractive. It does, however, trade on a philosophically interesting principle. If there are divisions in nature, there are natural kinds. If, on the contrary, there is a continuum, there are no natural kinds.

If we are to find such divisions, and therefore natural kinds, a good place to look would be at the elementary subatomic particles. They are purportedly few in number, have few basic properties, and have exact qualitative identity across all kind members. This last point means that they are what Ellis calls the infimic species, which are at the base of the hierarchy of natural substantial kinds. Every member of the kind is exactly like every other member. The elementary particles, as they are currently understood, fall into three groups. Their properties – their 'vital statistics' – are given in Tables 7.1 to 7.3 (from Isaacs 2000: 150–1).

We must not, however, be persuaded of a metaphysical thesis solely on such empirical grounds. For one thing, there is still a highly theoretical look about some of these kinds. The sixth quark, the top quark, was 'found' as recently as 1998, though its existence had been believed for twenty years before that as six leptons were known and it was assumed nature would be symmetrical. The mediators retain their theoretical status

Table 7.1 The leptons

Name	Symbol	Charge (electron charges)	Rest mass (MeV/c^2)
electron	e^-	-1	0.511
electron neutrino	v_e	0	*
muon	μ^-	-1	105.7
muon neutrino	v_μ	0	*
tauon	τ^-	-1	1784
tau neutrino	v_δ	0	*

Note:
* = neutrino masses are not yet estimated.

Table 7.2 The quarks

Quark symbol	Name	Charge
u	up	$\frac{2}{3}$
d	down	$-\frac{1}{3}$
c	charm	$\frac{2}{3}$
s	strange	$-\frac{1}{3}$
t	top	$\frac{2}{3}$
b	bottom	$-\frac{1}{3}$

Note:
Mass cannot be assigned to individual quarks.

Table 7.3 The mediators

Interaction	Mediator (exchange particle)	Rest mass (GeV/c^2)	Charge
strong	gluon	0	0
electromagnetic	photon	0	0
weak	W^+, W^-, Z^0	81, 81, 93	$+1, -1, 0$
gravitational	graviton	0	0

in the current view of the standard model, which was proposed in 1978. Further, the standard model is not unrivalled. Some who lean towards quantum theory, in its many varieties, are tempted to dispense with the notion of an object altogether and replace it with the notion of a field.[1] Though it is credible that if there are fields, instead of objects, there can be natural kinds of fields, the danger of drawing conclusions from the current state of science has been illustrated. Any claims of certainty about the infimic natural kinds to be found at an elementary level are bound to be challenged. While we can note that there is some good empirical evidence for the existence of natural kinds, therefore, it seems rather perilous to take it as decisive.

Perhaps aware of such peril, Ellis also offers us a philosophical argument. The argument is for the indispensability of kinds in our metaphysics. The most plausible reduction of kinds would be in terms of properties, or classical universals. The reductive position would be that there is no natural raven kind nor electron kind but, instead, properties of *ravenhood* or *electronhood* that are instantiated by substantial particulars in the usual way. In other words, one would say that there was no *kind* electron, but only the property *being an electron*, which is instantiated by every electron. But Ellis uses an argument, which he states more than once (for example, 2001: 75, 92), that there is not a property *being an electron*. Classical universals logically can be instantiated by any object. But being an electron would be a property that could be instantiated only by electrons, so it does not seem a genuine property. Further, such a property could not be instantiated *in* anything. What is the thing that supposedly instantiates the property *being an electron*? It cannot be an electron because all that makes something an electron is that it has the property *of being an electron*. The subject of instantiation would be either a nothing or a bare particular.[2]

Is this argument persuasive? The problem with it is that it seems simple to construct analogous arguments for uncontroversially classical universals. Thus, if one stipulates for ease of statement that being red means being red all over, and a red object is therefore an object that is red all over, then one could argue that being red is instantiated by all and only those objects that are red. Hence, it is no wonder that all and only electrons have the property of being an electron because all and only red objects have the property of being red. However, there may be a disanalogy that Ellis has in mind in stating the argument. It could be said that there is no necessity in the redness case but that there is in the electron case. It is possible that an object that is red is not red because being red is not essential to being what it is. In the language of possible worlds, we could say that an object *a*, that is red in the actual world, could have been not-red in another possible world. However, we cannot say the same for electrons. We cannot say that an object *a*, which has the property of being an electron in the actual world, could, in another possible world, not have had the property of being an electron. We cannot say this because there is nothing at all, short of a *haecceity*, that would allow us to identify this as the same object (or the object's counterpart) in these two worlds. If this thing is not an electron in this other world, we cannot say that it is the same particular (or counterpart) as *a* in this world. However, the problem for this response is that it might have to assume the very notion of a natural kind that the argument was intended to establish. The reason we supposedly cannot identify the two particulars is because they are not members of the same kind.

Lowe presents the *linguistic argument*, briefly, when he defends his four-category ontology (2002b: 231–2). This is simply that there is a division in language between substantial and non-substantial universals. Substantival general terms denote not a property or cluster of properties but things that bear those properties. Lowe admits that there would not be much power in an argument that rested solely on a division in language, even though there might be reason to expect the structure of language to reflect the structure of the world. The linguistic argument is not his main argument, therefore.

Lowe's chief defence of the four-category ontology is *pragmatic*. He shows how ontologies that attempt greater simplicity, with fewer categories of thing, encounter difficulties because of that. The four-category ontology can yield theories of laws, dispositions, trope individuation, and property perception. By eliminating one (or more) of the four categories from one's ontology, one becomes unable to offer credible accounts of one or more of these phenomena.

Such a pragmatic justification might also be thought to be short of a proof, like the other arguments encountered in this section, but much of metaphysics seems to be justified in this pragmatic way. David Lewis's modal realism, for example, contains no direct argument for the reality of possible worlds. Rather, he shows how much can be gained by assuming them.

While there is doubt, in varying degrees, about each of the empirical, philosophical, linguistic and pragmatic arguments, collectively they might yet have the necessary strength for us to accept the reality of natural kinds. None of the arguments depended on the notion of essence, however, so we are at liberty to consider this next commitment separately.

7.4 Essential properties

As it appeared in Aristotle, essence was associated with the fixedness of biological species and might have brought associations with the divine, with God bestowing a soul-like essence to each creature. Such an association would not have been fair to the subtlety of Aristotle's analysis, however (see Ellis 2002: 9–12). Many of the conceptual distinctions that Aristotle drew have survived, particularly the essence/accident distinction, even though biological species have not been thought to have fixed essences since the Darwinian revolution.

It is Kripke (1980, originally 1972) who is regarded as mainly responsible for the revival of the notion of an essential property and there is nothing mystical about the notion as he employs it. His account starts from individuals, showing that reference through proper names is rigid, referring to the same individual in all possible worlds. These considerations are then extended to natural kinds and other issues. The upshot is that natural kinds are said to have essential properties: properties they must have in all possible worlds. Kripke asked the question 'Given that gold *does* have the atomic number 79, could something be gold without having the atomic number 79?' (1980: 123), to which the short answer was *No*. This negative answer means that it is a metaphysical necessity that gold has atomic number 79.

Ellis articulates the position thus:

> some things . . . hold some or all of their intrinsic properties necessarily in the sense that they could not lose any of these properties without ceasing to be things of the kind they are, and nothing could acquire any set of kind-identifying properties without becoming a thing of this kind. These kind-identifying sets of intrinsic properties are the ones I call 'the real essences of the natural kinds'.
>
> (2001: 237–8)

The following adds a little more detail: 'it is a necessary truth that a thing of kind K has the property P if P is an essential property of K. It is, of course, a posteriori what properties are essential to a given kind' (ibid.: 219). Kripke is thus seen as vindicating the category of necessary *a posteriori* truths. Many of the truths of science are necessary but *a posteriori* including, according to Ellis, truths about the laws of nature.

While Ellis speaks, above, of the essential properties being kind-identifying, this seems to be understood in a strong metaphysical sense, rather than merely epistemological. Wilkerson is more explicit that the notion of a natural kind must go with the notion of essential properties. He says: 'the notion of a natural kind must first be tied to that of a real essence, understood as a property or set of properties both necessary and sufficient for membership of the kind' (Wilkerson 1995: 30), and again, 'I believe that the commitment to natural kinds is a commitment to certain real essences that permit scientific generalization' (ibid.: 62).

This position, of attachment between kinds and essences, is very clearly declared by Wilkerson and only slightly less so in Ellis.[3] Natural kinds must come with essential properties; you cannot have one without the other. But this seems far from proved and there has been a line of argument through Quine, Mellor and Dupré that denies it. I will present their views as a precursor to the problem of the universal accidental, which is a problem that challenges the coherence of the essence/accident distinction.

Quine is the best representative of the empiricist response to natural kinds and essences. He says that kinds, and the general notion of similarity, have a 'dubious scientific standing' (1969: 116). Similarity just means sameness of kind so is no use in defining kind. Almost any two things could count as members of the same kind. Nevertheless, the notions of kind and similarity are fundamental to our thinking. But they have 'non-logical roots' (ibid.: 121). There are no fixed or eternal natural kinds, as Aristotelians might think, for instance. Our notions of similarity and kinds can change as science progresses. Kinds get differentiated in language, which is an evolving thing, learnt through trial and error. Quine's theory is thus embedded in his empiricist account of knowledge and concept acquisition. This assumes, without any direct argument, that there are not fixed kinds in nature. Moreover, it does not consider cases of exact similarity or type-identity, as we found in the cases of the elementary particles. Such particles have all properties shared by all members of a kind and nothing else has all these properties that is not a member of the kind. Instead, Quine's notion of similarity admits of degrees or is a purely comparative thing. In general, Quine has no truck with metaphysics. He does not consider whether such things as natural kinds might be there, existing mind-independently. Instead, he considers our evolving use of kind concepts based on our ability to recognize similarities and quality spacings (though this ability could have an innate aspect in 'animal expectation'). Standards of similarity and natural kinds are revised over time, with new groupings formed if they are more useful in our inductive practices. Nothing is solid or fixed about natural kinds.

Mellor follows a similar line of scepticism but here the focus is on essential properties rather than natural kinds. He says: 'So-called essential properties are thus really no more essential than any other shared properties of a kind' and 'their status is evidently more a feature of our theories than of the world itself' (Mellor 1977: 135). Similarly, Dupré (1993) accepts many natural kinds but not essential properties. A problem for realism about natural kinds seems to be what Quine called 'the promiscuity of sets' (1969: 133). This seems to have been taken up by Dupré when he calls his position on natural kinds 'promiscuous realism'. He pleads for 'categorical empiricism'. This means that one can discover a kind and discover the properties that are characteristic of that kind, but there is nothing that promotes these characteristic properties to a higher status. Nothing empirically warrants the ascent from common characteristic properties to essential properties. Dupré's challenge to essentialism hinges in part on our alleged inability to distinguish between shared properties of a natural kind and essential properties. The argument is summarized thus:

There is certainly no harm in calling a set of objects that are found to have a substantial number of shared properties a natural kind. The discovery of such a kind, however, provides no basis for the supposition that some particular properties can nonarbitrarily be singled out as essential.

(Dupré 1993: 83)

It is this last point that I take as the near definitive statement of scepticism about essentialism, as developed through Quine, Mellor and Dupré. It prompts what I call the possibility of the universal accidental.

7.5 The universal accidental

Essentialism requires a division between essential and accidental properties. The essential properties are those in virtue of which something is a member of a kind. A further distinction can be drawn between the individual essence and kind essence; the primary concern here is with kind essences. These are the kind-identifying properties: those the possession of which determines which kind a particular belongs to. Essential properties for the kind K are thus necessarily possessed by every member of K.

As well as the necessary, essential properties, members of K can have accidental properties. These would be intrinsic properties that could change over time, could come or go, without that individual losing its membership of the kind. It is contingent, therefore, whether members of K have an accidental property. This last statement could be taken as definitive of an accidental property so should have no counter-examples. (A class of exceptions to this, however, seems to be where there are properties that are not essential for K and which are incompatible with some essential properties for K. It may, then, seem that it is not a contingent matter whether such properties are possessed.[4] The best response, in such a case, is to say that such properties are not accidental, because it is necessary for K-members not to have such properties, but not essential either because such necessity consists only in incompatibility with an essential property.)

The contingency of a member of K possessing an accidental property Q permits, however, the possibility of the universal accidental. This is a possibility that corresponds to the accidental regularities raised against the regularity theory of causation and laws. If it is contingent for any member of K, $a, b, c, \ldots z$, at any time, whether or not it possesses Q, then one possible situation is where all of $a, b, c, \ldots z$ possess Q at all times. In such a case, Q would be among the properties shared by all kind members. Thus, we have no way of knowing that among the properties $P_1, P_2, P_3, \ldots P_n$, of all K-members, there doesn't lurk a universal but accidental property. Given the contingency of accidental properties, nothing seems to rule out the possible universality of the accidental.

This possibility could be very serious for essentialism. It suggests that there must be more to being an essential property than simply being a property possessed by every kind member. But essentialists have failed to say what this extra something must be. They have failed to show how we ascend from being a property universally possessed, by all kind members, to the status of being an essential property. Without such an account, which must not be question-begging, a central distinction of essentialism – the one that permits talk of essential properties – cannot be upheld. An essentialist, therefore, must either deny the possibility of universal accidentals or must claim that it is not really a problem. I can only guess how an essentialist might deny that universal accidentals are possible and I cannot come up with a plausible argument that overcomes the difficulty.

The latter kind of strategy might produce the response that in the imagined case there is another way to distinguish accidental from essential properties. Ordinarily, we need consider only the actual kind members. If a property Q is possessed by only some and not all actual members, then we know that Q is accidental for K. But where properties are possessed by all kind members, we must distinguish the accidental from essential ones by considering all actual *and possible* kind members. In other words, we should consider all possible worlds in which K members exist. An essential property would be one that was possessed by every K member in every possible world. But this will not do. To assume that Q is not possessed in some worlds is to assume the very essentialism that the universal accidental problem has cast into doubt. The response will not convince the sceptic about essences, therefore. The essentialist is not entitled to assume any essentialist facts in their attempt to distinguish accidental and essential properties. They cannot simply assume that there are K-members without Q in other worlds. They must have some positive, non-trivial reason for that being so.

There is one position that technically might offer a way of avoiding the problem, but not in any way favourable to Ellis's New Essentialism, nor any other serious form of essentialism. This would be the modal realism developed by David Lewis. In this view, all the other worlds are real, hence the facts about these worlds effectively fix the essential properties by simple extension: the essential properties of K simply are those that are possessed by every K-member in every world. This once more illustrates the considerable advantages that follow from making the grossly counter-intuitive assumption of Lewis's modal realism. But Ellis wants all possibility to be immanent and all essences to be this-worldly. Talk of possible worlds is not to be understood in the worlds-realist form that Lewis has developed. It is best avoided altogether as our own world contains all the necessities and possibilities.[5]

A further case needs to be distinguished: the infimic case where there is exact similarity of all kind members, as we saw in the case of the elementary particles. These seem strong candidates for actual natural kinds and the essentialist argument appears strong. If we found a particle that did not have negative unit charge, for that very reason we would say that it was not an electron. Can we say, then, that with infimic species, we have found real cases of essential properties? I think not. Given the exact similarity of all kind members, the essence/accident distinction just seems inapplicable. One might deem all the properties of the infimic species essential, trivially, but this would be based on nothing but the principle of universal extension: that each member has each of the properties. We have already noted that we need something more than universal extension for properties to achieve the elevated status of being essential.

It should be noted that neither Wilkerson nor Ellis, defenders of essentialism, consider a problem like that of the universal accidental. Wilkerson does not even refer to the contributions of Quine, Mellor and Dupré. Ellis refers only to Dupré, briefly. Nor do they give any other direct argument for the existence of essences. I must conclude that, as yet, there is no adequate distinction between essential and accidental properties.

If there is no direct argument for the existence of essences, are there indirect arguments? Next, I will consider two such arguments.

7.6 From reference to essence?

It seems that Kripke has vindicated some non-trivial truths about metaphysical essences in his influential account of naming and necessity. Does this show that we can discover actual essential properties in our world? I think not. I am sympathetic to Nathan Salmon's (1982) diagnosis that what Kripke has is a theory of reference that he mistakes for a metaphysical theory. Kripke shows that reference can be direct, instead of mediated via Fregean senses. From this insight, he attempts to solve a whole host of metaphysical problems. But as Salmon argues in detail, there is no way of getting metaphysical truths from the philosophy of language. There is no direct path from direct reference to essentialism. Only a trivial essentialism follows from Kripke's theory: that each individual is essentially itself. Non-trivial essentialist claims, such as claims about the essences of natural kinds, can be got only by adding to the theory of reference some non-trivial metaphysical assumptions. We do not yet know what might justify these metaphysical assumptions, but it is not the theory of reference. This finding should not be a surprise. Metaphysics is one of the primary parts of our philosophy. We should never have expected a metaphysically interesting result to come out of a theory of reference. Nevertheless, after Kripke, it became common to believe precisely that.

7.7 From science to essence?

There is an argument from science to essences. It is the suggestion that much of science is made sense of by essentialism and would be left mysterious without it.

Molnar notes that generalizations are often made in science from a limited number, sometimes single number, of experiments (2003: 183). This is explained by an assumption of *methodological essentialism* on the part of science. One of the jobs of science might indeed be seen as the discovery of the essential properties of natural kinds.

What justifies the assumption of methodological essentialism? There is the instrumentalist justification that can be found in Cartwright (1989: 147). But instrumentalism does not justify the realism about essences that the essentialists want. Molnar has another answer. That essentialism is a success in science is best explained by it being true (2003: 184). This move from a useful practice to its metaphysical basis is bound to be controversial, however, and Salmon's analysis is again relevant. Why should essentialism be taken as anything greater than a theory of reference fixing? Why should it be understood as a metaphysical truth?

This is not to deny that science might indeed be posited on an essentialist assumption. But then essentialism would be like one of Russell's postulates of science (Russell 1948: Pt VI). As Russell describes such postulates, they are the basic assumptions on which the practice of science is predicated. They have, however, no independent justification. It is just that science would not be possible without them. If essences have nothing but this justification, then it seems close to the pragmatic justification that has already been considered above in relation to natural kinds. Our metaphysics can do more work, it is claimed, with essences than without them. The essentialists are thus saying: 'give us essences and we will give you the world'. Ellis comes close to this when he compares his metaphysic with Hume's. He says:

> The form of the argument is ... an argument by display. You show your wares and invite people to buy them. If your system strikes your readers as being simpler, more coherent, or more promising than any alternative for dealing with the recalcitrant difficulties of other systems, then this may be a good reason to buy it.
>
> (2001: 262)

This kind of approach is common in metaphysics. David Lewis has no positive argument for his metaphysic other than 'give me all the worlds and I will give you everything you want in return'. This looks a very high price to pay, especially as *all the worlds* includes the actual world, which, according to some, contains all that is needed anyway. Ellis's position might, then, be a better deal than Lewis's.

But, if the argument of this chapter carries any weight, Ellis has not yet delivered a decisive reason to believe in the existence of essences. Such essences are endowed by Ellis with many powers. His theory of laws of nature depends on them crucially. But the case for them has not been made adequately and if the possibility of the universal accidental is real, it is not even certain that essential properties can be distinguished in all cases from other properties.

We may not yet be persuaded that there are essential properties but I side with Dupré in seeing this as an insufficient reason to give up natural kinds. We saw that there are independent reasons to believe there are natural kinds. None of the empirical, philosophical, linguistic or pragmatic arguments for kinds invoked essences so they could be used to defend a notion of kind that was without essence. The no continuum argument points to cleavages in nature, for example. This employs a notion of a kind that is minimal and free of essentialism.

7.8 Essentialist laws?

While I have concluded that no adequate case for essential properties has been made, I grant that they may yet exist and that a more persuasive case for them could yet be advanced. This study of the essentialist view of laws could not be considered complete, therefore, unless it included consideration of whether Ellis's account of laws would be adequate as long as there were essential properties of natural kinds. In this section I assume, therefore, that there are both natural kinds and their essential properties.

We saw earlier that Ellis's theory was simply that we had a law of nature where there was an essential property of a natural kind. Ellis has showed how this can be a very wide-ranging theory, if one accepts the Basic Structural Hypothesis, and that it makes the laws of nature *de re* metaphysical necessities, thereby solving many of the problems associated with the Humean account of laws and Humean metaphysics in general. While I accept that, if there are essences, this would be a good account of the workings of nature, I claim that it does not vindicate the old concept of a law and nor does it establish a useful understanding of laws.

Ellis's account, as I understand it, is a reductive one. Because of that, it gets caught on the second horn of the Central Dilemma. Ellis presents a remarkable and persuasive argument against the old external or transcendent view of laws, showing that it will not do simply to say that laws are in nature but still outside the properties they govern. Instead, Ellis's laws are meant to be within the kind-members, in virtue of being kind-members, so that the units of Ellis's ontology are self-directed instead of directed from outside. His are active, dynamic particulars and he goes to lengths to contrast them with the 'dead' world of the old mechanistic philosophy. But if the activity and dynamism of particulars are provided entirely by the having of essential (dispositional) properties, then there is no job left for laws to do. If they have no job, there is no distinctive role for them to play and, it seems, no need to posit them. Such laws are no addition of being.

Natural kinds and essences provide a reductive grounding for laws. A successful reduction would still maintain the reality of the reduced phenomena, as reduction is to be contrasted with eliminativism. Nevertheless, the reducing phenomena provide all the reality that the reduced phenomenon can claim. Reduction is more than just identity. It is also a claim about an asymmetrical ontological dependence. As laws are reduced to things that are not laws – natural kinds and essential properties – in the essentialist view, laws are thereby dependent on these more fundamental things. But if the reduction is right and successful, then it is the reductive grounding that does all the work. It is in virtue of their essential (dispositional) properties that particulars act as they do. The laws merely ride on the back of these properties but, unlike jockeys on horses, cannot claim any credit for the direction the properties take. Likewise, the hands of the clock do not drive the mechanism within. They move with the mechanism but in virtue of it. Any metaphysical determination goes from properties and kinds to laws. This is significant because the notion of a law, according to nomological realism, is supposed to be precisely the notion of something that controls, governs, moves or plays at least some role. But you cannot claim credit for compliance with a law if everything already acts that way and is already bound to do so.

According to this horn of the dilemma, laws that play no part in determining what happens are not worthy of the name. They are contrary to one of the core connotations of the concept of a law: that laws must play at least some role in the history of the events. This connotation is a tacit claim of the direction of dependence between laws and events. Real laws in nature determine what events happen, not vice versa. Hence, there is something about the notion of laws, at its very centre, that is resistant to reduction. You cannot reduce something to a more fundamental base when it is meant to determine that base. That would leave us with the reduced determining its base but its base also determining it, which is a mystery.

Is there a way for the essentialist to avoid this problem? There might be an attempt to say that laws do have some governing role in nature. Perhaps the laws fix what the essential properties are for the kinds and what the essential properties will naturally do. But this would be to concede far too much altogether, and would be tantamount to giving up the essentialist strategy. It would be a return to laws directing the behaviour of kind members and of properties. It would be taking laws back out of particulars and making those particulars, again, powerless. It would also find, of course, the first horn of the dilemma waiting to trap it, which is a kind of danger we considered in the previous chapter.[6]

I cannot see how there is something between these two problems. An essentialist might try to develop a position in which laws are somehow within the properties of kinds, thereby avoiding the first horn, but not reducible to those properties, thereby avoiding the second horn. But I am not sure there really is a space here, between Scylla and Charybdis. If the laws are not reducible to properties and have a degree of ontological independence from them, I do not see how we can exclude the possibility of them varying independently of those properties, which is the very problem of the first horn. However, because I cannot find a way out of this difficulty does not mean that someone more sympathetic to the reality of laws will not be able to.

The two horns of the Central Dilemma are meant to catch primitivism and reductionism about laws respectively. Our last two chapters have provided case studies of these positions. If they are indeed embarrassed by the Central Dilemma, eliminativism is waiting in the wings, ready to step in. Part III of this book is designed to extol the positive case for that eliminativist stance.

7.9 Necessary laws?

If the essentialist view of laws is rejected, either because it is inadequate as a theory of laws or, more fundamentally, because of its dependence on a yet to be vindicated notion of essence, does that mean that the case for the necessity of laws of nature is defeated? It does not. The case for the necessity of laws has been made, by Swoyer, Elder and Bird, in a way that does not depend only on essentialism.[7] But while the necessity of laws in those accounts may remain when essentialism is given up, they still have a problem in explaining why it is laws that are the bearers of necessity, rather than other things in nature.

In Swoyer (1982), for instance, we are told that laws are necessary relations between universals. If the contingency of laws is renounced, many problems are solved.[8] Swoyer argues that the essential feature of a property is its relationship to other properties (ibid.: 213–14). This seems best viewed as a reductionist rather than primitivist account. Only the properties are needed as the nature of a property is supplied precisely by its relations to other properties. Only they are needed because, as Swoyer says:

> the only things constant in all these worlds that could explain why g cannot occur without f are just the properties themselves. In short, lgf does not hold because '$\forall x\ (xg \supset xf)$' is true in every world; the latter is true in every world because the very natures of g and f make it impossible for there to be a world in which it is false. So lgf obtains, when it does, not because some contingent, primitive relation happens to hold between g and f, but because of a far more intimate, internal relationship grounded in the properties themselves. This relation is not some third entity over and above the two properties.
>
> (ibid.: 216–17)

This sort of view is endorsed in places of this book. It is taken, however, as a good reason why laws are not needed. The relations are *internal* to the properties. They are no addition of being, so are not the real laws in nature of nomological realism. The relations of a property, P, with other properties, Q, R, S, . . ., fix the nature and identity of P. Those relations determine what the property is, so that anything with a different causal and relational role is a different property. This is only denied on pain of quidditism, the first horn. But note here that no essence/accident distinction is being maintained. We are not saying that some of a property's causal roles are essential and some accidental. All are on a par. It might be best, therefore, to describe these causal roles as necessary to the property, rather than confusing things with the term *essential*.[9] It is where we attempt to make the further distinction that the problem of the universal accidental strikes. This is why I am sceptical of a connection between natural kinds and essential properties and, thereby, Ellis's theory of laws. It depends crucially on a distinction between the essential and accidental properties of kinds: the laws are the essential properties of kinds and not the accidental ones.

7.10 Essentialist laws not proved

What can we now conclude about natural kinds and their essential properties? I find in favour of natural kinds where these are understood as distinguished by their properties. At the level of elementary particles, at least, there are cleavages in nature. The notion of essential properties seems far less clearly established, however. Ellis, the new essentialist, has not yet vindicated the notion, despite its pivotal role in his metaphysics. A theory of natural laws that depended on such a metaphysical conception of essentialism would still have work to do, therefore. Moreover, if such a theory is entirely reductive about laws, claiming that we need natural kinds and their essential properties only, then it has a serious problem in defending the realist commitment that laws play a role. On the contrary, such laws seem redundant. Finally, the essentialist path to the necessity of natural laws may have been blocked off for us, but there still may remain other sources of necessity in nature. Whether these sources of necessity should properly be thought of as laws, remains to be established. That there are necessary connections between properties, for example, does not seem to entail that thereby there are laws.

Part III

Realist lawlessness

8 Are natural laws a natural kind?

8.1 Conclusion

If there were real laws in nature, we might expect that they would be a distinct class of phenomena that could be the subject of our philosophical and empirical scrutiny. We might expect the natural laws to form a natural kind of their own, distinguishable from other classes of phenomena in nature: phenomena such as events, kinds, species, associations, and so on. I conclude in this chapter, however, that, on the contrary, there is no distinct kind to be found in nature that fits well our notion of a natural law. The concept of a law of nature, in addition to its other faults, is elusive and vague. Consequently, it permits an unhelpful diversity of phenomena. Following Quine's famous dictum, no entity without identity, this gives us reason to doubt the existence of laws. There is *such* vagueness in the concept of a law that it fails to refer.

On an autobiographic note, this conclusion was perhaps prompted by my failure to find a reference book that gave me a definitive list of all the laws of nature.[1] I had seen books of philosophy, in contrast, that had given me the laws of the various systems of logic. Perhaps this gave me the foolish hope that the laws of nature were as clearly distinguished as the laws of logic. But after finally concluding that the desired book was nowhere to be found, I began to wonder whether it was sufficiently clear within science what it was for something to be a law of nature and whether it was at all useful to endow a truth with the status of a law. This was a question quite independent of the general epistemological problem of how we would know certainly that we had discovered, proved, or established a law. Even if we knew all the facts, it seems we might remain unsure which of those facts do and do not count as laws.[2] Furthermore, if no definitive list of natural laws existed, it seemed to show also how easily science could get along without such a list. This prompted the question of whether laws really are so important to science, after all. Do practising scientists ever discuss laws among themselves? Are laws just an easy way of expressing more difficult ideas to non-specialists?

I conclude that metaphysics has no right to invoke scientific authority on the issues of whether there are real laws in nature and what it is to be a law. There does not seem to be a warrant for the claim that metaphysics is being scientifically minded where it attempts to provide a philosophically acceptable theory of laws.[3] Science has, hitherto, rarely contained a clear commitment to metaphysically real and naturalistically acceptable laws in nature. Science certainly involves an attempt to find truths about the world but it is far from clear that these sought truths are truths about laws in the world. Science is often concerned mainly with what we know. When or whether something is granted the status of a law seems just as much determined, in science, by an epistemic relation to it than by what it is. It is not clear, therefore, that metaphysics is doing a service to science when it supports nomological realism.

But just as the scientific notion of a law remains elusive, so does the philosophical one. Different philosophical theories of law may not be different theories about the same thing but, rather, theories about different things. And because science offers us no clear statement of what a law is, it is not clear which features of the world a valid metaphysics of laws must ground. In part, this is why I said there was no definitive list of features *S* that laws accounted for in the nomological argument NA (§5.3).

This vagueness in the scientific and philosophical notion of a law is damaging to nomological realism, I claim. It counts against the claim of laws to be a natural kind. But if laws are not a distinct, well-defined kind of thing, it is not clear what the criterion of success for a metaphysical theory of laws will be. This is reflected in the diversity of theories of laws that we have available. Some fundamentally different things can be called laws. Most of them, we have already encountered. Laws may variously be thought of as statements, empirically well-confirmed theories, fundamental universal truths, theoretical identities, relations between universals, or real essences of natural kinds. These theories may not be at odds: there may be all these things. A claim that one of these theories has successfully identified or characterized the class of laws looks very suspect, however. More plausible is the view that because of the vagueness of the concept, philosophers have been at liberty to construct theories of diverse things and call them laws. But adding the name *law* to a truth about the world does no specific extra job, so I maintain.

8.2 The elusive and ineffable nature of laws

When looking for a metaphysics of some phenomenon, we may often want to begin by reference fixing. If we establish the concept, fix its reference, we will then know what features the metaphysical theory is supposed to provide. This division between conceptual analysis and substantive metaphysics has a Lockean derivation.[4] In Locke, it appears in the distinction between nominal and real essence. As a generalized philosophical technique, it would make the nominal essence the target for conceptual analysis and the real essence the target for substantive metaphysics. With this approach, identification of the nominal essence is the prior task as it identifies the phenomenon of investigation. The metaphysics then provides a theory that grounds that phenomenon. The problem with the case of laws of nature, I claim, is that the prior task is insufficiently completed. This undermines the attempts to provide a metaphysically substantial nomological realism. No nominal essence has been universally accepted so it is not clear what the various metaphysical theories are meant to be metaphysics for. I speculate further that the task of finding such a nominal essence is incomplete because it is incompletable: there is no nominal essence to find. The existing concept of a law is so uncertain, vague and elusive, that a purely descriptive conceptual analysis is not going to uncover something metaphysicians can work with.

What we lack are clear and uncontroversial necessary and sufficient conditions for lawhood. It is not settled what the conceptual constraints are on X in statements such as it 'It is a law that X'. Can we put any old fact or truth in place of X and still have a statement that is a fact or truth? Or can only some truths take the place of X? All theories of nomological realism would maintain that only some truths are admissible. Truths such as 'John was born in 1966' and 'punctuality is a virtue' will not do. 'It is a law that X' is not a simple truth-function of X, therefore. Conversely, there seem also to be examples of laws that, taken literally, are false (according to Cartwright 1983) or, as in the case of Newton's First Law of motion, are vacuous. The conceptual constraints on X, that make it apt for being a law, are likely to be complicated, therefore. I claim they are not clear and not agreed.

To take a survey of all the things that physics, for instance, calls laws, would reveal a variety of things, the essential features of which are not obvious. Nor is it immediately obvious why some of the other statements of physics, that are not called laws, are not of the law kind. Hence, while we have laws (Curie's law, Dalton's law, law of conservation of mass, Newton's laws, etc.), we also have principles (Fermat's, Heisenberg's uncertainty), theorems (Bernoulli's, Goldstone's, KAM), rules (Hund's), equations (Einstein's $E = mc^2$, Klein-Gordon) and hypotheses (ergodic). It is far from clear that there are metaphysically significant differences between these classes. *The Oxford Dictionary of Physics* admits some overlap and vagueness but also tries to define a purely epistemic distinction in some cases. A hypothesis may not be known to be wholly true, though Avagadro's hypothesis is known to be true yet still called a hypothesis 'for no clear reason' (Isaacs 2000: 260). Science seems to contain little direct reflection, therefore, on the conditions under which something should be called a law. The Dictionary's own definition throws little light on the subject. A law in science is said to be 'a descriptive principle of nature that holds in all circumstances covered by the wording of the law' (ibid.). But this leaves a plethora of questions unanswered.

Given such a lack of clarity in the paradigm science, it might be wondered what the metaphysicians have thought they were doing in providing a philosophical theory of laws. They may have thought themselves scientifically-minded but, according to van Fraassen (1989), such thinking does not at all inform current science. The analysis presented by van Fraassen is that the idea of a law in nature is a solely metaphysical notion. Laws are not taken all that seriously in science and are certainly not among the most fundamental facts in which science deals.

Why, then, might one support a nomological realist thesis? We have seen with the nomological argument (argument NA) that the starting point of many such theories is the view that there are certain features in reality, such as order and uniformity, that stand in need of a grounding or explanation. Laws are then said to be the things that provide that grounding. I take this explanation of nature's orderliness to be weak and give my arguments in the rest of this Part. But these arguments will be helped if, in the first place, the vagueness of the class of things called laws is illustrated.

8.3 Laws as a kind?

It might sound odd to speak of laws being a natural kind. Might it be that I am casting doubt on the concept of a law only by, in the first place, setting unreasonably high expectations on the laws, namely, that they form a natural kind? But Ellis has argued plausibly for a broadening of the notion of a natural kind. Classically conceived, a natural kind means a natural kind of object. But there is no reason why we cannot have natural kinds of events or processes as well. A natural kind could be understood simply but broadly as any kind of thing that exists naturally. Understood so broadly, nomological realists must be claiming that laws are a natural kind of existent. Laws exist naturally, in that they are what they are whatever we may think of them, and they are a kind in that they are a distinct class distinguishable from others (at least epistemically), such as properties, events, objects and causes.[5]

There are two challenges to this view, however. These would be challenges that attempted to claim that there were laws but they were not a natural kind. The first comes from Nancy Cartwright, who says that laws are a kind but not a natural one. The upshot of a recent theory she has proposed (1999) is that laws can be artefacts. Laws are meant to be about exceptionless regularities, she suggests, but such regularities occur rarely in nature. Instead, they have to be made in the artificial and ideal conditions that she calls *nomological machines*. As we create the nomological machines, by creating the experimental set-ups, we create the exceptionless regularities. Thereby we create the laws. We thus have a basis for saying that laws are a kind (the class of exceptionless regularities) but they are an artificial rather than natural one.

This contrasts with a second challenge to the thesis of laws as a natural kind, namely a position, inspired by the later Wittgenstein, that the concept of a law of nature might be a family resemblance concept. Hence, while each thing we call a law might be a perfectly natural thing, the set of laws might not constitute a well-defined kind with necessary and sufficient conditions for membership. There is no identity running through every law in virtue of which it is a law, just as there is no single feature running through every family member that makes them a member of that family. With family resemblance concepts, there are no necessary and sufficient conditions for inclusion within the concept. The idea in the case of laws, therefore, would be that vagueness in the concept of a law would not be a proof that there was no such thing, as laws might form this kind of loose group of more or less resembling phenomena.

Neither of these responses is helpful to nomological realism. Realism about laws is not aided by saying that laws are an artificial kind, nor by saying that laws are only a loose grouping of under-defined phenomena.

In the first case, Cartwright's account of laws has virtues, among which one might say that it is an accurate account of the scientific discovery of laws. However, it is questionable whether such an account of laws is of use to the nomological realist. Cartwright's laws do not seem to be fully in nature in the way the nomological realist wants. If laws really are artificial, then they do not have the kind of independent existence realists have traditionally wanted. If they exist only when we manufacture an exception-less regularity, it would be possible to have a world like ours but which contained no laws. Similarly, there might have been no laws before humans created appropriate nomological machines.[6] These are not consequences easily acceptable to the nomological realist. Their laws are in nature, whatever human beings do in relation to them. I recognize that Cartwright might try to say the same about her laws because she says also that laws are about the causal powers of things which should be understood as there whatever we do in relation to them. But, as I have argued elsewhere (Mumford 2000b), there is a tension in Cartwright's position between the idea of nomological machines creating laws and laws being about the causal powers of things. If laws really are about the causal powers, then, given that those things have such powers whether or not they are manifested, we do not need the power to manifest itself in a regularity in order to say that there is a law. Cartwright should choose between a thesis of laws as causal powers of things or laws as outputs of nomological machines. I would prefer the former view but, in that view, causal powers (hence laws) are in no way artificial creations of the nomological machines.

In the second case, while Wittgenstein has gone some way in identifying circumstances under which different things could belong to a class even though there is an absence of necessary and sufficient conditions, I cannot yet accept that the notion of a family resemblance concept has been fully exonerated. There are causes for concern in Wittgenstein's suggestion, in the bare way it is presented, that indicate that something more is needed than resemblance for laws to constitute a genuine family. In this, I follow concerns raised by Pompa and apply them in the case of laws. But I will not do so in detail until I have further argued that the search for a common nominal essence for laws is fruitless. For the moment, I simply observe that nomological realism is undermined, rather than supported, if laws fail to constitute a clear and distinct kind.

8.4 Disagreements

While it cannot be denied that there are substantial disagreements among the main theories of laws, the question raised here is whether these disagreements concern laws specifically.

Following from the analysis already presented of the individual theories, and of the nomological argument, I surmise that it has not been adequately established that the theories offered by Armstrong and by Ellis are specifically theories of laws. Each has presented a metaphysic intended to account for some features *S* that are found in reality. But, according to my analysis of argument NA (Chapter 5), it is not proved that it is laws, and only laws, that can account for *S*. The question to be answered in each case, therefore, is why we should accept that it is a theory of laws specifically that has been offered. The main disagreements between Armstrong and Ellis, I argue, arise because Armstrong is advancing a theory of universals while Ellis is advancing a theory of natural kinds. These two theories are talking about different things, therefore, and neither has an adequate demonstration of why their theory is specifically a theory of laws rather than a theory of something else.

This provides corroboration of the claim that there is a lack of clarity over what laws are supposed to be. Are they supposed to be relations between universals, functional equivalences, theoretical identities, or characteristics of kinds? These are quite different things yet it has been claimed of each that it is the proper subject matter of a law of nature. In some cases, it has been claimed that only one of these things, and none of the others, is the correct subject of a law of nature. But what is the argument for that?

Armstrong denies, for instance, that there are so-called laws of composition. In N(F,G), N must always relate distinct universals (1983: 138). Armstrong rules, therefore, that theoretical identities, such as water $= H_2O$ are not laws of nature even though some have spoken of laws of composition or bridge laws, which would be exactly such identities. But what good reason does Armstrong have for excluding such things from the class of laws? He has nothing independently decisive to offer but instead he shows that such laws of composition would be inconsistent with his own theory and then states that such identities are not truths about laws but truths about the relata. Hence, water $= H_2O$ is not a law, it is 'only' a truth about water or about H_2O, if true.

The accounts of laws based on natural kinds, as we have found in Ellis, Lowe and Bird (2001), appear initially to be very different things from Armstrong's laws. Electrons have spin $\frac{1}{2}$ and ravens are black could qualify as laws of nature. But other than providing some order, regularity and universality to the world, or whatever other features are identified as constituting S in the theory, it has not been demonstrated sufficiently that these are specifically laws. Given the doubtless high number of natural kinds, and the doubtless even higher number of their characterizing qualities, the theory would permit a vast number of laws of nature. Natural kinds and their properties are ubiquitous. This would raise the question of whether such laws are available far too freely.[7] It is hard to answer this question, with certainty, as we do not yet have a definitive statement of how many laws of nature there are supposed to be.

What Armstrong has said of the theoretical identities, however, could now be said of the natural kinds theory of laws. Has it really been shown by the proponents of this theory that they are talking about laws? What we discover when we discover such facts are truths about kinds. Armstrong's diagnosis that water $= H_2O$ is a truth about water, not a truth about a law, would apply equally to electrons have spin $\frac{1}{2}$ and ravens are black. These are truths about electrons and about ravens. It has not been sufficiently proved that they are truths about laws (laws about electrons and laws about ravens). We can state these truths simply by mentioning these kinds and their characterizing qualities. We do not have to mention in addition that these truths have the status of laws. Hence we can wonder what justifies, for some truth X about a kind, adding to it the operator that gives 'it is a law of nature that X'.[8]

However, recognizing that natural kinds are themselves universals, and following up on the claim that the main difference between Ellis's and Armstrong's metaphysics is that Armstrong denies, while Ellis allows, a division of universals into substantive (kind) universals and non-substantive (classic) universals, it should be apparent that Armstrong's objection to theoretical identities being laws can be applied easily to his own position. If water $= H_2O$ is a truth about water, not about a law, and electrons have spin $\frac{1}{2}$ is a truth about electrons, not about a law, should we not say that F is N-related to G is a truth about the universal F rather than a truth about a law? I think this would be an appropriate thing to say, despite Armstrong's stipulation that the N-relation is the *lawful* relation. What Armstrong has, therefore, is a theory of how universals are related to each other. That this is a theory *of laws*, is a stipulation of the theory.

The existing theories, on the current analysis, each identify a feature of the world, of universals, of natural kinds, or something else, and then make the claim that the feature provides the laws. But this part of the argument it seems is undetermined. Hence it is not clear that there is in each case a substantial disagreement about the nature of laws. Rather, the disagreements seem to be about which features of the world deserve the name of laws. Given the insufficient grip we have on the nominal essence of the law-kind, a decisive conclusion on this issue seems a remote prospect.

There is an even greater disagreement among philosophers that is a case of conflicting intuitions over what laws are supposed to be about. We require from laws a governing role but we also require that they be, in some sense, descriptive of the observable facts. We want laws to account for regularity and regulation, but can a single thing provide both these features, which seem to pull us in different directions (Mumford 2004)? Those who emphasize more the idea of laws as descriptive of regularities are likely to favour a Humean treatment of laws. Those who would emphasize more the regulative role for laws are likely to favour a nomological realism such as necessitarianism. An attempt to forge a synthesis is fraught with difficulties.

8.5 The diversity of laws

Although Armstrong claims that it is a 'scientifically-minded' supposition that there are laws of nature that play a role in determining particular causal sequences, it is far from clear that science subscribes to anything like the metaphysical conception of laws. A scientifically-minded account might instead rule that laws were well-confirmed statements of universal scope, that support inductive inferences, and which can be used in explanation and prediction. A metaphysical conception of laws cannot accept any of these epistemic considerations as being *constitutive* of laws, however. The metaphysical concept allows that there were laws before there were people. Hence, a law is a law regardless of the use we make of it in our epistemic practices and any attitude we take towards it.

What would it really be to be scientifically-minded? The main claims I wish to illustrate here are that science does not use a unified and sufficiently well-defined notion of law nor, it seems, does it lay too great an importance to attaching the status of law to a claim. Hence, science does not give to its laws the same fundamental importance that is given to them by the metaphysical conception employed by nomological realism.[9]

First we can note the relatively arbitrary and almost certainly not metaphysical considerations that lead to something being called a law. Both historical and epistemological considerations would seem to play a role in the naming of something as a law, which could have no role in determining whether something is a law according to the nomological realist's position.

Thus, we have many claims of science that are called laws. Here are some famous examples:

Coulomb's law

$$F = -\varepsilon_0(pq/r^2)$$

Where ε_0, is a constant and F is the force between two charges whose values are p and q and whose separation is r. The law concerns electrostatic attraction and states the force between two charged objects.

Boyle's law

The volume (V) of a given mass of gas at a constant temperature is inversely proportional to its pressure (p), i.e. pV (after Robert Boyle, 1662). This is true only of ideal gases.

Kepler's laws

Three laws of planetary motion (from Johannes Kepler, $c.$ 1610):

1   The orbits of the planets are elliptical with the sun at one focus.
2   Each planet revolves around the sun so that an imaginary line connecting the planet to the sun sweeps out equal areas in equal times.
3   The ratio of the square of each planet's sidereal period to the cube of its distance from the sun is a constant for all the planets.

These are cases of false laws. At least, Newton's laws superseded Kepler's, showing that something else could deliver to the world all the facts Kepler thought his laws were necessary to provide.

Newton's laws of motion

1   That every body continues in its state of resting or of moving uniformly in a straight line, except insofar as it is driven by impressed forces to alter its state.
2   That the change of motion is proportional to the motive force impressed, and takes place following the straight line in which that force is impressed.
3   That to an action there is always a contrary and equal reaction; or, that the mutual action of two bodies upon each other are always equal and directed to contrary parts.

If one were to infer from these examples that a law is always a weighty and vital truth of science, one would probably be mistaken. There are plenty of relatively obscure laws in physics. For example:

Henry's law

At a constant temperature, the mass of gas dissolved in a liquid at equilibrium is proportional to the partial pressure of the gas (William Henry, 1801): a special case of the partition law that applies only to gases that do not react with the solvent.

Hess's law

If reactants can be converted into products by a series of reactions, the sum of the heats of these reactions is equal to the heat of the reaction for direct conversion from reactants to products (Germain Henri Hess, 1802–50).

Kirchhoff's (electrical circuit) laws

1   The current law: the algebraic sum of the currents flowing through all the wires in a network that meet at a point is zero.
2   The voltage law: the algebraic sum of the e.m.f.s within any closed system is equal to the sum of the products of the currents and the resistances in the various portions of the circuit.

I do not want to suggest that these lesser-known laws are unimportant in their respective fields. I want to suggest instead, that there is not a very small and restricted number of laws and the status of law is not reserved for the *great truths* of science. The deeper one delves into the details of a discipline, the more laws one is likely to unearth. Further, these cases are taken mainly from the example of physics. Each science may be expected to employ its own set of laws.

The examples show two further noteworthy things. First, that a law can be falsified but still retain its status as a law. I speculate that this is related to the epistemic considerations in the scientific conception of law. A law is some general truth that is thought to be proved, to a reasonably high standard of proof. From such an idea, it seems a relatively small step to allow that something is a law because it was *once* thought to be proved, to a reasonably high standard, but it is now known to be false. Hence, Kepler's laws can still be called laws because of the historical consideration that an important pioneering cosmologist thought they were proved, even though we now know them to be false or superseded.

Second, the common and high level of idealization can be noted. This is a feature that Cartwright (1983, 1989) has made much of. The gas laws are in many cases said to be true only for ideal gases, where an ideal gas is some imagined gas that obeys the gas laws perfectly because its molecules occupy negligible space and have negligible forces between them. The idealization in Newton's first law of motion is notorious: every body is driven by impressed forces to alter its state so no body ever continues in its state of resting or of moving uniformly in a straight line.

These two features stand as problems for any purely descriptive account of laws. The metaphysical realist is likely to rule that there is no such thing as a false law of nature in the metaphysically real sense (Carroll 1994; Swartz 1985). Being called a law, or being believed to be a law, is insufficient for being really a law. Hence, Kepler's laws are not false laws. They are not laws at all. But, if all laws must be true, what is one to say of the cases of idealization such as Newton's first law? Literally, idealized laws are false so in what sense are such idealizations laws? Only theoretically or only counterfactually?

Rather than pursue these questions, I will compare the list of laws with a list of apparent non-laws.

Goldstone's theorem

In relativistic quantum field theory, if there is an exact continuous symmetry on the Hamiltonian or Lagrangian defining the system, and this is not a system of the vacuum state, then there must be at least one spin-zero massless particle called a Goldstone boson.

Fermat's principle

Not called a law but figures in laws, suggesting that it is more fundamental than a law: the path taken by a ray of light between any two points in a system is always the path that takes least time. This 'leads' to the law of the rectilinear propagation of light and the laws of reflection and refraction (after Pierre de Fermat, 1601–65).

Ergodic hypothesis

A hypothesis in statistical mechanics concerning phase space: 'the orbit of the representative point in phase space eventually goes through all points on the surface', (there is also a quasi-ergodic hypothesis).

Einstein's equation

Simply, $E = mc^2$: the mass-energy relationship announced by Einstein in 1905. ($c =$ the speed of light. Energy is defined elsewhere as a measure of a system's ability to do work. Entropy is a measure of a system's inability to do work.)

Gravitational constant

G: the constant that appears in Newton's law of gravitation. It has the value: $6.67259(85) \times 10^{-11} \, \mathrm{N\,m^2 kg^{-2}}$. Though assumed to be constant usually, on some models of the universe it decreases with time as the universe expands.

Hund's rules

Empirical rules in atomic spectra that determine the lowest energy level for a configuration of two equivalent electrons (that is, with the same n and l quantum numbers) in a many-electron atom. They are:

1   The lowest energy state has the maximum multiplicity consistent with the Pauli exclusion principle.
2   The lowest energy state has the maximum total electron orbital angular momentum quantum.

(after Friedrich Hund, 1925)

Pauli's exclusion principle

A principle of quantum mechanics applying to fermions but not bosons: no two identical particles in a system (such as electrons in an atom or quarks in a hadron) can possess an identical set of quantum numbers (after Wolfgang Pauli, 1925).

Bernoulli theorem

Where a fluid flows through a pipe, the sum of pressure energy, kinetic energy and potential energy of a given mass of the fluid is constant (after Daniel Bernoulli, 1738).

The main point I seek to exploit, from these two lists, is why the first list is a list of laws when the second list is not? Why is Pauli's exclusion principle not a law? It appears to state the same kind of general fact as a law. Is it something more fundamental, like symmetry principles are supposed to be (see van Fraassen 1989)? But if there are things that are more fundamental, that perhaps apply to or constrain less fundamental laws, why are they not the necessities that philosophers are interested in? Why is the ergodic hypothesis not a principle or a law? It can be treated as an axiom from which other things follow, just like many laws. It is, however, said to be 'difficult to prove'. This suggests that the scientific distinction between a law and a hypothesis is nothing more than epistemic. Why are the many fundamental constants not laws? They figure in many laws. Are they more fundamental than the laws in which they figure? Why can we not say 'it is a law that the G in $<F = GM_1M_2/d^2>$ has the value $6.67259(85) \times 10^{-11} \, \mathrm{N \, m^2 kg^{-2}}$'? Why is an equation such as Einstein's not a paradigmatic law of nature? The interest of the Bernoulli theorem is that it is said to be *equivalent* to a conservation law. Does this make it a law?

8.6 A family resemblance between laws?

Given both the diversity of the things called laws and the alleged vagueness in the notion of a law, it might be thought that an obvious response
of someone who nevertheless seeks to defend nomological realism is a
move to a family resemblance notion of a law. This would be to follow the
well-known sections of Wittgenstein's *Philosophical Investigations* where he
considers what could be common to all things that are called games.
Finding only diversity, with no single defining feature throughout all the
different games, he says:

> And the result of this examination: we see a complicated network of
> similarities overlapping and criss-crossing: sometimes overall simil-
> arities, sometimes similarities of detail. I can find no better expression
> to characterize these similarities than 'family resemblances'; for the
> various resemblances between members of a family: build, features,
> colour of eyes, gait, temperament, etc. etc. overlap and criss-cross in
> the same way.
>
> (Wittgenstein 1953: §66, §67)

There is no textual evidence that Wittgenstein was proposing that all concepts are of the family resemblance variety but some are, such as game
and number. In *The Blue and Brown Books* the idea of a family resemblance
concept is offered as an alternative to the 'craving for generality', one
source of which is a 'tendency to look for something common to all the
entities which we commonly subsume under a general term' (1958: 17).

We might speculate, therefore, that there is no single feature in
common to all laws – no single defining essence – but nevertheless there
are lots of particular laws with only a family resemblance between them.
One might still seek to support nomological realism on this basis while
conceding that the conceptual analysis had failed to reveal a nominal
essence for laws.

However, like much of Wittgenstein's later work, his writings are suggestive but not immensely detailed. Can the notion of a family resemblance concept be taken seriously? Will it withstand scrutiny?

There is a criticism of the notion that was presented by Leon Pompa
(1967) which seems relatively unscathed by the criticism of Huby (1969)
and Llewelyn (1969). Pompa notes (1967: 65) that there can be a family
resemblance between x and y if and only if x and y resemble and x and y
are from the same family. The criteria for the latter are based on the laws
of heredity and are independent of the criteria for the former. Therefore,
to claim a family resemblance one would have to claim membership of the
same family, which must be independent of resemblance.

Suppose one said, in response, that Wittgenstein did not mean family
in this strict biological sense and he intended that the particulars that fall

under a family resemblance concept have only a rough pattern of resemblance, backed by no independent criterion such as heredity. The problem then would be that the pattern of resemblance alone would be insufficient to make individuals members of the same family. I may resemble my next-door neighbour more than I resemble my sister. Resemblance is such a weak notion that any two people may be said to resemble each other such that, on the basis of resemblance alone, any two people could be said to be part of the same family.

Wittgenstein may not have been intending his discussion of family resemblance concepts as an explanation of why two particulars are classed under the same concept. But, if not, his 'analysis' comes to look much weaker and less helpful than at first it might have been hoped. If Wittgenstein was saying that there is no single common feature, or no necessary and sufficient conditions, that explain why a number of distinct particulars fall under the same concept, but that the particulars have a rough resemblance, then not only does this say very little but it will also be little help to us in the case of laws. If the nomological realist was saying something as weak as this, they would have said nothing at all about why something, *a*, is a law. On the weaker interpretation of Wittgenstein, this would mean only that *a* resembled some other law *b* (to be a law is to resemble another law). If *a* would thereby be a law, so too would be anything that resembled *a*. It is clear that this will be far too weak to offer any explanation to us of why something is a law. But it seems equally difficult to see how anything more substantive can be got from Wittgenstein's discussion because it rules against any independent criterion of lawhood that identifies a common feature of all laws.

There is another way of understanding family resemblances, for which no historical accuracy is claimed. It is the idea of the quality pool from which each member of the family – each particular under the concept – draws its qualities. In the case of laws of nature, we could attempt to describe what that pool of qualities was. But for a family resemblance concept, it is not necessary, to be a member of the family, that any one feature from the pool be possessed. It is only necessary that *some* of the qualities are possessed but with no strictures on how many are possessed.

This may suffice for a description of *similarities* among laws but, again, it in no way explains what the concept of a law is and how it differs from other concepts. There may be things that are not laws, such as principles, equations, fundamental constants and accidental constant conjunctions that have some, if not many of the qualities in the law quality pool. No explanation is provided at all of why these things are not laws and yet Guass' law, for instance, is a law.

This brings us to the primary worry about the shift to the idea of a family resemblance notion as a fallback position when the conceptual analysis seems to have failed. If there is no plausible account of what it is to be an *X*, then there seems to be no justification for saying that *a* is an *X*, *b* is an *X* and *c* is an *X*. But this seems to be the claim of the family resemblance idea. We are asked to believe that there is nothing at all definitive of being a law, for instance, yet that *a* is a law, *b* is a law and *c* is a law. But if there is nothing that has to be satisfied for something to be a law, what is the basis for the claim that *a*, *b* and *c* are laws? If it is merely that they have the name 'law', then that is no help to nomological realism at all. To repeat, nomological realism is a strong, metaphysical claim. It is that there are real laws in nature that play a distinctive, one would say *nomological*, role. If we fail to say what is distinctive about laws, that distinguishes laws from other things, nomological realism is surely undermined. To say, instead, that law is a family resemblance concept, is a claim that offers little hope once subjected to a little critical scrutiny.

Bearing in mind the few comments Wittgenstein made on family resemblances, and how vague they were, I think we should be cautious in granting an uncritical shift to such resemblances when a conceptual analysis has failed. We should be cautious, in like proportion, of permitting that the vagueness of so important a concept in metaphysics is harmless (or even virtuous). Vagueness might be permissible for a concept such as baldness, but not for a concept that we are urged to accept as one of the most central of all those we use to explain the world.

8.7 Modernization?

The claim I have made in this chapter is old. Nagel said something similar: ˙

> The term 'law of nature' is undoubtedly vague. In consequence, any explication of its meaning which imposes a sharp demarcation between lawlike and non-lawlike statements is bound to be arbitrary.
>
> There is therefore more than an appearance of futility in the recurring attempts to define with great logical precision what is a law of nature – attempts often based on the tacit premise that a statement is a law in virtue of its possessing an inherent 'essence' which the definition must articulate. For not only is the term 'law' vague in its current usage, but its historical meaning has undergone many changes.
>
> (1961: 49)

Apart from the emphasis on laws *qua* statements, I am happy to endorse this view.

A further response should also be acknowledged, however. One may admit that the existing concept of a law is vague. But this shows only that it stands in need of revision or modernization. It might then be claimed that it is one of the tasks of philosophy to undertake such modernization: to regiment our concepts after identifying the existing flaws.

While I acknowledge that there are cases where philosophers can and should undertake such a modernization of a concept, to do so should be for a reason. Some concepts may be irredeemable or so useless that we can get along without them. We update a concept when we think that there is still some work for it to do, or for something recognizably close to it to do. But is that the case with laws of nature? I will argue not, in the following chapters of this Part. For this chapter, I end by claiming only that, from a look at laws in science and metaphysics, the status of a law does not appear to have such significance that we could not manage without this category. What counts is the various truths about the world, in science and metaphysics, rather than whether these facts are correctly classified as laws.

9 The Central Dilemma

9.1 The Central Dilemma: introduction

The idea of there being a dilemma facing nomological realism has come up in relation to the theories of laws discussed in Chapters 6 and 7. It is now time to take this dilemma as a topic in its own right. I aim to formulate a more precise version of the dilemma and to show in what way, and how seriously, it threatens realist claims about laws in nature. In stating the dilemma, a number of the things that are said might seem puzzling and strange. I think this is because the claim that there are real laws in nature is indeed puzzling and strange once an attempt is made at a clear articulation. The problem I call the Central Dilemma exploits this very point.

Before formulating the dilemma, it will be useful to set it in the context of the book's argument as a whole. Often in metaphysics, alternative ontologies are presented and a judgement between them is made by weighing up the relative advantages and disadvantages. In such a way, one might consider the start-up cost of the metaphysic and the benefits to be gained for that cost. Ellis offers such an evaluative model of decision-making in metaphysics when he says 'You show your wares and invite people to buy them' (2001: 262). One might offer an alternative to laws, then. One might develop a metaphysics that was law-free and try to show that it is at least as good as a lawful metaphysics. This has been one of the tasks of the present book: a law-free metaphysics gives us everything we thought we wanted laws for, and might do so in a better way. But while it is one thing to offer an attractive alternative, it is another thing to offer an actual argument against the metaphysic of laws. If such an argument were to be successful, this would be a far more decisive blow against laws than merely showing that there were attractive alternatives. The most powerful such argument would show that a metaphysics of laws is unworkable, hence that it is no longer a viable option.

This chapter is an attempt to provide an argument that, if successful, would have this conclusion. The argument comes in the form of a dilemma that results from the claim of nomological realism. The realist claim has already been developed in earlier chapters. The Central Dilemma is designed to show what strange metaphysical beasts real laws in nature would have to be. If we take law-talk to be more than mere metaphor (see Chapter 12), we face the difficulties that the dilemma identifies. More specifically, the dilemma aims to show how hard it is to find a credible role for laws to play in nature. The nomological realist is committed to the view that laws have at least some role so the Central Dilemma pushes the point of what that role is and how laws are supposed to fill it. No sensible and plausible account can be given of how laws are supposed to do their work, I will claim, so there is no acceptable way to solve the Central Dilemma. If there is no such solution, then this will oblige us to return to the view that prompted it. If that view has saddled us with an irresolvable problem, then we should reconsider it. The alternative response, however, is metaphysical lawlessness, which is the response I recommend.

If the argument goes through, it will be a powerful blow against realism about laws. In practice, I acknowledge that things are seldom cut and dried in philosophy. There will be plenty of room for argument at almost every stage. Certain steps will have to be accepted on the overall balance of evidence. There may be other steps where there are other possible answers that are yet to be considered but which might avoid the consequences I am trying to force upon my opponent. We may come up short of certainty, therefore. But with such a cautionary note, I might nevertheless hope that the reader's mind is influenced at least a little against the metaphysical plausibility of realism about laws.

9.2 The argument: summary formulation

The preceding makes it clear that the Central Dilemma plays a role in a bigger argument. The bare structure of the bigger argument may be presented as follows:

> I   Either laws have [1] some (governing or determining) role or [2] not.

To answer [2] is to have a lawless metaphysic, as I have tried to show in Part I. To answer [1], is to allow nomological realism: that there are laws in nature. But the Central Dilemma strikes against those who answer [1].

> II   If [1] there is a (governing or determining) role for laws, then such laws are either [A] external to the things for which they play that role (they govern or determine) or [B] they are internal to them.

The decision to be made between [A] and [B] is the Central Dilemma for laws.

III If [A], then an account of an external (governing or determining) role must be given that is plausible and avoids quidditism. If [B], then an account of an internal (governing or determining) role must be given that is plausible.

9.3 The governing role of laws

Before going further into the detail of the argument, I should explain something that might seem controversial about it at the very beginning. Otherwise, it might seem that the argument has no initial appeal.

It might be said that the idea of laws 'governing' the world's events, or any other things in nature, is an outdated and archaic sense of law that went out of philosophy and science centuries ago. Perhaps, then, the attempted argument may have no force as it starts with such an unrealistic sense of law that no nomological realist would want to defend. The Central Dilemma would thus only be a problem because it stipulates such a strong sense of laws – governing laws – in an attempt to force an unreasonable position on the nomological realist. If the argument works, therefore, it defeats only a straw man.

In response, I would say that throughout the argument I am prepared to use the term *governing* in as loose a sense as possible while still saying something meaningful. The governing in question might, as Armstrong says, have 'an element of metaphor' (1983: 106), which comes from the comparison with legal and moral laws. It might be an extremely weak sense of governing. However, any nomological realist must allow that laws play *a* role, I would maintain. Laws must add something to nature such that the world would be significantly different were they not there. According to the realist position, a world that lacked laws would be a very different world from ours.[1] What would the difference be?

Real laws in nature, it seems plausible to say, would play some role in determining the world's history, rather than vice versa. We saw in Part I that the opposite view – Humean supervenience – claims that laws play no distinct and irreducible role at all. They are entirely supervenient on, or determined by, what happens in the world. They supervene upon the contingent, non-modal facts of the world's history: a four-dimensional history of events or property distributions. The argument of Part I was that this is a lawless metaphysic, in spite of there being a so-called 'Humean theory of laws'. The nomological realist, therefore, is obliged to deny that the direction of determination is this way. If the direction is the other way, from laws to events, I claim this is all that is necessary to allow some sense in which laws govern.

It is very easy to be tempted by the idea of laws playing this determining function. One might wonder why a property or state has the particular role that it has. The answer easily suggests itself that the property or state has this role because of the laws of nature that govern it. It is natural to think that such laws could have been different or could have not applied at all. The model of metaphysical explanation that is provided is that from properties *plus* laws we can get events or causal roles. Without the laws, nothing would produce anything else.

There must be some sense, therefore, which the nomological realist would have to explain, in which the history of the world, or the connection between properties, was determined by the laws rather than vice versa. For something really to exist, as the nomological realist claims for laws, it must do something; it must make a difference. And whatever it is that laws do is what I am calling their governing role.

For those whose concerns are still not assuaged, the argument built on the Central Dilemma could be formulated without giving a name to the role of laws. If it were preferred, wherever I say 'governing role', you could substitute 'x-role' and leave the nature of x entirely open. The argument would then question the detail of what exactly this x-role is and whether a coherent account could be provided of how laws play the x-role. The nomological realist is committed, I claim, to the view that laws play some role, x. If they do not say this, they have not satisfactorily shown that their position is genuinely realist about laws. They have a burden to show that they are claiming something that lawlessness does not.

These notes of caution are to be borne in mind throughout the rest of the chapter. They will apply henceforth but will not be repeated. I move, now, to the detailed explanation and justification of the Central Dilemma. I will take each horn in turn.

9.4 The Central Dilemma, first horn: externalized laws

If laws are external to the things they govern, we need an account of how they govern those things externally. Laws might govern properties or particulars, for instance, without being themselves, or being internal to, the properties or particulars governed. If the nomological realist favours this option, they owe us an account of what the relation is between such laws and that which they govern and how something can determine something else to which it is external.

For such laws to be taken seriously, the account must be plausible. The relation or mechanism involved could not be simply a *deus ex machina* and it should not have any highly implausible consequences. The first horn of the Central Dilemma is that no acceptable and credible account can be given of how laws of this kind could govern their so-called instances externally. The situation may be even worse than that, however, for any account of external governance, that treated laws and their instances as distinct existences, would thereby allow that they could vary independently. As we will see, this may lead to a position of quidditism, which is a highly undesirable consequence.

It will be useful to provide two examples of such real but externalized laws. This will illustrate how the first horn might strike against actual theories. There is a real problem for such accounts of how the gap is to be bridged between laws and the things that they govern. That there is such a gap is an inevitable consequence of taking laws to be external to their so-called instances.

A classical example of external laws is to be found in a Newtonian model. This is the idea of nature as a mechanism for which God is the mechanic. Although it is suggested in remarks in Newton's Preface to the first edition of the *Principia* (1687), I am not claiming that this account has historical accuracy or is a contribution to Newtonian scholarship. Newton rarely discussed these issues directly or in great detail so it might be better to claim the account to be no more than a speculative reconstruction. (We will see, with the second horn, that there is a later passage in Newton that suggests a possible model for internalized laws.)

Each individual object in the natural world has the same inertial state unless impressed by other forces to alter its state, in accordance with Newton's First Law (1687: Axioms or Laws of Motion). The law itself, however, is something outside such objects. God, the perfect mechanic, has made (or decreed) such laws and has made them apply to every object. But because laws are external to the things that they govern, thus independent from them, they could have been different or could have applied to different things.

We are permitted to say that Newton's laws could have been different though this is a logical 'could'. There is also a sense in which they could not have been different. Because God is the perfect mechanic, the world – the mechanism – is also perfect, we may deduce. God's perfection thus placed a constraint on him and means that the laws could not have been otherwise, in this sense; that is, could not have been less than the perfect ones they are.[2] Such perfection takes the form, we might infer from reading the *Principia*, of a simple mathematical system in which the laws are the axioms. The perfection of this system is evident in its simplicity.[3] It needs just three basic *Laws of Motion* but applies them universally. Hence, logically laws could have been less than universal but the world would then have been a less than perfect creation. Through the need for simplicity, therefore, Newton made universality an essential part of the notion of a law.[4]

How do such laws relate to the things they govern? It is clear, in this example, that the laws are external; indeed, not only are they outside the objects they govern, they are also outside nature. God's decrees may have their manifestations in nature, and can be known by their effects, but how they come to be manifest in nature remains unexplained. They are essentially supernatural, so how do laws have effects in nature? One theory of miracles is that a miracle is a natural event with a supernatural cause (Mumford 2001). By this definition, this would make any effect of a law upon nature miraculous. This is not a compelling model of how laws govern. This relation between laws and the world is a paradigmatic *deus ex machina*. The Newtonian model emphasizes the gap between laws and the objects, properties, or events they govern. The gap is unbridgeable naturally so it is bridged supernaturally.

The second model of externalized laws is a more recent and naturalistic one. This is the Dretske–Tooley–Armstrong (DTA) theory of laws that was discussed in Chapter 6. Such laws are perfectly natural, as opposed to supernatural, so at least such laws would not have to cross this metaphysical boundary in order to have their influence. Without unnecessarily repeating detail, we can characterize the DTA theory for present purposes as the theory that laws are the holdings of external relations between universals. Although one major obstacle has been removed, however, we still have some way to go to find an explanation of how these laws govern in the required way.

We saw in the earlier examination of the DTA theory that it provides a metaphysically neat account of how laws relate to the rest of the natural world. Laws are taken to be higher-order universals: they are relations whose relata are first-order universals or properties. Because laws are universals themselves, they are subject to the same requirements as others in our general theory of universals. If you have an Aristotelian, immanent conception of universals, this means that laws must be instantiated. The instantiations of laws are to be found, in Armstrong's theory, in the particular causal sequences that involve the instantiated first-order universals.[5]

The theory has such simplicity and neatness. However, the Central Dilemma raises problems for it, which appeared initially in Chapter 6. While it is plausible that if laws are universals they would bear the relation of instantiation to particular causal sequences, it is not clear that this relation is also a governing one or any other that is appropriate to, indeed required by, a nomological realist theory. The relations X is instantiated in Y and X governs Y are not obviously the same and, it might be argued, do not sit together well. If Armstrong is to claim that the relation between a law and its instances is just a case of the metaphysically ubiquitous relation that exists between a universal and its instances (the instantiation relation), then he has to say that there is nothing more to X governs Y than X is instantiated by Y. But we have seen that this is a difficult thing to say where universals are understood in the Aristotelian sense as having no existence beyond their instances. That laws govern their instances is said only to be a 'likely supposition' (Armstrong 1997: 227). Having experienced particular causal relations, one might ascend to nomic relations, directly between the universals involved, then throw away the ladder and treat this as the primary relation. But despite these words, it seems very hard to maintain the nomological realist commitment to [1], laws playing a (governing) role in determining their instances, while seemingly treating those instances as metaphysically prior. Indeed, Armstrong's theory instead seems to have some commitment to a limited Humean supervenience as it will be a law that N(F,G) only if some x (or an x and a y) instantiates F (and thereby G) at some time t (or t_1 and $t_{1+\phi}$). This is a threat to the claim of realism, that laws play a (determining) role in the world's history rather than vice versa.

The DTA theory provides an account of how a law relates to the rest of nature, therefore, but it does not provide a plausible account of how a law governs or plays any other role. Without the latter, the establishment of (this form of) nomological realism is jeopardized. I leave it open, however, that there might be a better theory of externalized laws that can explain the relation of a law to its instances at least as well as the DTA theory but can improve upon the DTA theory's account of the governing role of laws.

While the foregoing was an attempt to show that there remains a problem in what I take to be the best version of an externalized theory of laws, others may disagree with my estimation. Perhaps another external theory does better. There remains a quite general problem with any theory of externalized laws, however: the entailment of quidditism. I now return to that subject, therefore, noting also that if the DTA theory were amended in such a way as to avoid the problem raised above, as Tooley's version might do, it would still retain a major shortcoming.

9.5 External laws and quidditism

A major shortcoming of an external conception of laws is that it appears to have no likely way of avoiding the implication that laws could vary independently of properties. This entails a thesis that is called quidditism that seems highly undesirable. I will recapitulate the nature of this thesis, which was introduced in §6.10, and add more detail. To set up this objection we need to be aware of a number of assumptions. I maintain that they are assumptions that on the balance of argument are acceptable.

We must assume that by an external conception of laws we mean that laws are wholly distinct existences from the things that they govern. It is simplest, in light of the arguments for the DTA theory, to assume that it is *properties* that are related by laws though, if it is something else, it might be possible to show an analogous form of quidditism.[6] If laws do relate properties then, on the external conception, there is no intrinsic connection between them. Despite the relation N, in DTA laws, being called nomic necessitation, for instance, it is contingent which properties nomically necessitate which other properties. There is nothing in the essence of F and G, or a necessary part of F and G, where it is a law that N(F,G), that makes it a law that N(F,G). What is a law might not have been a law and vice versa.

We can now note the upshot, which is almost but not quite the quidditist position, that the nature and identity of a property (or whatever else it is that is governed by laws) are, on the external conception, entirely independent of the laws in which they feature. If laws and the things they govern are independent existences, then there seems nothing that could rule out the independent variation of them. Hence, we may have different laws to the actual ones governing the actual properties (or the actual laws governing a different set of properties). This is explicitly accepted in Armstrong's combinatorial theory of possibility (1989, 2004c).

We can state this view more precisely. It does not, of course, require an actual change in the laws; rather, it can be put in terms of what the theory of external laws allows as a possibility. Where there is a property F, that features in a law L_1, the external conception allows that F could have not featured in L_1 yet still have been F.[7] This is to say that the identity of a property is independent of its nomic role.

It might be that the property F features in a number of different laws, such as N(F,G), N(F,H), N(F,I), ... N(F,X). The external view allows that F need not feature in any of them. F would still be F if there were none of these laws or if F features in a different set of laws instead, N(F,G*), N(F,H*), N(F,I*), ... N(F,X*).

Why is this a problem? There is a second main assumption of the quidditist objection that makes it a problem; namely, the view that the identity of a property is dependent on its nomic or causal role. This assumption can be justified, I believe, and I argue for it in Chapter 10. The view that connects the nature and identity of a property with its nomic or causal role was defended in modern times by Shoemaker (1980) though arguably it has a history going back to Plato's Eleatic Stranger (*Sophist*: 247d–e). Shoemaker's discussion is in terms of properties and their causal roles. Are we permitted to extend his point to the question of properties and their nomic roles? There is clearly a close connection which, it is arguable, justifies the extension. One might agree with Armstrong, for instance, that causal role is merely the instantiation of nomic role. One might think, independently of Armstrong's view, that nomic role and causal role supervene on the powers of a property or that nomic role supervenes on causal role. With either view, what is said of causal role should also be said of nomic role. If the causal role of a property can vary, so can its nomic role.

The view that closely connects properties and their nomic or causal role can be considered on its own merits, independent of the current context. One might say simply that the nomic roles provide the identity criteria of properties, which thereby makes the nomic roles essential to properties, and this would clearly allow no independent variation of properties and nomic roles. One might say that properties just are powers, which is what Shoemaker said at first (1980: 213) though he has recently offered a more cautious view (1998). My own preferred view is that causal powers (and other connections) are *exhaustive* of properties. This allows that a property might be constituted by a cluster of more than one causal power (or connection), though it allows also that a property might be constituted by a single power. This view is developed in Chapter 10 where the merits of the theory are assessed. If we do not accept such a view, of causal or nomic role fixing the identity of a property, what else does fix a property's identity?

While I do not wish to claim that there is no other serious account of the identity conditions of properties, there is reason to think that any alternative identity conditions may also be vulnerable if a change of laws is permitted. One might argue, for instance, that the identity of a property is fixed by its phenomenal role. The identity of redness, for example, is fixed by its appearance of red to a normal observer in ideal observational conditions. A possible change of laws, in the external conception, would seem to allow a change of the phenomenal role of a property. Any alternative conception of properties might similarly be affected by a change of law. If you accept nomological realism, you accept that nature is governed by laws, so any natural explanation of the identity of properties is subject to the reign of law.

We arrive, finally, at quidditism. If one accepts that laws are external to properties, then the identity of a property must be entirely independent of laws. As we have seen, this means also that a property's identity must be independent of anything that is in turn dependent on laws. The only thing that seems to escape this web of laws, that could determine the identity of a property through a change of laws, is an individual essence of a property, a quidditas.

Robert Black (2000) has developed the notion of quidditism, though only to show its undesirability. Lewis famously denied haecceitism (Lewis 1986a: §4.4) – the primitive identities of individuals across possible worlds – but his position permits, if not requires, the primitive identities of properties across possible worlds. 'Quidditism' is Black's term for this latter kind of primitive identity: of properties rather than of particulars (Black 2000: 92). This seems to be the only view that would allow the identity of a property to survive a change in its nomic or causal role. Such an identity is not affected by a change of law nor change of anything that a change of law would change. Anti-quidditists think that something *constitutes* the identity of a property and it is hard to see how this, whatever it is, would not be affected by a change in laws.

Quidditism is not simply an invention. Though the notion may not have been given serious consideration prior to the work of Shoemaker and Black, the view is certainly there, in the neo-Humean metaphysics of Lewis and the contingent and external theory of laws of Armstrong. It does not require too much work to bring it out, as Black has demonstrated in the case of Lewis. Such views have the existence and identities of properties standing wholly apart from the laws they feature in, so are either committed to a form of quidditism or owe us a very good explanation of why not. Ellis has identified the metaphysical background of the view. The view is an essentially Humean one where the laws animate an otherwise inert world of discrete qualities and particulars. Such a Humean metaphysics should not be attractive for a nomological realist and, indeed, Armstrong is criticized for attempting to keep a foot in both camps (Ellis 2001: 216).

That the identities of properties are primitive seems unnecessary and even counter-intuitive. Black starts with the question of whether two qualities could swap their nomic roles. Could F and G swap their roles and still be F and G? If F took the place of G in all its nomic connections with everything else, and G took the place of F, why would F not thereby actually be G and G thereby be F? Our answer to this question is revealing of our intuitions. These would be anti-quidditist intuitions, if we follow Black. But is there also a direct argument against quidditism? Black thinks so. It is not conclusive but it is damaging to the extent that it challenges the intelligibility of quidditism. The argument is that the quidditist could give no non-arbitrary answer to the question of how many (fundamental) qualities there are in the totality of possible worlds (Black 2000: 96). For any world, there will always be another just like it except that its (fundamental) properties are replaced by others. Quidditism allows that a property could be replaced by another that takes on its causal role. Hence, there could be two worlds that coincided in their histories but differed by having different fundamental properties – different because of their individual quiddities – playing the same nomic roles. But, then, for any number of (fundamental) properties you think there might be, the quidditist has no principled reason why there could not be one more than that number. More properties can always be generated simply by substituting for a property another that plays the same role but differs in its quidditas.

Black presents quidditism as an embarrassment for concrete modal realism. It is so because it takes the identities of properties to be primitive rather than constituted by their nomic role. For this reason, I argue, quidditism is also an embarrassment to any theory of laws that allows laws and properties to vary independently. This applies, therefore, to any external conception of laws. If laws govern properties from outside or beyond, such difficulties lie in wait.

9.6 First horn: summary

This has been a lengthy diversion into some deep issues of metaphysics. Before moving on, therefore, it will help to summarize the argument so far, as it has contributed to an understanding of the first horn of the Central Dilemma.

I have tried to show that the nomological realist must say that laws play some role. This role may, in a loose sense, be called a governing role. It means that the laws must, to a degree, determine the world's history: a history of events or distribution of properties. To not allow this would be to have a lawless metaphysic such as Humean supervenience. But if laws are to play a determining role in the world's history, the nomological realist must give us an explanation of how they do so. They must say that laws either govern externally or internally. If they govern externally, we need an account of how they are suitably related to the things they govern. The DTA theory, I claim, is one of the best attempts to answer this question. But it has a problem explaining how this relation can correctly be thought of as a governing relation for laws. It also faces the problem, which it seems would apply to any theory of external laws, that it entails the deeply problematic thesis of quidditism.

A simple statement of the first horn of the Central Dilemma can now be offered:

> *First horn:* a theory of external laws [A] is in need of an account of how laws relate suitably to the things they govern. The most plausible such account, the DTA theory [A_T], still has difficulty in explaining this relation and entails an incredible thesis (quidditism). Any other theory of external laws would need to avoid the problem of A_T but in a way that provides an account of A that is at least as plausible as A_T.

We can now move to consider the second horn, where laws govern internally.

9.7 The Central Dilemma, second horn: internalized laws

The second horn of the Central Dilemma is an attempt to show problems with the reductive accounts of laws that nevertheless profess nomological realism. Ellis (2001, 2002) has such an account, I argue, and so does Lowe (2002b). The second horn shows that there is a problem with any account that attempts to be realist about laws while nevertheless conceding that they are not primitive elements of an ontology. Rather, such laws are constructed from other elements that are not laws. They are *reducible* to such elements. If laws *supervene* on things that are not laws, or are *constituted* by them, then the same sort of considerations apply.

If laws are internal to the things they govern, we need an account of how they can govern or play any role from within, from the inside. There will be at least two things we will want to know. First, we will want a plausible account of how laws could be internalized in properties or events. Second, we would want an account of how such laws could govern or play a determining role in the properties or events in which they were internalized. I will argue that these two requirements are at odds and that a satisfactory answer to one will almost certainly preclude a satisfactory answer to the other. We can show how laws could be embodied in properties or events but then it seems very hard to maintain that they can govern those properties or events in which they are embodied. Alternately, we can attempt to give an account of governing, but any such account is likely to make it highly implausible that such governing laws are internal to the things they govern. I will give an example of each such case to illustrate how difficult it is to satisfy both demands on the internal theory. First, I will describe Lowe's recent account of laws, which builds them from other categories in his four-category ontology. Lowe shows that laws are reducible to, or constituted by, elements that are not laws. But then can he really claim that the laws govern or determine anything? If not, what claim do they have to be real laws in nature? Second, I will consider another Newtonian model of laws. This is the view that there are internal governing forces within individual bodies. While we might concede the governing role of such forces, the concession will then be grounds for thinking that such laws are not really internal to what they govern, so the account might slide back to an external conception of laws.

Lowe has presented recently a new theory of the metaphysics of laws (2002b). This can be understood independently of his normative account (Lowe 1980, 1982), though in its core features it is consistent with it. Lowe says 'A law simply consists – in the simplest sort of case – in some substantial universal or kind being characterised by some non-substantial universal or property, or in two or more kinds being characterised by a relational universal' (2002b: 235).

The key point about Lowe's theory, for our present argument, is that such laws are accounted for entirely by the existing metaphysical resources that Lowe thinks his four-category ontology describes (see Figure 9.1). Lowe presents this as an advantage of his theory of laws. The DTA theory had been accused of relying on a 'mysterious' tie of nomic necessitation between universals (van Fraassen 1989: Ch. 5). Lowe is able to avoid this charge because, though he has a theory like the DTA theory, he has a richer ontology. Substantial and non-substantial universals are distinguished (see Chapter 7 for the justification of this richer ontology). Once this distinction is made, laws can be accounted for purely in terms of the universals involved, which are sometimes substantial universals or kinds. We have a law simply when we have a characterizing attribute of a kind.

Lowe's theory may fairly be described as a reductive theory of laws. Laws are reducible to kinds and their characterizing attributes. Reduction

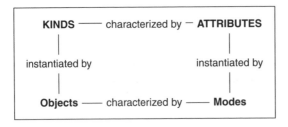

Figure 9.1 Lowe's four-category ontology.

is a strong claim, however. Should one offer a more modest account, such as laws supervening upon these other elements or perhaps being merely constituted by them? I think there is good reason to class Lowe's theory as reductive. But the applicability of the second horn would not hinge on this. The second horn of the Central Dilemma would be applicable to each of reduction, supervenience and constitution. The way that it strikes against reduction, means that it will also strike the weaker claims.

Lowe's theory is reductive because it allows that *Ks* are *F* is a law (2002b: 236). Laws are identical with a kind having a characterizing attribute so there is the one-to-one correspondence that is required by reduction but not by supervenience. In the case of constitution, there is a one-to-one correspondence but without identity. The statue and block of marble could coincide without being identical as it may remain the same statue even if some of the marble that constituted it was replaced. This could not be said of laws, as understood in Lowe's theory. We could not replace one characterizing attribute of a kind with another and still have the same law.[8] Nor could the law survive a change in its component kind and still be the same law it was.

Could we make sense of a law that was reducible to other things that are not laws? There are plenty of accounts that assume so. Both Lowe and Ellis offer accounts that they take to be theories of laws. Their theories are not primitivist about laws but they are supposedly realist. They offer analyses of laws in terms of other categories, which are taken to be realized or non-empty. But if the claimed identity is a fact, and such other categories indeed exist, how could one not then concede that laws exist by being identical with something (else) that exists? A correct reductive analysis of laws might, therefore, be considered a proof of the existence of laws.

This argument would appear plausible but it is a bit too early to proclaim its victory. The Central Dilemma says that there is a problem about how the role laws are supposed to play – the governing role – could possibly be realized. The second horn applies to such reductive accounts and effectively questions whether laws could be reduced in the intended way.

The simple question raised by this side of the dilemma is how something could govern, or play any determining role in, that to which it was reducible. It can be seen that precisely the same can be asked of supervenience and constitution. How could something govern, or play a role in determining, that by which it was constituted? How could something govern, or play a governing role in, that upon which it supervened?

I started this chapter by saying that if laws are real, they must do something. Otherwise, they are just loose wheels, which are thereby not part of the mechanism.[9] Attempts have been made, within broadly reductive accounts, to say that laws nevertheless do something. Lowe has said, in his earlier theory of laws, that they have a normative force (1980, 1982, 1989: Chs 8, 9, 10). But would this count as laws actually doing something? Are they determining what ought to be the case?[10] How could they do this while still being reducible? The second horn leads to the charge that they could not. The law that ravens are black (one of Lowe's favourite examples from his normative account) cannot make it that ravens are black if the law is reducible to blackness being a characterizing attribute of ravens. The law says only *that* blackness is a characterizing attribute of ravens, it cannot *make it* that blackness is a characterizing attribute of ravens. And, if laws are reducible, it seems there is nothing else that they can do.

This sort of criticism may sound familiar. It has been made before in the context of the regularity theory (for example, Armstrong 1983: 40–1). If you take the regularity theory to be a theory *of* laws (rather than the Humean interpretation, which I prefer, that it is the theory that there are no laws), then you take laws to be reducible to exceptionless regularities of events. But laws are supposed to explain, we might have thought. A regularity-law does not explain its instances. It does not explain *why* $\forall x$ $(Fx \rightarrow Gx)$; it only states *that* $\forall x$ $(Fx \rightarrow Gx)$. Regularity-laws do not explain because they play no role in determining or governing their instances. They are reducible to their instances. They would, thus, constitute another example of what I wish to emphasize: that there is an inconsistency in the idea of something determining that to which it is reducible. For real laws, we need such a governing role, so a reductive account is not an option.

Note that this is not a general attack on the notion of reductive analyses, which are often the main business of philosophy. The argument is only that there is something unacceptable about the claim that a reductive analysis of laws is a credible realist account of laws. If real laws are supposed to be things that govern or play some determining role, they cannot be also reducible. They are the things that cannot be reducible and still have a claim to be what we supposed. Other reductive analyses may be perfectly successful.

9.8 Newtonian spirits

The subject of the second horn was internalized laws but the attack, so far, seems to have been on reducible laws. Might there be a sense in which a law could be internal to the phenomenon it governs without being reducible to it, supervenient on it, or constituted by it? It is hard to imagine an alternative to these options but perhaps one is suggested by a reading of Newton. This is another Newtonian theory, based on a reading of different texts from the first Newtonian theory, above. Again, I claim no historical accuracy for the theory.

In *De gravitatio*, Newton suggests that there are inherent powers in bodies. According to Stein (1995: 355), Newtonian bodies may be nothing more than powerful fields. In the *Principia*, bodies are said similarly to contain forces. What might be the sources of such powers and forces?

A suggestion is provided in the General Scholium to Book Three of the *Principia* (see Densmore 1995: 402–6). Bodies are inhabited by spirits that control their movements. Might we be able to say that the actions of such spirits could constitute the laws that govern those bodies and which are, thereby, internal laws but not reduced laws?[11]

Regardless of the merits or otherwise of this theory of laws, it is not what we are looking for. It appears to be a theory of internal laws only in the sense in which we allow that spirits can inhabit a body. But although such spirits are supposed to reside within bodies, it is also true that they are not a part of those bodies, hence not truly internal to them in the pertinent sense. They are independent existences and it is no essential part of the body that it is inhabited by this spirit imposing these forces in accordance with these laws. The laws could have been different, if God had decreed it so, in which case the same bodies may have contained different forces.

This Newtonian account appears to slide unavoidably back to an external conception of laws, therefore. The only way to have a properly internalized conception is to have laws as at least a part of what they govern. Newtonian spirits cannot properly be thought of as a part of what they govern, in the required way. In general, it is hard to see how we could have the required sense of internal laws that was not provided by a reductive or similar account that was thereby subject to the second horn of the Central Dilemma.

9.9 Second horn: summary

Just as we did with the first horn, it will now be useful to have a simple summary statement of the second horn of the Central Dilemma.

The nomological realist must say that laws play some role. This role may, in a loose sense, be called a governing role. It means that the laws must, to a degree, determine the world's history: a history of events or distribution of properties. To not allow this, would be to have a lawless metaphysic such as Humean supervenience. But if laws are to play a determining role in the world's history, the nomological realist must give us an explanation of how they do so. They must say that laws either govern externally or internally. If they govern internally, we need an account of how they are suitably related to the things they govern. A reductive theory, I claim, is one of the best attempts to answer this question. But it has a problem explaining how something can govern that to which it is reduced.

A simple statement of the second horn of the Central Dilemma can now be offered:

> *Second horn*: a theory of internal laws [B] is in need of an account of how laws could be suitably internal. The most plausible such account,

reduction [B_T], is an implausible account of governance. Any other internal account would need to avoid the problems of B_T but in a way that provides an account of B that is at least as plausible as B_T.

9.10 Full statement and conclusion

We can now bring together the two horns of the Central Dilemma to give the full version of the argument. This is it:

Either laws have [1] some (governing or determining) role or [2] not.

If [1] there is a (governing or determining) role for laws, then such laws are either [A] external to the things for which they play that role (they govern or determine) or [B] they are internal to them.

If [A]: a theory of external laws is in need of an account of how laws relate suitably to the things they govern. The most plausible such account, the DTA theory [A_T], still has difficulty in explaining this relation and entails an incredible thesis (quidditism). Any other theory of external laws would need to avoid the problem of A_T but in a way that provides an account of A that is at least as plausible as A_T.

If [B]: a theory of internal laws is in need of an account of how laws could be suitably internal. The most plausible such account, reduction [B_T], is an implausible account of governance. Any other internal account would need to avoid the problems of B_T but in a way that provides an account of B that is at least as plausible as B_T.

Neither [A] nor [B] look good. Therefore, [1] doesn't look good. The alternative is [2], lawlessness.

The Central Dilemma has been designed to highlight a weak point in any nomological realism. In much of the philosophical discussion that has supported a realist stance on laws, it has not been satisfactorily described what laws are supposed do and how exactly they are supposed to do it. This has become an embarrassment for the traditional notion of a law of nature. So difficult has it been to maintain the stance that laws play some role in metaphysics that it has been considered instead whether they have a role only in epistemology. Laws thus became the statements of a theory that were foundational of it or statements that played a certain robust explanatory role. But this is to give up on the project of taking laws metaphysically seriously. Any such existence for laws has been accounted for in terms of other things that we were more confident existed and fully deserved their place in our ontology. We could only claim that there were laws if we weakened the notion of a law considerably from its Newtonian origin. But this has required that the concept has changed out of recognition.

I have been considering whether a more traditional concept of a law – where a law plays at least some role in determining phenomena – can be redeemed. The Central Dilemma is offered as a major obstacle for anyone who thinks it can be. It might, thus, be a good reason to give up on laws. If laws cannot do the work they were originally intended to do, there seems little attraction in retaining them. But the lawless metaphysics I advocate needs more than that. As well as finding that laws can do no work, it would also be reassuring to find that there were things other than laws that were capable of providing what we thought laws could give us. This will be the subject of the next chapter.

10 Modal properties

10.1 Necessity in nature

Although Wittgenstein was a thinker of great originality, he nevertheless stuck to the standard Humean attitude to necessity when he wrote in the *Tractatus* that 'There is no compulsion making one thing happen because another has happened. The only necessity that exists is *logical* necessity' (Wittgenstein 1921: §6.37). I have shown in earlier chapters how this lack of necessity in things has produced a strategy of subsumption under laws. Some philosophers take these laws to be real and responsible for the world's regularity. Humeans take these laws to be nothing more than the regularities. Wittgenstein was in the latter camp, and he seemed to profess his anti-realism about real laws in nature in the next section of the *Tractatus* (ibid.: §6.371): 'The whole modern conception of the world is founded on the illusion that the so-called laws of nature are the explanations of natural phenomena.'

Both the nomological realists and Humeans invoke an image of nature that is intrinsically free of necessity. The realists argue that unless there are laws, the necessity that there is in the world would be lacking. Therefore, there must be laws. The Humeans, in contrast, are happy with the idea of there being no necessity in nature. They are happy to allow *talk* of laws but only in the attenuated sense. The pattern of events determine what the laws are. Realists claim that the direction of determination is the other way round.

A verdict must now be passed on this issue. We must decide whether there is necessity in nature and, if so, whether it is provided by laws. The position of realist lawlessness, which I advocate, is that there is necessity in nature but that it is not provided by laws. Realist lawlessness is the view that both of the existing main positions are wrong in part. The Humeans are wrong to suppose that nature contains no necessity. We have already seen some of the weaknesses of the Humean position but now a more positive case for there being natural necessity will be mounted. The nomological realists are wrong to think that laws deliver, or could deliver, the necessity they think nature contains. I have argued that there is something deeply problematic about the putative ability of laws to deliver any such necessity.

But if laws do not give the world necessity, what does? I will argue the positive case for it being properties, and properties alone, that do the job. Accordingly, we might call them *modal* properties, taking the lead from Cartwright (1993). I must, however, concede a certain redundancy in this expression as I am not sure any sense can be made of a non-modal property. Given the wide-scale and enduring view that properties are intrinsically modally impotent, however, I think it is worthwhile emphasizing the idea that properties come modally loaded. This means that they can provide at least some of the world's necessity and possibility.

This chapter is about natural necessity and possibility and its natural source. There are four main views to be defended. First, I will argue that recent claims about the necessity of laws rest almost entirely on as yet unproven Kripkean essentialism about kinds. Second, even if such essentialism is granted, the necessity about laws it provides is not too different from the much-maligned contingent natural necessitation of the Dretske–Tooley–Armstrong theory of laws. Essentialist necessitation still falls far short of logical necessitation and it retains a significant degree of contingency. Contrary to the claims of most essentialists, therefore, there still remains use in the notion of contingent natural necessitation. Third, I will argue that there can be *de re* necessities or natural necessities even if Kripkean essentialism is rejected. This will depend, however, on acceptance of the fourth main claim of the chapter, that properties provide real causal powers. Modal properties are the grounds of the world's necessity and contingency, and therefore of the world's patterns and order. If one believes in truthmakers, such properties are thereby fit to be the truthmakers of some modal truths. They would make true the *de re* modal truths, which are the modal truths that are *non-logical* and *non-analytic* modal truths. I will outline the basics of a restricted combinatorial theory of possibility that gives an indication of the sort of modal truths modal properties could make. This will not be a reductive theory of possibility, therefore. I will permit certain classes of natural modal facts. Necessity and possibility, therefore, are real features embodied in the actual world and they are not reducible to non-modal features.

10.2 Full strength necessity in laws

The claim that the laws of nature are necessary has, since Kripke, had a steadily growing popularity. To recapitulate, Kripke (1972, 1980) showed that a truth need not be contingent just because it is discovered empirically. His primary conclusion was that true identity statements were necessary a posteriori truths. Once this category of truths was vindicated, however, Kripke and others started thinking what other types of truth might fall within the category. The necessitarian view is that laws do.

Contingency theorists are said to be confused and are perhaps making an elementary mistake of thinking that just because we cannot know a law a priori, it cannot be necessary. Most confused of all is thought to be Armstrong for his misconceived attempt to marry contingency and necessity in natural laws. But contingency and necessity cannot be combined: it just cannot be done.

Chris Swoyer (1982) was one of the first to raise this view. He accepted the chief insight of the DTA theory that laws involved a relation between universals. But he dissented in arguing that the relation involved was one of metaphysical necessity. He had some arguments against Armstrong's view that the relation was contingent. If it was a contingent relation, it would not support counterfactuals (ibid.: 209). It would be questionable, therefore, whether laws would warrant predictions. Further, this view of laws was offered as an alternative to Humeanism, but it is actually a second-order form of Humeanism: 'according to which it is simply a brute fact that given properties happen to stand in the *I*-relation to each other' (ibid.: 211). Third, Swoyer has a poor view of the attempt to use a notion of physical or nomological necessity. The notion has never been sufficiently clarified nor explained.

Crawford Elder (1994) followed the necessitarian clarion call. He thought unwarranted any attempt to distinguish types of necessity. We cannot accept a notion of physical, nomological or natural necessity that is less than 'full strength'. The necessity of laws must be accepted as being as strong as logical, conceptual or metaphysical necessities. Elder's chief reason for saying this is, like Swoyer's third, that no acceptable account has been given of how physical necessity would differ from contingency (ibid.: 656).

It is in Ellis (2001: §6.8), however, that the notion of contingent necessitation receives the most scorn. Ellis is not so much dismissive of the idea of natural necessitation as such, only of the attempt to make it contingent. Those who, like Armstrong, defend this line, are trying to 'have their cake and eat it too' (ibid.: 215). Armstrong's hybrid relation is supposed to be contingent in one sense and yet hold necessarily between the universals so related. But, he says:

> There is no possible account of natural necessity that is compatible with the view that the laws of nature, and hence the law-making relation, is contingent ... If the relation between the universals is contingent, then the laws are contingent; if it is logically or metaphysically necessary, then the laws are logically or metaphysically necessary.
>
> (ibid.: 216)

This difficulty is inescapable, according to Ellis, so we must declare our laws to be either wholly contingent or wholly necessary and must not attempt to fudge the issue.

The positive argument for necessitarianism comes straight from Kripke's essentialism, which has already been considered in some detail (Chapter 7). While some necessitarians are clear about this, for example Bird (2001), Ellis is keen (2001: 54–5) to emphasize his differences with Kripke. Despite such caveats, Ellis, along with Bird, Elder and Swoyer, all employ the Kripkean essentialist insight as the crucial premise in their necessitarian argument. The core of this insight can be simplified in the following way.

> *Simplified essentialist claim E*: All members of some type F must have some property G because if something did not have G, it would not be an F.

To say that G is an essential property of an F is to say nothing more than that the claim *E* is true. *E* makes it necessary that every F is a G. However, it must be discovered empirically that something that does not have G is thereby not an F. Science has the job of uncovering the essential natures of kinds. Where G is (part of) the essential nature of F, it is a metaphysical necessity that any F is G. But it is an a posteriori necessity.

Despite his desire to seek a modern version, Ellis is very clear that his position is essentialist, calling it *Scientific Essentialism* or, in another place, the *New Essentialism.* Commitments to essentialism can also be found in key places in Bird (2001: 267, 270; 2002: 258), Elder (1994: cf. 664) and Swoyer (1982: 213–14).[1] I have already argued (§7.5) that there remains an unresolved difficulty in essentialism concerning what justifies the elevated status of a property being essential. Unless an improved account can be given, we can only claim that science discovers the properties of kinds, not their essential properties (see Mellor 1977). But I have said that an improved account cannot be ruled out. What I claim here is only that the positive case for the new necessitarianism about laws rests, as yet, solely on this essentialist insight. Those who seek to defend the positive virtues of necessitarianism, ought, I believe, to attend to the existing weaknesses of the basic Kripkean position, especially as it is extended to natural kinds.

10.3 Contingent natural necessity

We might yet adopt a position in metaphysics even though a conclusive positive argument for it has not, so far, been discovered. If the alternative is so bad, it might win as the last theory left standing. But have the attempts to malign the contingent necessitation theory been sufficient to destroy it? There remain problems with Armstrong's view, including the attempt to marry contingency and necessity, but is the position of the necessitarian theory much different or much better? The necessitarians attempt to distance themselves from the contingency theorists by forcing the choice between contingency and necessity for laws and refusing to acknowledge great differences between types or modes of necessity. We do not have different necessities, according to Ellis. Rather, 'The difference ... is not so much a difference in the kind of necessity as a difference in the kind of grounding of the necessity' (ibid.: 37). Hence, logical, analytic and metaphysical necessity all mean the same but differ in virtue of what grounds them. Logical necessity is distinguished in virtue of being grounded in (logical) form alone, and holds independently of the meanings of the terms involved. Analytic necessities do depend, for their necessity, on the meanings of their terms. But metaphysical necessities are grounded in reality – in the real essences of things (2001: 11). If we are not allowed different types of necessity but only one type of necessity and three different ways it might be grounded, Armstrong's attempt at a distinctly contingent natural necessitation looks a bad idea from the start.

Has Ellis succeeded in collapsing all forms of necessity into one or (depending on which side you take) reuniting an incorrectly divided concept? Necessitarians have been disposed to speak of the laws of nature as necessary, without qualifying the necessity involved, probably because they have a view similar to Ellis's. Ellis avoids such a qualification when he says, 'Both [analytic and metaphysically necessary] propositions are, as logicians would say, true in all possible worlds' (2001: 37). But can we say that a metaphysically necessary truth is true in all possible worlds without qualifying what sort of possible worlds we mean? Can we say that a metaphysically necessary truth is true in all *logically* possible worlds? Surely, we cannot. Ellis has stated, reasonably, that what is logically possible is dependent solely on its logical form. A proposition's *logical* possibility, in simple terms, is determined by whether or not it contains a contradiction.[2] The negation of a true natural law statement, however, is almost certainly not going to be a *formal* contradiction. Hence there will be some logically possible world where the negation of a metaphysical necessity is true. Note that we are not saying that we are identifying a metaphysical or naturally possible world here, only one that is logically possible because it contains no formal contradiction.

It can very quickly be seen that the negation of a law statement is logically possible. The most widely accepted contenders for the correct logical form of a law statement are (1) a universally quantified conditional, $\forall x$ $(Fx \rightarrow Gx)$; (2) a second-order relation between first-order universals, $N(F,G)$; (3) a functional equivalence, $G = f(F)$; and (4) a dispositional characteristic of a natural kind, φF (following Lowe 1980, 1982). Even if we assume the metaphysical necessity of such laws, we cannot say that their negations are logically impossible, that is, on the basis of their form alone. Hence, $\neg(\forall x\ (Fx \rightarrow Gx))$, $\neg(N(F,G))$, $\neg(G = f(F))$, and $\neg(\varphi F)$ are logically possible even if they are negations of metaphysical necessities. We may grant the metaphysical necessity of electrons having spin (or intrinsic angular momentum) $\pm\frac{1}{2}$ while accepting its logical contingency because its negation is not formally self-contradictory.

There is a sense in which the negation of a law is self-contradictory but this would not help the case for metaphysical necessitarianism. One might say that by an electron one *means* something that has spin $\pm\frac{1}{2}$. Hence in negating the law, one is effectively saying that something with spin $\pm\frac{1}{2}$ does not have spin $\pm\frac{1}{2}$, which *is* self-contradictory. But this move cannot be employed by the essentialists as they distinguish sharply between a statement being necessary and it being analytic. Crucially, they claim that the necessity of laws is *de re* necessity – necessity in the things themselves – rather than *de dicto* necessity, which is mere necessity of words, grounded in meaning. The move from metaphysical to logical necessity, via analyticity, is not a move open to the essentialist, therefore, on pain of the self-destruction of essentialism.[3]

The metaphysically possible worlds are plausibly, therefore, a sub-set of the logically possible worlds, simply because the constraints on logical possibility are so weak. We can say on the basis of extension alone that any P that is metaphysically possible will be logically possible, but not vice versa.[4] It is wholly plausible, therefore, to speak of something being metaphysically necessary but logically contingent.[5] It seems, therefore, that we cannot deny that there are different *modes* of necessity. But to endorse such a view is already to concede that a notion of contingent necessitation is not so hopeless, as long as we are not saying that something can be contingent and necessary in respect of the same mode of necessity.[6] There was no reason to think Armstrong and other contingency theorists were ever claiming something quite so contradictory.

What were they claiming? Something, I shall argue, that is not so different from the view Ellis must hold. Indeed, the chief difference between Ellis's natural necessitation and the contingent natural necessitation view comes down not to different views over the modal nature of laws but to Ellis having a richer ontology than Armstrong. Ellis admits natural kinds as an irreducible class, which Armstrong does not, and this allows him to make the case for a more restricted view of natural possibility. First, though, how can Ellis's view be close to that of Armstrong's contingent natural necessitation?

Ellis defends, as we saw in Chapter 7, a natural kind structure throughout nature, up to and including the whole world itself. The world is one of a kind. However, 'What is naturally *necessary* in our world is what must be true in any world of the same natural kind as ours' (2001: 253). There are, however, alien worlds that contain alien kinds. Consequently, these worlds have different laws of nature. Because of that, they are not worlds of the same kind as ours (ibid.: 255).

It can be seen from this that Armstrong and Ellis do not differ in respect of their attitude to necessity but in respect of their attitude to kinds. Armstrong thinks that kinds are reducible to complexes of properties or classical universals (1997: 65–8), so we do not need a separate category of substantive universals or kinds. Because of this, he steers clear of the issue of essentialism about kinds and is able to say that it is logically possible that the laws of nature are different. Because Ellis thinks there are good reasons to believe in kinds, reasons I reviewed in a Chapter 7, the essentialist move is open to him. But this leads merely to the transformation of Armstrong's intuition of the contingency of laws. While Armstrong says that laws are naturally necessary but no law is logically necessary, Ellis says that laws (understood as essences of kinds) are naturally necessary but that no kind is a necessary existent. The logical contingency of laws is thus transformed into the logically contingent existence of natural kinds. While Armstrong supports 'necessitation, given the contingent relations there just happen to be between universals', Ellis supports 'necessitation, given the contingent kind of world we have'. All that is required for this difference in conclusion is the acceptance of natural kinds and essences by one position and their denial by the other. And, although Armstrong has little to say on the modes of necessity, we are nevertheless entitled to say that the different statements of the logical contingency of laws depend in no crucial way on a difference in attitudes to necessity and contingency.

We may conclude, therefore, that nothing absurd has been proved in the notion of contingent necessitation that the new necessitarians scorned. Indeed, the necessitarian position contains a number of structural similarities with the contingent necessitation theory. The chief difference concerns the acceptance of natural kinds, linked with essentialism, by the necessitarian theory, which leads to a more constrained view of what is naturally possible and necessary. But what is logically possible is wholly unaffected by essentialism and, unless distinct modes of necessity are improperly conflated, the category of a naturally necessary but logically contingent truth remains justified. The claims we saw in Swoyer, Elder, and Ellis, that Armstrong's contingent natural necessitation is a wholly mysterious and puzzling relation, are not fully convincing therefore. Perhaps Ellis has succeeded in providing a better account of logically contingent natural necessitation but, if not, his position would be no less mysterious and puzzling than Armstrong's.

10.4 *De re* necessity

De re necessity means necessity in nature: in things, rather than in words or logical form. It is the sort of necessity that is denied by Humeans and by the *Tractatus*-Wittgenstein. They think there are no necessary connections in nature between distinct existences. We have seen how this standard empiricist account of the world has been challenged by essentialism. But there remain enough concerns about essentialism to justify a reluctance to have the whole anti-Humean case rest upon it. I claim, however, that essentialism is just one possible source of *de re* necessity so we might yet accept necessary connections between distinct existences in nature even if we eventually reject essentialism. I will also call *de re* necessity natural necessity or sometimes metaphysical necessity. I do not restrict metaphysical necessities to essentialist necessities. Let us consider some of these other sources of *de re* necessary connection.

First, there seem to be necessary connections between distinct properties that cannot be put down to form or meaning and, more plausibly, should be considered *de re*.[7] These necessary connections are not obviously anything to do with essentialism, nor is it obvious that they are merely analytic. Examples are the non-symmetrical relation of necessitation between being coloured and having shape and the symmetrical necessitation between having shape and having size.[8] No plausible case can be made for these being examples of single properties – for example, being the single property of shape–colour – as it is a datum that variation of one of the related properties can occur independently of variation in the other. Thus, something may change its colour while retaining its shape, or vice versa. These two properties thus qualify as distinct existences.[9] Could one deny that there really is a metaphysically necessary connection between them? I do not think plausibly so. Colour requires an area to be coloured, but every area is bounded. A bounded area must be of some shape. There is thus a chain of necessary connections through colour, area, boundary, to shape. At no point does the chain appear weak. And we cannot reasonably maintain that the necessary connections are merely logical or analytic. They must be grounded in the natures of the properties involved.

Second, there are necessary exclusions between properties, the paradigm examples of which are determinate properties that fall under a determinable. Ellis prefers to speak of species that fall under a genus, rather than determinate properties of determinables, because all instances of having a mass of 2 grams are also instances of having a mass, though this is hardly conclusive against the alternative distinction.[10] It seems that a particular cannot instantiate two different determinate properties (of the same level of determinacy[11]) under the same determinable. For example, if a particular weighs exactly 5 grams, it cannot at the same time weigh exactly 10 grams. Having charge $\frac{2}{3}$ is incompatible with having charge 0. A particular cannot be all red and all green. Breaking down the apparent metaphysical necessity of these exclusions into smaller necessary steps, as above for necessary connections, does not seem quite so easy. This may be because it is a necessity that permits no further analysis. Indeed, Johnson thought that such necessary exclusion could actually be constitutive of the determinable.[12] A determinable would then be a group of incompatibles – a mutual detestation society.

Armstrong discusses such incompatibilities (1989: 78) and says that they do not threaten his theory of unrestricted compossibility. More on what this means later – for now we need only consider his claim that such examples are not genuine *de re* incompatibilities. His theory of unrestricted compossibility applies only to distinct properties but the incompatibilities between determinates do not involve (wholly) distinct properties, he says. Being 10 grams has being 5 grams as a proper part so these two properties are not compossible. Armstrong acknowledges (ibid.: 80), however, that if there are irreducible qualities, as opposed to quantities, then the foregoing response cannot apply. Colours are the most obvious examples of incompatible qualities. Whether they can be reduced to quantities is controversial.

A third source of *de re* necessity might prove to be the most important but also the most contentious. These are the necessary connections that dispositions or causal powers bring to the world. Being soluble and being dissolved are distinct existences, it is to be maintained, yet they are *de re* connected and the connection is, contrary to claims by the enemies of the dispositional, more than mere analytic necessity. Such properties may prove to be the most important modal properties to the extent that they evidently abound but they are also typically dynamic. By dynamic, I mean that the causal powers of particulars are the properties that are responsible for, or productive of, changes in those and other particulars. Such dynamism, if it can be justified, would be a crucial feature for properties to have. The previous two classes of metaphysical necessity do not have this dynamic aspect. They appear static in that their kind of exclusion and connection between properties does not involve, determine or afford change.

Some more traditional accounts of properties depict them as intrinsically passive, sometimes 'categorical' or causally inert (Ellis 2001: §3.2). If properties are like this, then it seems that laws are needed to provide the world with animation – to make things happen (see Armstrong 2004a). But we have already seen the weakness of the nomological argument (Chapter 5) that it makes the unwarranted assumption that laws, and only laws, can provide the world with certain evident features. In the idealized nomological argument, NA, one of the characteristic features of S, the set of so-called nomological features of the world, is *de re* necessity. Perhaps the world has something else that can provide it. It would be hoped so as the Central Dilemma shows that it is not easy to see how laws can supply S, including the required necessity. It seems a good idea, therefore, to investigate the idea that dispositions or powers supply the world's necessity and possibility through being intrinsically modal: affording, grounding or instigating change. There are, however, some serious attacks on whether powers can do this job.

10.5 Is a power's necessity merely analytic?

There is a line of attack against powers or dispositions that states that any necessity between a disposition and its manifestation is merely analytic. Worse than that, this objection might be pushed further to the claim that a disposition and its manifestation are not even distinct existences and, for that reason, a disposition cannot be the cause of its manifestations.[13] If the connection between a disposition and its manifestation is only analytic, then the claim that dispositions can deliver metaphysical necessity to the world, instead of it being laws that do so, faces serious difficulty.

The objection starts from the observation that a disposition term means something that causes manifestations of a certain kind. Further, for any particular kind of event, a disposition term can easily be generated that means a property for that kind of event. This could be done merely by attaching a suffix '-ible' or 'able' to the event-kind term. Hence we could create 'bendable', 'breakable', 'flexible', and so on (see Quine 1960: 223). This has led to the *virtus dormitiva* objection, which is that dispositions are only trivial or spurious causes of anything (see Mumford 1998a: §6.6). They might not even be real things at all.

It should be conceded that there is analytic necessity involved in the case of dispositions. Like other analytic necessity, this is grounded in meaning. One of the central meanings of disposition terms is of the form 'the cause of F', at least according to a functionalist account but also, arguably, on a physical intentionality account of powers as well.[14] But this does not demonstrate that there is *only* analytic necessity involved. Indeed, it would be absurd to say that *the cause of F* could not cause F because it means *the cause of F*. It is reasonable to argue that *the cause of F* and *F* denote distinct properties and likewise for a disposition and its manifestation. Dispositions, it seems, can certainly be said to exist independently of their manifestations (Molnar 2003: Ch. 4). For example, something can be soluble without ever dissolving. Dispositions and their manifestations thus pass an obvious test of being distinct existences. Further, if they are causes of their manifestations, and we have a non-reductive, non-Humean account of what such causation is, then they are *de re* necessarily connected to those manifestations. This view takes causal language at face value and gives up on the recalcitrant problem of reducing causal concepts to non-causal, non-modal concepts: a problem the counterfactual dependence account persists in trying to solve.

This view would, however, require that we be realists about dispositions and some philosophers have thought the existence of dispositions to be far less certain than the existence of laws. Increasingly, however, the reality of dispositions or powers is accepted (Ellis 2001; Molnar 2003; McKitrick 2003). Those who have doubted the existence of dispositions have assumed the availability of laws that might do all the work dispositions would have done and explain the appearance of dispositionality besides (Armstrong 2004a). Hence, we could have non-powerful, categorical properties that are governed by laws. Laws somehow ensure that all categorical properties of the same kind have behaviour of the same kind and there is nothing more to dispositions than this. There are certainly not irreducible dispositional properties besides. But such an account of laws is not as easily available as empiricist philosophers have thought. How laws exercise their power seems far from clear (Chapter 9), and no more clear than the powers account that it is supposed to avoid. One of the chief purposes of this book is to defend this point.

Instead, many realists follow an idea that was voiced by Shoemaker (1980): that properties are intimately connected with powers and have *de re* connections with other properties in virtue of those powers. If this is defensible, the laws view would be redundant and we would not have to tackle its problems.

10.6 Powerful properties

Properties are powerful. In virtue of being powerful, they provide natural necessity and possibility and are 'fit to be truthmakers of modal truths.[15] They are not the truthmakers of all modal truths: only the natural or *de re* modal truths.[16] But in what sense are properties powerful? Their power has been denied. Many philosophers have had, what Nancy Cartwright has called, a de-modalized view of properties (Cartwright 1993). On this view, properties are not intrinsically powerful, though they may be powerful extrinsically in tandem with laws of nature. What reason do we have, then, for claiming that properties are intrinsically modalized?

The view of properties I find most attractive is one in which they are natural clusters of, and exhausted by, powers (plus, as we will see in §10.8, other connections to other properties). The considerations I prefer in defence of this view are metaphysical. There is also a linguistic argument for the view and an epistemological one. The linguistic argument is simply that property terms and verbs are modalized, in that they indicate possibilities and necessities (Cartwright 1993). The epistemological argument is that we can experience the causal powers of properties – indeed that is all we experience of properties – and that we distinguish properties by their powers (Shoemaker 1980). But neither of these considerations can prove the metaphysical thesis that properties are powerful. Perhaps they assume a metaphysics of powerful properties but a direct discussion of the metaphysical position would be better.

There are two metaphysical reasons in favour of powerful properties as a metaphysical commitment. The first is the negative one. The alternative view is implausible. The alternative, in this case, would be the metaphysics of impotent particulars with a world animated only by laws. No account has provided the necessary detail that would explain how this could work. The second reason is a positive one. It is that by accepting powerful properties, the other metaphysical difficulties we have encountered are solved or dissolved. The account has, therefore, metaphysically useful implications. As well as positively recommending the view, however, we need also to defend it. There is an attack on the notion that properties are clusters of powers that claims nothing would be actual. The world would consist of a constant shifting round of powers with everything being mere potential.

Before offering the required defence, we need to understand better what is meant by the claim that properties are powerful. On this view, powers are not regarded as further properties of properties, at least not directly. There is such a view, which sees powers as second-order properties of properties. Instead, properties are understood as clusters of powers. This view is inspired by Shoemaker (1980), who finds something similar in Locke (1690: Bk II, Ch. 8, Sec. VIII). Properties are to be regarded as clusters whose identities are thereby fixed by extension. Because of this, a property's causal roles are necessary to it.

There are various interpretations of how properties might be connected with their powers or causal roles. Perhaps properties are sets of instantiated powers. Perhaps they are mereological sums of them. Perhaps property terms merely plurally denote multiple powers.[17] A full development and defence of any of these options will require much work. Fortunately I do not have to provide it here. My claims are neutral on these options. The cluster view is that there is nothing more to a property than its powers and that the powers fix the identity of the property. We don't need to commit on exactly what a cluster is.

Swoyer's essentialism comes from similar considerations. Unlike Ellis's essentialism about natural kinds, Swoyer's is an essentialism about the causal roles of properties. I say more or less the same but I would again downplay the essentialism. We can say merely that a property's identity is fixed by the (causal) role it plays in relation to other properties. Though its identity is fixed by relations with other properties, its existence has no ontological dependence on those properties (Molnar 2003: Ch. 4). The power and its manifestation are distinct existences between which there are *de re* connections. No essential/accidental distinction can be drawn among a property's causal roles as all are equally important and all jointly fix identity. One might say that this makes all of a property's powers essential, as Shoemaker (1980, 1998) does, but given that 'accidental powers' is an oxymoron on this theory, this leaves only a trivial essentialism. Instead of a redundant notion of essence, therefore, we need only extensionality to provide the identity conditions for properties.

Understanding properties in this way would immediately explain what is undesirable about a theory of properties that entailed quidditism. Powers, and the other metaphysical connections that will be described in §10.8, exhaust the properties. There is no remaining residue or other feature of a property in addition to its powers and other connections. This seems entirely the right thing to say as any such residue would be superfluous and unapprehensible. If the residue is not a power, complex of powers, or connection with other properties, it is unknowable. Would it be, again, an unknown property essence? We would certainly want an explanation of what this extra feature was and, more importantly, why it was necessary for our theory of properties.[18] With such an essence, the categorical properties-*plus*-laws view might have a glimmer of credibility. But there seems no other reason to believe in such things.

Do the clusters that constitute properties always contain many powers? Could there be a property that had its identity fixed by a single power? Either option is consistent with the general realist lawless metaphysic being developed and there could be a mixture in which some clusters of powers are complex and some are simple. This would be consistent with a view that permitted a hierarchical ordering in nature in which some properties are very specific, or low level, and some are very general or high level. At a theoretical lowest level would be the single power properties. As a possible example we might take a property invoked in particle physics that is meant to belong to an elementary particular. Some such properties, like spin, charge and mass, relate to precisely defined single powers. Hence, when we say that a down quark has a charge of $-\frac{1}{3}$, we are speaking of a property that seems to be related to (exhausted by) a single kind of power that makes exactly the same contribution to interactions with other particles. (Exactly what the interaction will be will depend also on the different charge powers of the other particle(s) involved in the interaction.) We can test for this power and there might even be more than one test for the very same power. Test results do not constitute the power, as they concern only what we know of powers, so we would not thereby be justified in concluding that we have more than one power merely because we have more than one test for it.

A one-to-one relation between properties and powers would seem neat and simple, so why should we complicate things by allowing one-to-many relations as well? The reason is that it seems plausible for more general, higher-level properties that they involve more than a single power. That is what makes them less specific. In such cases, a property has powers to do more than one thing. Being elastic, for example, affords many different possibilities. This case is different from that where we have different tests for a single power. An ability to bounce (when dropped) is different from an ability to bend (when pressured) though both might reasonably be thought powers of something that is elastic, in virtue of its elasticity. When something has a particular dimension of extension, a variety of behaviour is thereby grounded. A sphere with a 5 cm diameter, for example, would have the power to pass through a 6 cm round hole, but a sphere with a 7 cm diameter will not. But having a 5 cm diameter does not involve only this power, which was arbitrarily selected, and each such power is a part of what it is to be that property.

Viewing the relations between properties, powers, their manifestations, and tests for them, this way might clarify the confusing issue of multiply manifested dispositions. Molnar (2003: 198–9) thinks the distinction between single and multi-track powers is troublesome and has little use. That distinction may now be understood in the following way, which seems relatively unproblematic. Each power is always a power to a single manifestation, as Molnar says ('manifestations are not polygenic'), but a property might involve a multiplicity of powers that can thereby issue in a multiplicity of manifestations. Manifestations are understood in an objective sense: they are not test results that are manifest to an observer's mind but rather events that may exist unobserved. In cases where a property is a complex cluster of powers, therefore, it might be reasonable to speak of it, in this way, being multiply manifestable.

If there are properties that are clusters of distinct powers, however, what is the bundling relation that ties the powers together and makes them all powers of the same property or trope? In short, there is none. There is not an extra bundling element, or external relation, in addition to the powers. This is the answer we would give for any set, in set theory, that is exhausted by its extension. There is not a tie connecting the members or binding them into the set. I propose a similar treatment for properties *qua* clusters. There is no extra element holding a causal power within the cluster or tying the individual powers together. But were one of the powers absent from the cluster, we would have a different cluster so different property. Hence it is possible that a cluster of ten powers exhausts property F and that property G is just like F but differs in respect of just one of the powers. Among other things this might explain why properties can resemble other properties and in different degrees.

But this is not to deny that there can be real and important connections between powers. Something cannot have the power to break easily unless it has the power to break, for example. We are, after all, allowing *de re* connections in nature. And many of the connections between properties will hold in virtue of the connections between the powers that exhaust those properties. But note that, according to the proposed view, those connections are entirely internal to the powers involved. They are not some additional element, extra to the related powers, which would resemble the view of laws being external to that which they govern. Instead, they would be internal relations, which are relations that exist solely in virtue of their relata or relatum existing. In this way, some of the powers in a cluster may be internally connected.

Given that there can be such connections between powers, we might have hope of explaining the notion of a *natural* cluster of powers. The properties that are instantiated in our world do seem to be clusters of connected powers, rather than any odd disparate grouping of them. In the case of elasticity, for example, a detailed understanding of the property could well be expected to reveal a web of interconnected powers. This could explain why some properties (or clusters) are instantiated in our world but not others.

A note should be added to say that this cluster theory of properties is wholly independent of a cluster theory of substances. A rich ontology is favoured in which a category of substance is required over and above the category of properties. Just because one thinks properties are exhausted by powers, one is not committed to viewing substances as exhausted by properties.

Finally, commitment to the view of properties as clusters of powers should be independent of the issue of whether properties are tropes or universals. If they are universals, a cluster is an instantiation of that universal with an exact type of identity of powers running through all such instantiations. If they are tropes, each cluster is a particular, related to other such particulars by similarity relations.

10.7 Shifting potencies

There is one major objection to the claim that properties are exhausted by powers. This has been called the 'always packing, never travelling' objection by Molnar (2003: §11.2). Armstrong, who endorses the objection, explains it thus: 'Causality becomes the mere passing around of powers from particulars to further particulars ... the world never passes from potency to act' (2004a). As a result, he thinks that to give some actuality to the world at least some properties must be non-powers. But if some properties must be non-powers, it would be best to say that they all are non-powers so that a relation between powers and non-powers does not need explaining. Armstrong concludes in favour of the categorical properties-*plus*-laws view, therefore.

But should we grant that if all properties are exhausted by powers, all there will be is shifting potencies and nothing would pass from potency to act? I think not.

First, this view assumes that a power is a potential only and not at all actual in its own right: a power's actuality resides only in its manifestation.[19] A fine example of this assumption is to be found in Howard Robinson's (1982: Ch. 7) argument for idealism, where the only non-power properties are said to be mental. But if a power to F is deemed to be real only when F is realized, we are presented with a very puzzling interpretation of powers. If the power is not actual unless its manifestation is, then in what sense is it a power to F? In what sense is it anything at all? The danger of this view is that it treats powers as nothing more than mere potentialities but thereby ignores the obvious point that to be potent (as opposed to potential) is to be actual. On a causal criterion of existence (see §11.5), being potent is the mark of being actual. Potent means powerful, which is something very different from being potential, meaning not yet actual. Those who favour powers regard them as potent rather than potential. Hence, while powers are powers to do or be other things, they are also things in their own right. The shifting round of potencies is acceptable, therefore, as long as there are actual things doing the shifting.

Second, one might turn the tables on the objector to powers. Do the so-called categorical properties meet the reality test? The test is that something is real when it is powerful. If something can affect something else, then it passes the reality test. Powers pass this test instantly and if reality and actuality are taken to be equivalents, then powers are actual. But according to the theory of non-power properties, that attempts to draw a metaphysical distinction between the categorical and dispositional, categorical properties are by definition intrinsically impotent. No categorical property, taken alone, affects anything else.[20] The Armstrong-world, in which all properties are categorical, is animated only by the addition of laws. Without laws, nothing happens because properties are only extrinsically powerful. How the categorical properties would pass the reality test looks like a more serious concern that it does for dispositions, therefore.

I claim that a view of properties as clusters of powers makes them actual enough. There is more to be said in defence of the metaphysic being recommended but that will be a task for later (Chapter 11). Instead, in the remainder of this chapter, I wish to say more on the business of natural necessity and possibility.

10.8 Restricted combinatorialism

A version of Armstrong's combinatorialism (1989, 2004c) is the preferred way of articulating natural necessity and possibility. This is not intended as a reductive account of modal terms, however. Necessity and possibility are taken as two of the most basic and fundamental notions. What is more, these notions are accepted as propositional modifiers that are made true by things that exist, embodied in nature, as the following account will indicate. This contrasts with Lewis's account, among others. Lewis attempts a reductive analysis of necessity and possibility in terms of other worlds. I argue, in contrast, that the actual world already contains necessity and possibility as intrinsic features *de re*. Hence, I see the combinatorial model as a way of cognizing modality. It does not constitute it. The combinatorial model is a way of representing, understanding, and articulating modal truths and relations. The truthmakers of the natural modal truths would be features in the world, duly called modal properties.

The preferred version of combinatorialism is more restrictive, in a number of ways, than Armstrong's.[21] Though in another way, explained later, it is more liberal. The main principles of combinatorialism will be presented along with the differences between this version and Armstrong's. These principles are all illustrated in the model represented in Figure 10.1.

Following Armstrong, possibilities may be understood in terms of recombinations of existing elements or facts in the world. All the possibilities, including those that are actual, might be represented by listing all those elements in a table or grid. Armstrong's original grid (2004c) shows possible recombinations of particulars and properties. It allows that any particular could have any property, which is a claim that essentialists in particular would dispute. The grid as I present it is designed to show the

		A	B	C	D	E	F	G	H	I	J	...
							Second property					
	A	T			×			□^d			×	
	B		T		×	□^d		×		◇^m		
	C		□^m	T							□^m	
First property	D	×			T			□^d		◇^m	×	
	E	◇^d	◇^d			T		□^d				
	F		◇^d	◇^d	◇^m	□^m	T	□^m	×		×	
	G							T	×		□^d	
	H	□^m	×				◇^d		T	□^m	□^d	
	I	×				×			□^m	T	×	
	J	□^m			◇^m				◇^m	×	T	
	...											

Figure 10.1 Model of restricted combinatorial possibility.

de re connections and exclusions between properties, in virtue of their powers, that I have argued for in this chapter. Some notes are needed in explanation of how the model works.

First, connections between universals are often asymmetrical. One property, F, may necessitate another, G, but not vice versa. A property, G, may exclude another, H, but not vice versa. The model represents this asymmetry by listing each property twice, once along the vertical axis and once along the horizontal. The appearance on the vertical axis denotes the first term of an ordered relation; the horizontal axis denotes the second term. This, of course, does not indicate a specifically temporal priority. The 'first' and 'second' are used to indicate any asymmetrical relation that relates an ordered pair. Temporal priority would be such a relation but so would be necessary or probable connection. A symmetrical relation, for example mutual necessitation, can be represented where H necessitates I and I necessitates H. Mutual exclusion, for example, is represented where I excludes J and J excludes I.

Second, there is an assumption of permissiveness for the properties that can be connected and recombined. Some of the universals may be basic and fully determinate. Some may be what Armstrong calls determinables or Ellis calls more general kinds. Some universals may be kind terms or substantive universals, others classical universals.

Such permissiveness has to be admitted even at the risk of double counting. We have to allow the possibility of a relation holding between determinables even when it does not hold between any particular determinates under the respective determinables. There seems to be a metaphysical necessity, for example, that every coloured thing is an extended thing. This is to be understood as a connection between the universals involved, rather than the particulars that instantiate those universals. This relation between universals, however, cannot be reduced to relations holding between the particular determinates. While we might say that <colour $\Box^m$ shape>, where this means that being coloured metaphysically necessitates having shape, there is no similar relationship between any of the determinate colours and determinate shapes. It is not true, for example, that <red $\Box^m$ square>. Armstrong presents his combinatorialism (2004c) as holding between atomic properties and particulars and, so restricted, it would miss any such relations that hold only at the non-atomic level.

A second reason for such permissiveness is irreducibility. Lowe (2002b) and Ellis (2001) both argue that kinds, or substantive universals, cannot be reduced to clusters of classical universals or properties, contrary to Armstrong's view. Further, Ellis argues that more general kinds (determinables) cannot be reduced to their species (determinates). More general spectral, quantitative kinds, such as mass and length, cannot be reduced to their values because some values in the spectrum might be uninstantiated. We could, of course, have separate grids for substantive universals, determinable universals and determinate universals, if it was important for our purposes to keep them separated. Where not, we can mix them all together.

Third, the relations that hold asymmetrically between universals come in different kinds, as shown in the model. The model displays natural, modal connections. Natural possibilities are indicated by $\diamond^m$ and $\diamond^d$ connections and natural necessities by $\Box^m$ and $\Box^d$ connections. We may represent the individual connections in nature by formulae such as <F$\Box^m$G>, <A×B>, <G$\diamond^d$J>.[22] Where there is no connection or exclusion between universals, a blank on the grid, this is indicated by a formula such as <B○C>. Every universal is trivially connected with itself, hence <ATA>, though this is not to suggest that all connections of a property with itself are trivial or uninteresting. One token or trope of A may cause a distinct token or trope of A, for instance. The model shows, however, that each universal is at least trivially connected with itself. The easiest way to indicate the holding of one of these relations symmetrically might be to prefix a superscript ^{s} to the relation. For example, where <(A$\Box^m$B) & (B$\Box^m$A)>, we might just have <(A $^s\Box^m$B)>, and likewise for all the other relations when they hold symmetrically.

The model shows five sorts of basic asymmetrical connections between properties:

$\diamond^d$ *Dispositional possibility*: The having of one property may dispositionally make possible the having of another property. For example, being fragile makes possible being broken.

$\Box^d$ *Dispositional necessity*: The having of one property may dispositionally make necessary the having of another property. For example, having gravitational mass necessitates attraction of other objects.

$\square^m$ *Metaphysical necessity*: The having of one property may metaphysically make necessary the having of another property. For example, being coloured makes necessary being extended.

$\Diamond^m$ *Metaphysical possibility*: The having of one property may metaphysically make possible the having of another property. For example, being square makes possible being red; having length makes possible being 3 cm.

$\times$ *Incompatibility*: The having of one property may be naturally incompatible with having another property. For example, being square is incompatible with being triangular; being 100°C is incompatible with being 50°C.[23] Incompatibility means either dispositional or metaphysical incompatibility (appropriate superscripts could be added if required: $\times^m$, $\times^d$). Logical incompatibility is *not* intended by $\times$ as no property is logically, i.e. *formally*, incompatible with any other property.

We need also some explanation of a blank cell, which we can represent as $\bigcirc$ and explained as follows:

$\bigcirc$ *Compatibility*: The having of one property is compatible with the having of another property. For example, being five feet eight inches tall is compatible with being female. $\bigcirc$ and $\times$ are interdefinable as each other's negations. Logical compatibility is *not* intended by $\bigcirc$ though it is entailed by it, trivially, as every property is logically, i.e. *formally*, compatible with every other.

Fourth, it might be wondered why the model displays the relations $\Diamond^m$ and $\Diamond^d$ in addition to the natural possibilities of the blank cells. This would seem to suggest that there is something more to $\Diamond^m$ and $\Diamond^d$ than $\bigcirc$. The suggestion is correct. A distinction must be made to allow for the complex relations between properties that there can be in nature. $<X\bigcirc Y>$ does not entail any other connection between X and Y other than that they are compatible. For example, while being five feet eight inches tall is compatible with being female, the two properties have no further metaphysically interesting connection. This contrasts with the connection between being fragile and being broken. There is a connection between these two properties that is more than bare compatibility although it is less than necessitation, as being fragile does not necessitate being broken. The connection is an asymmetrical one with a causal dimension, in that when certain events occur, fragility has a causal connection with being broken. We may assume that there are cases where the cause merely raises the chance or probability of the effect without necessitating it (for which we have the separate connection of $\square^d$). Thus we need a relation that represents connections in nature that are less than necessity, $\square^d$, but more than mere unconnected compatibility $\bigcirc$. $\Diamond^d$ is the connection.

The connection between fragility and being broken highlights the need to distinguish a direction of connection and allow that it may be asymmetrical. While being fragile makes it possible that something be broken, and raises the probability of breaking under certain conditions, there is no such connection the other way, from being broken to being fragile. Quite the contrary. Some dispositions manifest themselves once only and are lost as soon as manifested (Mumford 1998a: 53). Fragility may be a case in point. Its manifestation can destroy its object, one might argue, by destroying its unity and connectedness of parts.[24] Once manifested, the disposition can no longer be ascribed to the object. Hence, there would be an asymmetrical incompatibility between being broken (first property) and being fragile (second property). But this is consistent with there being a connection between being fragile (first property) and being broken (second property). Hence it is possible (naturally and logically) that $<(X \Diamond^d Y)$ & $(Y \times X)>$. This case shows why we cannot allow $\Diamond^d$ and the other such *de re* connections to entail $\bigcirc$. Two properties may be *de re* connected though they are incompatible. Solubility bears the $\Diamond^d$ relation to being dissolved but it is not the case that <soluble $\bigcirc$ dissolved> if nothing can be both soluble and dissolved. As two universals might, thereby, be both connected but incompatible, $\times$, would be best reserved for cases of universals that are incompatible and otherwise unconnected.

The requirement of metaphysical possibility, $\Diamond^m$, in addition to compatibility is still to be justified. Metaphysical possibility is something stronger than mere compatibility. In the case of being five feet eight inches tall and being female, there is no connection between the distinct properties, but also nothing that excludes them from being combined or co-instantiated. There is, however, a connection, in metaphysical possibilities, which amounts to the following. In the case of a metaphysical possibility, such as that from having length to being 3 cm, having the determinable first (or generic) property entails having a further determinate (or specific) property. But it is not entailed which exact determinate (or specific property) is had. We may say, therefore, that where there is the connection $<X \Diamond^m Y>$, X necessitates having one from a range of properties, R, and Y is one of the properties in R. The scope of the necessity should be noted. We are not saying that there is a range of properties and Y is the one in that range that X necessitates. Rather, what is necessitated is that from a range of properties, R, to have X is thereby to have one from R. A metaphysical possibility is whenever a connection of this sort exists between distinct properties. I am not, however, claiming that the relation between a determinable and a determinate is the only sort of relation that could count as metaphysically possible.

It is clear, then, that the model in Figure 10.1 is capable of showing a variety of modal relationships, including logical modal relations and six kinds of non-formal modal relation. Natural possibilities are a subset of the logical possibilities that are indicated at every cell in the grid. The natural possibilities are all the cells other than those where we have an incompatibility ×. Modal properties and metaphysical connections within nature determine what is naturally possible but logical form alone determines what is logically possible, hence there are many combinations that are logically but not naturally possible. Where <A × F>, it is nevertheless logically possible that <A & F>, and where <C □ᵐ H> it is logically possible that <C & ¬H>.

10.9 Possible properties

I said, at the start of the last section, that in one way this restricted combinatorialism was more liberal than Armstrong's original version. This is because it allows a relaxation of Armstrong's instantiation requirement. Recombination of only those properties that are instantiated, at some place or time, does not yield all the possibilities. This is because I accept, while Armstrong denied, that alien properties are nevertheless possible properties. (Armstrong does now grant the possibility of alien properties, see, for example, his 2004b. I am arguing only against his original position.) An alien property is one that is never instantiated anywhere in our world and nor is it a complex property whose components have all been instantiated in our world. If it were the latter, one might yet say that it is real because all the elements that could compose it are real and the property is possible because it is a non-actual recombination of real elements. Suppose, then, that we have a non-complex property that is ever uninstantiated. Because Armstrong has an Aristotelian immanent view of universals, rather than a Platonic transcendent view, he ruled that such a thing is not a property. A property must have at least one instantiation. I agree with Armstrong on this ruling. But I disagree with his verdict that it is not even a possible property. Our intuition is that such a thing could have been instantiated and it may be mere accident that it is not. While I am in favour of restricting what exists to what is actual, I am not in favour of restricting what is possible to what is actual. Armstrong's early combinatorialism limits possibilities to recombinations of the actual and is, for that reason, too restrictive. The more liberal view allows possibilities that are recombinations of possible as well as actual properties.

For this reason, I leave open the full bounds of the model in Figure 10.1. The properties that occupy the axes of our grid may go on indefinitely. It is appropriate to allow some metaphysical and even dispositional connections between merely possible properties. To be a possible property is to be a possible such cluster. Hence, a quantitative determinable – a spectral kind – makes metaphysically possible its values. But we have already come across the idea that certain values on a spectrum may be ever uninstantiated. Nevertheless, where the determinable or spectral kind is real, so is its metaphysical connection with its determinates, including those determinates that are never instantiated and, hence, merely possible. Similarly for the case of a dispositional connection, we may have a disposition whose manifestation is never actualized at any point in the world's history. Its manifestation may be a property that can be instantiated no other way. Our knowledge of such a manifestation and its property may be theoretical only but no less a real possibility for that.

10.10 Natural necessity

Although this chapter has been long, I fear that it has done little more than lay down a framework. The little that it may have done, however, is answer the charge that has come from Swoyer, Elder, Ellis and others, that no sense has been made of the notion of natural necessitation and how it could be something different to plain necessity or plain contingency. We were asked to jump one way or the other and state that the laws, or other connections in nature, are either fully necessary or fully contingent. Because of the well-known problems with wholly contingent laws, if laws had to be stronger, they had to be wholly necessary. But this encouragement to conflate different modes of necessity is inappropriate. It is an over-reaction to the problems of Humeanism. We can acknowledge the modal strength of some connections in nature – those that make other properties necessary or possible – without collapsing this necessity and possibility into logical possibility. The category of logically contingent but naturally necessary is respectable after all, I conclude. By carefully distinguishing between the different connections that may hold in nature, and the relations between these different connections, we can make reasonably good sense of something being in one way contingent but in another way necessary.

This has been an important step in explicating realist lawlessness. I have no doubt that more could be said on this metaphysics of modal properties. But a start has been made. I hope it has shown that laws of nature do not have to be added to properties to make them connect with each other. A little more detail must now be added and some objections pre-empted.

11 Objections and replies

11.1 Responses

The core of the theory of realist lawlessness has been presented. In this chapter I attempt to anticipate some of the likely responses and objections to the account and to the claim that it offers an alternative to a metaphysics of laws. As well as anticipating objections, I am also using this chapter to reply to actual objections that the theory has provoked when it has been presented.[1] In replying to these objections, some of the finer points of the account can be brought out.

Replies to a number of objections have already been given or have been tacit in what has been said before. It will nevertheless be useful to collect them all together one last time. Some of the problems, however, are raised for the first time here.

11.2 Holism versus discreta

First, it may be observed that the account of properties, articulated in the grid of Chapter 10 (Figure 10.1), indicates a holistic view of the world. Am I happy to accept the holism?

On balance, I accept that a holistic view of the world is more attractive than its alternative, which would be a metaphysics of discreta. Some general considerations in its favour are that a property cannot stand alone, unaffected by and unconnected with anything else. A world comes with a whole, connected system of properties. This system is not everything that constitutes the world, as there will be particulars that instantiate those properties and events that those particulars undergo when they instantiate further properties. Properties can plausibly be viewed as properties for something else, however: their effects. Properties are powerful and the particulars are thereby powerful when they instantiate properties. The properties that are real in a world must, therefore, form an interconnected web: a system with no property standing alone or outside.[2] It is implausible to say that anything could be outside the system and still be a property. If something is not a part of the web, it would be difficult to see how it could do anything. Having such a property would make no difference at all to what other properties a thing did, did not, or could possibly have. What would such a property be? What would fix its identity if not the relations borne to other properties? The only answer would seem to by a primitive property essence, a quidditas.

There may be other possible systems of properties to the system we have or, as some would say, other possible worlds. These would be worlds that were filled with properties other than ours. They could not be other worlds that were inhabited by our properties that, for some reason (a different set of laws?), had a different set of relations to each other from the relations they bear in our world. Bearing different relations makes them different properties. These other-worldly possible properties must also come as complete packages of properties.[3]

This prohibits certain possibilities. It says that they are not real possibilities. There is no possibility of a world just like ours but which has a property swapped with a different one that plays the same role. There is no real difference in the imagined world. This seems to be a good consequence of the theory. Indeed, this theory is not the only one that generates this consequence.

If B bears all the same relations to all the other properties that A bears, A and B are identical. There is no further real possibility of a world in which two properties swap their relations, such that B bears all the relations that A bears in the actual world and A now bears all the relations B bears in the actual world. This is really just imagining our own world again but with two names of properties swapped. We cannot even permit a wholesale name swap. Our world contains properties A, B, C, D, and so on, each bearing relations to each other. If we systematically swap A for A*, B for B*, C for C*, and so on for all properties, but preserve the relations such that if $<A \Diamond^d B>$ in the actual world, then $<A^* \Diamond^d B^*>$ in our imagined world, and so on for all relations, then we have not imagined a new world. We have imagined only the properties of our world but we have changed all their names. Such cases are real possibilities only if you either accept quidditism or reject holism. The intuitive implausibility of these cases instead confirms that we should reject quidditism and accept holism.

Lewis uses a metaphor in describing the world, according to his Humean theory, as a vast mosaic (1986b, ix). The point of the metaphor is that the world contains only discrete particulars.[4] Each mosaic tile is completely self-contained, has all its properties (shape, colour, etc.) intrinsically, has no connection (metaphysical, causal, necessary) with any other tile, and may fit alongside any other tile or tiles to make any picture. Hence, in the Humean account of causation, an event is self-contained, its qualities are entirely intrinsic, it has no internal connection with any other event and it may be a part of any pattern of events. Such patterns of events are all there is to causation in the world that gives us an idea of what causes what. But the same events could have fallen in a different pattern. The mosaic tiles could be rearranged to form a completely different picture.

Lewis's metaphor is not precise but it does convey what is peculiar about the Humean view. It is a metaphysic that, because it contains independently existing units, allows the possibility of recombination of those units into any order and arrangement. To extend the idea into three dimensions, the units are like the toy bricks from which children can make lots of different things. One day a brick may be part of a toy house and the next day the very same brick could be part of a toy dinosaur.

Here is another metaphor. In respects it is also imprecise but no more so that Lewis's and it provides a more accurate metaphysical picture, I maintain. The world is more analogous to a jigsaw puzzle. Each jigsaw piece can fit with the rest in only one way. It can connect with a number (all) of its neighbouring pieces but its shape and colouring allow only a single place for it in the complete picture. Furthermore, the entire sum of pieces will fit together only in one way to form one picture. The puzzle has a single solution due to the complexity of its interconnections (I assume this and am ignoring the obvious possibility of jigsaw puzzles that have been cleverly designed to have more than one solution). It is impossible to lift two pieces out of the complete picture and swap their places. Only something of a determinate shape and colouring will fit the vacant spaces (again I employ simplifying assumptions, though true of most actual puzzles). In this sense, the place in the whole picture is necessary to the piece.

The metaphor is inexact in a few ways. The most significant ones are that each piece still has intrinsic qualities, which you could describe if you found a single piece that was separated from the rest of the puzzle, and each piece still has a self-contained identity. In the metaphysics of Chapter 10, each property has an essence and identity only in relation to the other properties. Of course, we could say that only with the other pieces does the individual jigsaw piece make a picture but the same is true of the mosaic tiles.

The point of the inexact metaphor, however, is to illustrate some of the important features of the holistic view of the world. The world is a single whole, composed of properties whose essence and identity are determined by their place in that whole. Such units connect with other units only in certain ways and cannot be a part of another picture. The metaphor of the mosaic suggests unconnectedness and the possibility of the recombination of these very same units.[5] I have given various reasons to reject this metaphysic of discreta. The alternative is a holism, which I therefore recommend.

11.3 Relativity

The theory of properties developed in Chapter 10 involves a kind of relativity that may appear alarming. Such relativity emerges from the rejection of quiddities or individual essences for properties. Instead of quiddities, the essence and identity of a property are determined by its relations to other properties. To be F is only to bear certain relations to all the other properties, G, H, I, and so on. A property was said to be nothing more than a set of connections to, and causal powers for, other properties. The worry naturally arises, however, that if the essence and identity of every property reside only in the relations borne to others, then how can any of the properties have any essence, nature or identity at all? All the other properties, in relation to which F has its entire nature, also have their whole natures relative to further properties. Effectively, we have a gigantic circularity of the kind also found in a dictionary. Every word is defined in terms of other words. Hence, if one begins by understanding no words, as when one picks up an unknown foreign language dictionary, one cannot break into the circle and understand even one of the words. Arguably, then, in this theory of properties, no property can have an essence or nature.[6]

Here is a miniature world that illustrates the difficulty. Let us suppose a world containing just five properties: A, B, C, D and E.[7] A is the property that bears the following relations: $<A \times B>$; $<A \square^m C>$; $<A \bigcirc D>$; $<A \diamond^d E>$. The nature of A is fixed in part, therefore, by a relation it bears to B. But B's nature is given in terms of the relation it bears to the other four properties, for example: $<B \times A>$; $<B \bigcirc C>$; $<B \bigcirc D>$; $<B \diamond^m E>$. The nature of B, therefore, is defined in part by a relation in bears to A. This interdefinability looks like circularity. As exactly the same can be said also of C, D, and E, it is clear that the circularity is global, for this limited world, and nothing at all appears to get its nature fixed. This miniature world differs from ours, if at all, only in the number of properties involved in the interdefinability, so no property in our world has its nature fixed.

There are two points to be pressed into service in assuaging this concern. The first is that an entirely relativistic conception of properties may not be quite so counter-intuitive as at first seems. Indeed, the alternative may be even less acceptable.

There is a clear analogy to be drawn between absolute and relative conceptions of spatial location. Prior to Einstein's relativistic revolution in physics, position in space was thought of as absolute, for instance by Newton and Descartes. Even though there were relations between various positions, a position was thought of absolutely, having a nature and identity independently of the relations it bore to other positions. Its identity could be given in terms of Cartesian co-ordinates, for example. A priori sense could be made even of a single position in a micro-world. Sense could also be made of a world in which an object retained, for a time, its absolute position while its relations with other objects changed. Furthermore, the whole universe could have a position. But this idea of position has been replaced after a widespread acceptance of Einstein's cosmology. There is now nothing like absolute position. The position of everything is given only in terms of the relations it bears to other things. Hence, in another imagined miniature world, where there are only five particulars, f, g, h, i and j, the position of f can be given only relative to g, h, i and j, for example: $R_1(f, g)$; $R_2(f, h)$; $R_3(f, i)$; $R_4(f, j)$. The positions of all the particulars must be so-given in terms of all the other particulars. In the case of particulars, therefore, we have come to accept that relative position is the only position. The alternative cannot credibly be upheld. Absolute positions would require undefined positional essences: spatial haecceities. This would seem less appealing than the idea of the position of f being given in terms of its relations to all the other particulars there are.

What can we say when we return from the example of spatial location back to our original case? First, the alternative to a relativistic conception, once considered, does not appear attractive. The alternative would require a property to have an absolute nature, irrespective of the relations the property bears to other properties. But we have seen (in §6.10 and §9.5) that this appears to entail the unacceptable thesis of haecceities for properties. The idea of properties having a relative nature, rather than absolute one, may not be so counter-intuitive then. We have the Einsteinian model of position as an example of an entirely relativistic system. We can learn to live with relativity. We also have the attractions of the Shoemaker theory of properties to consider and the Eleatic Stranger's reality test. These considerations suggest that an acceptable theory of properties precisely should have properties defined in terms of relations they bear to each other. Properties must involve (or are exhausted by) modal relations to other properties. This entails a relativistic conception of properties while the alternative treats them as intrinsically inert and intrinsically and internally unrelated to each other, which would mean that they would fail the preferred reality test.

There is also a second point about our relativistic conception of properties. It may help to return to the dictionary analogy. This analogy was introduced to illustrate the circularity that arises when we have a global interdefinability of all terms. Nevertheless, there are cases where the words that appear in a dictionary are understood (as well as anything is understood). One explanation of this is the causal theory of meaning. We interact with the world and with other conscious beings. We come to understand the word *cat* not by reading its definition in the dictionary (at least not solely) but by causally interacting with cats and using the word in connection with those interactions. On this theory, it is such interaction that allows us to break into the circle of definition and for words to mean something in the world.

If we now return to properties, we can see that whatever can be said of objects can also be said of properties. We are able to interact with properties. Among the effects they have in their clusters of causal powers, are the effects they have on us, namely, their phenomenal appearance. We can thus know properties either by the phenomenal appearance they cause in us or by the phenomenal appearance in us of other effects that they cause. Some of the relations borne by properties are thus experienced and in this way we are able to break into the circle of interdefinability for the nature of a property.[8]

This idea should not be taken as a form of idealism or even epistemological relativism, however. There is no reason to think that properties are exhausted by their relations to us (see Langton 1998: 182–5). Even though these are the only such relations we will experience, it is a metaphysically persuasive hypothesis that properties bear relations to other things that are not perceivers. And it is not a matter of choice what relations a property bears to us, even though we could envisage those relations differing at different times and among different groups of people.

We may conclude, therefore, that a relativistic conception of properties or universals is not damaging to a theory. On the contrary, after due consideration it should be decided that this would be a desirable consequence of a theory of universals.

11.4 Do all properties have a causal essence?

While the preferred reality test for properties is the Eleatic Stranger's, the test does not entail that all properties have a causal or dispositional essence.[9] It might be wondered, therefore, whether the dispositional relations borne to other properties should be regarded as necessary to a property. In Chapter 10, it was argued that the relations borne to other properties were necessary to a property and fixed its identity. Hence, we might say that F partakes in the following relations necessarily: $<F \times H>$; $<F \Box^m I>$; $<F \bigcirc J>$; $<F \Diamond^d K>$. But if there is a property that is not essentially dispositional, then a $\Diamond^d$ relation cannot be included in its essence.

Whether there are properties that are purely categorical or non-powers remains a contentious point of metaphysics. Armstrong (1968: 85–8) argued that there were categorical properties. More recently he has said that there need only be categorical properties because if there are laws then their effects upon the categorical properties would give us the powers (2004a). I have argued (1998a) that all properties may be regarded as dispositional as all can be denoted in terms of what difference to the world they are capable of making. Molnar (2003: 158–62) argues, however, there are at least some properties that are non-powers. He calls them the S-properties, which include spatial location, spatial orientation and temporal location.[10] While Molnar says that these are not powers, because they do not meet his preferred criteria for being so, they nevertheless have some causal relevance (ibid.: 162–5). Powers exert forces but the forces they exert can be location-sensitive. The actual degree of force may involve a function that includes distance. So while S-properties are not powers, they can be causally relevant to how powers are manifested.

I confess to some degree of scepticism about Molnar's argument here. If one can regard the gravitational force as a location-sensitive power, with its sensitivity described by the inverse square function, then why could one not regard location as a gravitation-sensitive power, with its sensitivity described also in a function? The same function that allows us to derive force from masses and distances apart will allow us to derive combined masses from force and distance apart, and distance apart from force and combined masses. It is not clear why there can be nothing that counts as the manifestation of location if there are other properties that are sensitive to it.

I need not, however, settle the issue of whether all properties have a causal essence because there is no reason to insist that a $\Diamond^d$ or $\Box^d$ relation must always be among the relations that a property bears. Our only stricture is that each property must bear at least one type of connection to other properties, and there are other connections that are not dispositional. There is no requirement that every type of relation must be borne by every property to some or other property.

The S-properties listed by Molnar would indeed bear some relations to other properties. Being wholly located at position p_1 at t_1 excludes being wholly located at position p_2 at t_1, where $p_1 \neq p_2$. Being wholly located at position p_1 at t_1 is compatible with being wholly located at position p_1 at t_2, where $t_1 \neq t_2$. A non-power, if there is such a thing, would thus bear only metaphysical relations to other properties.

11.5 Epiphenomena

It might thus be wondered why there cannot be epiphenomena. An epiphenomenal property would be one that has no causal effects at all. It would have no powers and nor would it have the kind of non-powerful causal relevance that Molnar claims for the S-properties. The units of Humean metaphysics are epiphenomenal in the sense that, intrinsically, they are causally inert. I have presented an alternative to Humeanism but I have provided nothing that shows the impossibility of epiphenomenal properties.

Both Humean lawlessness and nomological realism admit categorical, non-power properties. I think it is fair to describe such properties as epiphenomenal. In Humean lawlessness, such non-modal distinct existences are all there is. There are no modal facts or beings (Figure 11.1). Nomological realism (Figure 11.2) is an attempt to add modality to an otherwise inert world of categorical properties. Intrinsically, such properties can do nothing. They have to be directed, therefore, by laws. The Central Dilemma concerned how something could be sufficiently modal

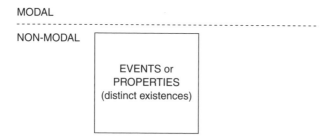

Figure 11.1 Epiphenomenal properties.

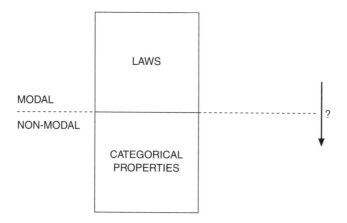

Figure 11.2 Epiphenomenal properties somehow directed by laws.

and sufficiently naturalistic to play the appropriate role in affecting the behaviour of the non-modal, categorical properties.

If to be epiphenomenal is to have causes but no effects, an epiphenomenal property could not be experienced. If such properties have no effects, they have no effects on us. The only case in which one could maintain that some epiphenomena can be experienced is if one thinks that experiences are themselves epiphenomenal. But even if experiences are, we would not thereby be able to experience epiphenomenal properties. All we would be able to experience would be epiphenomenal experiences. And if one coupled such a view with epiphenomenalism about properties, one could never explain how an epiphenomenal property caused an epiphenomenal experience.

Why, then, would one want to believe that there might be these inert properties? There is nothing intrinsically appealing about them and they violate at least one version of the Eleatic reality test. If they are supervenient epiphenomena, they do make a difference to the world because, if they were absent, that upon which they supervene would be absent.[11] But even supervenient epiphenomena violate what could be called the Eleatic *efficacy* reality test (EERT). The original Platonic formulation of the Eleatic test (*Sophist*, 1961b: §247d–e) is disjunctive: something must have causes or effects to be real. This disjunctive formulation permits the reality of epiphenomena, which are standardly taken to have causes though not effects. The efficacy test requires that something must have effects to be real, or at least possible effects. Hence I have formulated the following reality test:

> *EERT*: For any intrinsic non-abstract property *P*, *P* exists if and only if there are circumstances *C* in which the instantiations of *P* have causal consequences.[12]

Given that epiphenomena are not epistemically accessible and that they violate an otherwise appealing metaphysical principle, it seems that any reasons that recommend them will be broadly a priori. There will have to be good philosophical reasons to accept an overall view of which epiphenomena are an essential part. I know of no conclusive a priori reason to rule such properties out but I know of no good reason to accept them. There *might* be such things, even though we cannot know them. But there seems to be an onus of proof on those who tell us there are such things.

If it turned out that there was a good reason to accept that there are epiphenomenal properties, though I cannot imagine what that might be, mine would then be a theory only of the modally connected properties. The theory, like everything else, would be unaffected by the existence of some epiphenomenal properties. It would be only a theory of the connected properties of which we know; not a theory of the unconnected properties that dangle loosely, unknown and doing nothing.

Are all properties epiphenomenal? The aim of this book has been to show how unattractive such an account of the world would be. The most plausible account is one in which properties are inherently modal.

11.6 How might the account be extended to relations?

Can the account of properties be extended to relations? If not, why not; but if so, how? With only a little extra complication, I think that the account can be extended to relations. It is desirable to do so, given that both are universals and ought to be treated alike, *mutatis mutandis*. The only difference in the treatment is an acceptance that properties are instantiated in single objects while relations require at least two objects for their instantiation.

Certainly relations can hold between relations, such as necessitation, possibilification, incompatibility and compatibility. Hence, *a* being taller than *b* necessitates *b* being smaller than *a*. *c* being married to *d* necessitates *d* being married to *c*. *e* being older than *f* is incompatible with *f* being the same age as *e*. But *g* being the same weight as *h* is compatible with *h* being heavier than *i*. Any number of further examples of connections between distinct relations could be generated.[13] Are there any causal or dispositional connections between relations? In §11.4, I argued that it need not be a requirement that some of the connections between properties be dispositional or causal. But it is not inconceivable that there might be circumstances in which the holding of a relation has causal consequences. That *g* is the same weight as *h* would lead to them balancing on scales, for example.

Figure 11.3 provides a model of the metaphysical connections that there might be between different relations. It is only one variant on the theme, however. We might want to allow connections between relations of different orders. Hence, a dyadic relation might be connected with a triadic or a monadic relation. For example, *a* being taller than *b* is necessarily asymmetrical. Whenever this relation is instantiated, therefore, so is the property of asymmetry. Hence, we must allow cases such as $<R_1 \Box^m A>$, where R_1 is a dyadic relation and A a property, and $<R_1 \times R_2>$, where R_1 is a dyadic relation and R_2 is triadic. There are many other permutations. We may represent them either by mixing in universals of any order along the axes of our two-dimensional grid, or we may prefer a multiple-dimensional matrix with many axes. Both would have adequate representational power. Clarity is a matter of choice.

One thorny problem remains, however, if the account of properties and relations is to be complete. The connections between properties and relations themselves are relations. If the relational analysis is to cover all properties and relations, the basic relations used in the analysis – $X \times Y$,

		Second relation								
		$R_1(x,y)$	$R_2(x,y)$	$R_3(x,y)$	$R_4(x,y)$	$R_5(x,y)$	$R_6(x,y)$	$R_7(x,y)$	$R_8(x,y)$	...
First relation	$R_1(x,y)$	T		×		×		◇m		
	$R_2(x,y)$	×	T		◇m		□m		×	
	$R_3(x,y)$			T		×			◇m	
	$R_4(x,y)$	◇m	□m		T	□m		×		
	$R_5(x,y)$			×		T				
	$R_6(x,y)$	□m					T		□m	
	$R_7(x,y)$		◇m	×	×	◇m	□m	T		
	$R_8(x,y)$	×					◇m	◇m	T	
	...									

Figure 11.3 Connections between relations.

$X \bigcirc Y$, $X \Diamond^d Y$, $X \square^d Y$, $X \square^m Y$, and $X \Diamond^m Y$ – must fall under the same account. Were one to instead invoke them as primitive relations of the theory, one would be effectively admitting that there are at least six *relation quiddities*. As the theory is partly motivated by the desire to avoid such quiddities, it would have fallen at the final hurdle. We have to maintain, therefore, that the nature and identity of a relation are exhausted by the relations it bears to all other relations, subject to certain formal or logical constraints. Some of these relations borne might include bearing itself to some other relation; for example $<<A \times B> \times <A \bigcirc B>>$. The fear that this might generate one big circle, in which no property or relation can have a nature or identity, has already been addressed in §11.3. The formal or logical constraints will be significant, of course. Any relation that includes a modal aspect must respect the axioms and theorems of modal logic. The incompatibility relation, more obviously, is amenable to a precise logical definition.

11.7 Meinongianism

A metaphysics that accepts the reality of powers and propensities seems to raise the possibility, perhaps one should say danger, of Meinongianism (which has already been used against Strawson in §4.3). I am using this term to refer to the position parodied by Russell (1905) in which non-existent objects such as the golden mountain nevertheless have a secondary kind of existence called, perhaps, subsistence.[14] Russell's account was historically inaccurate, however. It was not what Meinong had argued, at least in the best-developed statement of his view (1902).[15] Nevertheless, at the risk of an injustice, I will retain the well-established term *Meinongianism* for the view that some non-existent objects can still, in a way, be. The historical Meinong was not, in this sense, a Meinongian.

Powers and real propensities have as part of their essence, it might be thought, events or states of affairs that need not be actual. A power is always a power *to do*, or a power *for*, something. For a power to be the power of *solubility*, it has to be related appropriately to the distinct property *dissolving*. But also, to be a power, being soluble cannot be dependent upon dissolving actually occurring. Powers can exist unmanifested. That which a power is essentially a power *for* need not, therefore, exist, so the charge goes. An unmanifested power is thus a power to only a Meinongian manifestation. *Reductio ad absurdum*.

Real propensities were discussed in Chapter 3. The problem there was how real chances related to actual frequencies of events. The Meinongian problem reappears. A real $\frac{1}{2}$ chance propensity is a propensity for a 50:50 distribution. But an actual 50:50 distribution in any sample is unlikely, even though more likely than any other distribution. There being a $\frac{1}{2}$ chance propensity is consistent with any actual distribution. That which the propensity is a propensity *for* may be, therefore, non-existent, so the charge goes. In such a case, that which a propensity is a propensity *for* would be a Meinongian entity. *Reductio ad absurdum.*

The first question that must be answered is whether realism about powers and propensities really does entail a commitment to anything like Meinongian entities. If the first question is answered affirmatively, we must ask a second. Is this really an undesirable or absurd aspect of the theory? Powers do at least some, though not all, of the work we thought we wanted laws for.[16] If the lawless theory requires powers, and powers require the acceptance of an absurdity, it looks bad for the theory. I argue that the acceptance of powers and propensities does not entail a metaphysically strong form of Meinongianism; but even if it did, it would not be fatal to the theory.

First, let us consider the reality of possibilities. Powers and propensities make possible other properties. In the case of propensities, I understand properties in a broad sense in which a proportional distribution could be thought of as an instantiation of a universal. Such other properties may, thereby, become actual but they need not. They may remain always possible. To be a possible thing is not, however, to be a thinner or ghostly kind of actual thing. When the possible becomes actual, there is not a transition from one state of being to another. A possibility is not yet anything at all. For example, one might *say* that one fears possible delays on one's journey but one need fear only an actual delay, for only that can make one late.

To reify powers and propensities is not to reify any unmanifested possibilities that they make. Nevertheless, we are prepared to allow that there are *real possibilities*. It was possible that Kennedy would have lived, had the assassins missed. It is possible that this ice cube will melt tomorrow. What can we mean by saying that such possibilities are real if they do not have a Meinongian existence?

Broadly, there are two ideas about what these possibilities are. The first is that such possibilities have an entirely logico-linguistic being. That this ice cube could melt on a certain day, is nothing more than a truth, grounded in some non-modal fact of the world or our linguistic practices. The second view grants that this is indeed a truth but looks also for something else in the world that the truth is about. According to Lewis (1973), the truthmakers of counterfactual truths are other-worldly. I prefer what might be called an immanent rather than transcendent theory of the possible. But there is more than one immanent theory. Armstrong (1989) thinks of possibilities as recombinations of the existing elements of our world. I think instead of possibility as grounded in powers, propensities and the other connections between properties, and thereby in the states of affairs in which properties, powers and propensities are instantiated.[17] There are states of affairs in the world, particulars bearing properties, that make other states of affairs possible (or necessary).[18] There is no need to accept the Meinongian reality of the possible states of affairs once one accepts the reality of the powers and propensities that the actual states of affairs instantiate. Among the things that powers do, therefore, is the grounding of possibility and necessity. By a real possibility, therefore, we can mean a possibility grounded in such immanent features of the world, which means being grounded in the real powers and the other connections between properties as shown in Figure 10.1. It does not require reifying a possibility in the Meinongian sense but it does require that acceptance of real powers.

This is background on how there might be real possibilities, but it has not shown specifically how one can answer the danger of Meinongianism. For that answer, we must consider in more detail what powers are powers *for* and we must enter a little into the theory of universals.

Our restricted combinatorial model is a model of how universals are related. When the first term of a relation is instantiated, this does not mean that the second term is automatically instantiated. In some cases it will be: where the relation is one of necessitation. But in some cases the second term is made only possible by the first, rather than being necessitated. This means that the first term could be instantiated but the second term not. How, if this second property is not instantiated, can we say that the first property is directed towards it?

A power, disposition or propensity is always a power or propensity for a manifestation of a certain kind and this is the key datum in answering the charge. In the case of powers, this is for a manifestation of a property. For a propensity, this is probabilistically for a certain proportional distribution. Where, when and in what way this property or distribution of events will be manifested is left indeterminate (Molnar 2003: 64) and becomes determinate only when instantiated. The properties these things are *for* are real enough. Can we say that the powers are directed towards the properties rather than the particular instantiations of those properties at particular times and places? In a significant sense, yes. For the power is indeterminate in respect of time and place of its manifestation. Each manifestation will be somewhere and somewhen but the somewhere and somewhen are not necessary for the having of the power. They are among the contingent details of its manifestation. What is necessary to its manifestation is the universal only. This universal exists, whether or not manifested by some particular power.[19] So if the universal is what a power is a power *for*, then its existence is *not* Meinongian.

This response may appear disingenuous, for surely a power is always a power for a particular instance, placed and dated, rather than for a universal itself. The following two considerations show, however, that this *is* a credible reply to the Meinongian charge. First, a power is not typically a power to manifest a universal in some very precise way, at a precise time and place. A power might be a power to dissolve, *when and wherever*, and rarely a power to dissolve at spatiotemporal location $p_1 t_1$.[20] Second, because a universal is fully present in its instances, we can note that the thing to which the power is directed will indeed be present whenever we have an actual and specific instantiation. Our universal F is present in the specific manifestation $F(p_1 t_1)$ and is the part of $F(p_1 t_1)$ for which the power was a power.

The case of probabilistic propensities would require a little more elaboration, though the same principles apply. A specific quantitative distribution can be regarded as a universal. Such a propensity is a propensity for a specific quantitative distribution – a proportion – to be manifested. But it is only probabilistically so. Only where the most likely distribution is actual is the universal instantiated. This may be rarely. But such a universal, the proportion, exists whether or not this propensity manifests it. It need not be Meinongian.

This seems to me the most plausible response to the Meinongian charge. I admit that there remains much in it that is troubling. I note, however, that mine is not the only metaphysics that is affected by such issues (see Handfield 2002) and I would welcome a more detailed account. Suppose mine does not succeed and nor does any other. What if powers and propensities were unavoidably Meinongian? If so, it might count against the theory but I am not sure fatally. Perhaps the world does include entities that are directed towards non-existent states. Perhaps Molnar would then be right to speak of physical intentionality, complete with intentional inexistence (2003: Ch. 3). This would be counter-intuitive but not obviously, contrary to the statements of the objection above, a *reductio* of the position.

11.8 Why is this not a theory of laws?

A common response that the realist lawless theory has provoked has been the question 'why is this not a theory of laws?'.[21] Much of what people thought of laws appears to be here. There is *de re* necessity, for one thing, as I have an account of how one property necessitates another. I have described a world in which counterfactuals and inductive inferences would be made true. So why should there be such an emphasis on lawlessness? Should we call laws whatever in the world provides necessity and makes true counterfactuals and inductive inferences? Is the dispute between my position and the nomological realist's merely a linguistic dispute?[22] Is it simply that they want to call these necessary connections in nature laws and I do not? Is there anything metaphysically substantial that divides us?

Let us recall some of the evidence presented thus far. I began by distinguishing two kinds of theory of law. The first was the Humean theory that, I claimed, was not really a theory of laws at all but, rather, a theory that there are no laws. There are no additional metaphysical entities over and above regularity. This is a Humean account in which there are no necessary connections at all so, on my classification, it offers us an example of a lawless metaphysics. Second, I looked at theories of genuine nomological realism. NA was the idealized form of the nomological argument that might be used to support the view that there are laws. The argument was that there are certain features in the world, the set of features *S*, that would not be there if there were not laws. But, as I argued in Chapter 5, the argument must be more than that laws are whatever it is in the world that grounds the features *S*. The theory of laws is one particular theory that explains *S*. *S* is not taken to be definitive of laws. The theory of laws offers a particular way that *S* might arise: through general truths or facts that are able to govern, or play some determining role, in their instances. I then went on to look at two purportedly realist theories and argued that there was a difficulty in providing a satisfactory metaphysics for laws. In Chapter 9, the general reason for this was articulated in the form of the Central Dilemma. The Central Dilemma strikes against the claim that something could be adequately naturalistic, sufficiently modal, and yet play a governing role for its instances. The Central Dilemma exploits the realist's difficulty in answering the question of how the modal laws affect the non-modal properties, if laws and properties are in that way seen as distinct existences (see Figure 11.2). This problem shows a weakness in the nomological argument. It was claimed that laws *could* do the job the nomological realist wanted them for. They could deliver the features *S* to the world. How do they do so? No adequate answer has been provided, I claim, and the Central Dilemma shows that there is a general obstacle in the way of providing such an answer. If there is a difficulty about laws providing the world with *S*, metaphysics might be in trouble as it seems hard to deny that the world does contain those features, such as regularity and predictability. I argued in Chapter 10, however, that this potential crisis can be averted as it appears that there are things in the world that are better placed to deliver at least some of the requisite features: powers and other necessary connections between properties.

Call these laws if you will, but let us not forget how we got here.[23] Laws, I have claimed, were a solution – and not even a good one – to a pseudo-problem. This problem was created by thinking of the world as inactive and containing discrete units. Those who wanted necessity and animation thought that it could only be added by laws. But laws were never needed in the first place. Had we seen first that properties were already modal, and the particulars that instantiated them were thereby already powerful, we need never have posited laws in the hope of them doing work that was already being done.

Once we have the idea of a law of nature it might be thought relatively harmless to retain it, perhaps in a more modern form. But I argue that it is not a harmless idea, certainly not metaphysically so (more on this in Chapter 12). Laws of nature accompany the powerless view of propertied particulars. If particulars are rightly seen as powerful actors, there remains nothing that laws could do. Could they direct a property to have a different power from one it actually has? Not so if properties are taken to be clusters of powers and other connections, for if a power were lost, we would have a different property. So laws can determine nothing more than what already happens, which is only a trivial sense in which to determine. They are, thus, a loose wheel that turns though nothing else turns with them. They are not, therefore, a part of the mechanism.

11.9 Why is this theory not subject to the Central Dilemma?

If the problem raised by the Central Dilemma is such a threat to the laws account, why does it not also threaten the powers and other necessary connections that usurp laws in the realist lawless account?[24] If laws are unable to produce regularities, how can powers produce them?

The Central Dilemma is effective against the view of laws that takes them to govern or determine their instances, where these instances are a distinct kind from the laws themselves. The Central Dilemma underlines the issue of how laws as a distinct class of entities can impose themselves on something else.

The causal powers of things, and other relations between properties, are not like this. They are *internal* relations that exist whenever the properties exist. If we are to cling to the governing metaphor, then we would say that such modal properties are self-governing. Being self-governing ensures that the Central Dilemma is not a problem for the realist lawless account. There is no gap across which such properties must exert their influence. They connect with or affect each other without the governance of an external and outside entity. Hence there is certainly no danger of quidditism, and so on.

An internal relation is something that exists when its relata exist. The internal relation is not, therefore, some extra element that has to be added to the relata, such as laws are supposed to be on the naïve realist account of laws or on the more sophisticated DTA theory. This is the sense in which modal properties are self-governing, therefore. The possibilities they make, are made from within. The reductive accounts of laws offered something like this. But the second horn of the dilemma exposed the problem that there was nothing left for such (reduced) laws to do that was not being done already. A reduced law was, therefore, unable to play the governing role.

The external account, instead, adds a further element N to the universals F and G to get a law that N(F,G). The objection to this account concerns how the N can make it that every thing that is an F is also a G? The Central Dilemma thus strikes at the same weak point in the realist theory that is exploited in van Fraassen's (1989: 38–9) inference and explanation problems.

11.10 Am I looking for the wrong kind of law?

The denial that there are laws in nature might provoke the response that I am looking for the wrong kind of law.[25] I began with a search for metaphysically real laws of nature, as existents over and above the world's events and properties, and which play some role in determining those events and properties. It might be objected that there are laws of nature of other kinds. Such laws are not distinct existences from what they govern but are patterns of observable behaviour in the world or scientifically useful heuristics. Lange considers laws as reliable inference rules (2000: viii), for instance, and it is hard to deny that there are such things. Lange may be right that this is the notion of a law with which science works and I am happy to allow that there are laws of nature in these senses.

Lange works with an epistemic view of laws, however. Laws are distinguished from accidents on the basis of counterfactuals, confirmations and explanations (ibid.: ix). But this cannot take the place of a metaphysically satisfying theory. Were it to be taken as a metaphysical thesis, it would entail that there were no laws of nature before there were thinkers. It would entail that the laws are what they are only because of what we think of them. It would clash with the traditional view of laws. For example, Lange says that laws govern their instances (ibid.: ix) but how can an inference rule govern something in the world?

Laws *qua* reliable inference rules are not the metaphysically real existences that have been sought, unsuccessfully according to me. There is a tempting view that the world contains something in it that makes for regularity and order and which could be the reason why there are some reliable inference rules. Since at least Newton, there has been the thought that there are laws in nature that play this role. Such a view came under attack from the empiricists because they denied all metaphysical connections. But the idea of metaphysically real laws resurfaced with the loss of confidence in empiricism. I do not think, therefore, that the idea I have been attacking, throughout this book, is a mere straw man.

In my account, there is no such thing to be found in the world that should be called a law of nature. But I do not deny that there is order and regularity that permits reliable inference. The explanation I offer for such phenomena is internal and immanent, as opposed to external and transcendent. Reliable inferences are based on other sources, for example kinds, properties and their connections. To deny metaphysical laws is not, therefore, to deny that there can be reliable rules of inference that some people may refer to as laws of nature.

11.11 Can all laws be replaced by powers?

Nomological realism might yet be saved if there is at least one ineliminable law of nature. Perhaps, therefore, it would be of significance if there were laws that could not be reduced to, or otherwise explained in terms of, powers. Chalmers (1999: 12–14) makes such a case. He claims that the laws of thermodynamics, and all conservation laws, cannot be reduced to powers; not even to causal powers of the global kind, as Ellis would have it.

Chalmers might be right. But whether a power can be put in place of every law is not what is at issue. If there was a power for every law, it might even (though I think ultimately not) be supportive of a reductive view of laws rather than the eliminativism I advocate.[26] But laws are a very diverse bunch, as I argued in Chapter 8, and it is hard to imagine that there might be a single theory that accounts for everything that has been called a law. Some causal laws might be best explained in terms of causal powers but others might be better explained in terms of metaphysical connections between properties and others might merely describe the structure of space–time or the nature and limit of energy. The case against nomological realism does not, therefore, rest solely on the issue of whether laws can be reduced to powers.

Perhaps more importantly, what has not yet been shown is that there is a case that compels us to accept metaphysically real laws as the only, or even best, explanation of some phenomenon in the world. Problems might be raised for any of the alternative accounts to laws that are offered. But this does not oblige us to accept the laws account, just as my inability to explain a strange natural phenomenon does not oblige me to accept the existence of ghosts. I have raised some difficulties for the realist view of laws. Such is the seriousness of those difficulties that I would avoid invoking them even as a last resort. My strategy is not simply to say that all laws are reducible to powers. Rather, I say that the class of 'laws' is not a significant or useful class. It was the wrong metaphor and can do no work.

The arguments that have been considered so far in this book might make us think that the onus of proof now lies with the nomological realist. When they make appeal to a real law in nature, there are some very basic issues that we might push. In what sense is there specifically a law that compels conservative (or any other) phenomena? Is there some universal force that makes conservation so? If there is, why call this force a law? If not, why claim that conservation is governed by a law? Is there some other way in which the law exercises its power? What work is done by the addition of the notion of a law? In what way does it ground or explain what we know to exist?

11.12 Powers are no better understood than laws

If powers are just as much a metaphysical mystery as laws, then it might be thought that realist lawlessness avoids the devil only to face the deep blue sea. The advocated position accepts powers but not laws. If powers are no better understood than laws, then no gain has been made.[27]

I dispute the claim that powers are no better understood than laws. There has been much new work on the metaphysics of powers, such as that by Molnar. We are now in a position to say some positive things about what they are. They are instantiated in particulars in virtue of their properties. Consequently, whether A has a power is purely a fact about A. Thus, we are able to test for their presence and gain symptomatic evidence for them through their manifestations. Such tests, though attempts to stimulate powers, are not failsafe, however. Powers exist independently of their manifestations so may be there even if their manifestations never are.[28] Because powers are instantiated in particulars they can be considered immanent. Any modal force they bring, therefore, is a part of the object itself. They make for inherently powerful particulars.

If we compare powers with laws, we find that laws have few of these attractions. A law cannot be found in a single particular or in any finite class of particulars. It is supposed to be something more than its instances and that has a completely universal scope. Whether A's behaviour is an instantiation of a law is something more than a fact merely about A, therefore. This makes laws difficult to test as a finite number of tests would not prove the universal scope of the law.[29] Hence we get left with the well-known problems of confirmation and induction. It is difficult for us to give an account of how such laws are immanent, though we have seen Armstrong's brave attempt. The modal force that laws bring is not a part of the particular objects that fall under it. The modal force belongs only to the law of nature and in the objects we find nothing more than the non-modal outcome of the law. In this sense, the particular objects of nomological realism are not inherently powerful. Without laws, there would be no compulsion for them to do anything for they are intrinsically powerless.

12 Conclusion

Law and metaphor

12.1 Law as metaphor

The prospects for a thoroughgoing realism about laws in nature look poor, according to the arguments I have presented. Nevertheless, in scientific and philosophical contexts, laws-talk remains common. Why do we persist in speaking of laws in nature?

Only those who have a particularly strong theistic view of the world are predisposed to take strong laws-talk literally. They might think that the natural world is governed by the laws that God has created and imposed. But, even then, it is far from easy to see how such laws would work (see the two Newtonian models discussed in Chapter 9). For the rest of us, however, it is most likely that laws-talk is intended only to be metaphorical. If something can be metaphorical in degrees, then laws-talk is arguably metaphorical to a high degree. Even theists, such as Aquinas (*Summa Theologiae*, 1964–81: 2–1; 91.2 ad 3; 90), have ruled that 'law' applied to nature is a metaphor.[1]

How is the metaphor supposed to work? Perhaps it is that the world is so regular and orderly that, whatever the true reasons (or even if there is no reason), it is *like* there is divine legislation making it so. This simile can then be condensed to a metaphor, by dropping the term *like*, to produce statements such as 'nature is law-governed'. The claim is not that nature is really governed by laws. Metaphor works by comparison, resemblance and association. A term is used imaginatively rather than literally. Hence, 'my manager is a rottweiler' associates the manager with a ferocious dog, perhaps comparing their traits. The truth-value of such statements cannot be determined by their literal meaning. If such statements can have truth-values at all, they would have to be determined by how appropriate or useful the comparison was. It is not literally true that my manager is a rottweiler but you might assent to the claim if you recognize it as an appropriate metaphor. In respect of law, therefore, it might be claimed that I have mistakenly interpreted claims about laws literally and this is my reason for rejecting them. If laws-talk is appreciated as an appropriate and useful metaphor, it might yet be right to use it.[2]

If 'law of nature' is a metaphor, what are the associations and comparisons of which it makes use? One might hazard that the order in nature can be compared with the order in a society. The metaphor makes use of the normative conception of law, from the legal and moral cases (Mumford 2000a). The reason why we stop our cars at red lights or return our tax forms is because there is a law of the land that says we must. The reason we refrain from killing people without good reason is because it is morally wrong to do so: there is a moral law. Metaphorically, then, objects attract electrostatically, proportionate to their charges and distances, because of the 'law of nature' that makes it so.

Could we say, then, that there is no need to exercise our thoughts on the issue of nomological realism? No one really proposes that talk of laws of nature is to be understood literally. Instead, laws-talk is supposed to be a useful and reasonably appropriate metaphor, making a comparison between an orderly world and the well-established sense of a law. If the metaphor is appropriate, it should continue.

12.2 Law as the wrong metaphor

There is nothing wrong with metaphor as such. In the case of laws of nature, however, I maintain that the metaphor is neither useful nor appropriate. It is not a good metaphor – not a helpful one – for understanding the world. There are a number of places where the comparison between natural laws and moral or legal laws breaks down. This suggests that there are few significant or important associations that can usefully be drawn.

First, moral and legal laws work through the mediation of a conscious and reflective intellect. After understanding the law, and deliberating on whether to act in accordance with it, we make a decision to comply with it. This story, of how a general law determines particular events, cannot apply in the case of laws of nature. As Robert Boyle said: 'I cannot conceive how a body devoid of understanding and sense, truly so called, can moderate and determine its own motions, especially so as to make them conformable to laws that it has no apprehension of' (1686: 181–2).

There cannot be, therefore, any credible comparison between natural and legal/moral laws in the way they determine order in nature and society respectively. If the comparison offers no help here, then how do laws of nature have an influence over the particulars they metaphorically govern? This leaves us with the problem exploited by the Central Dilemma. How does a law of nature govern the supposed instances of the law? Such instances may be consistent with compliance to the putative law but consistency with compliance does not prove compliance. Unless we have some theory of *how* the instances comply with the law, we cannot say that there is compliance nor even, by extension, that there is a law. In the legal/moral case, deliberative agents convert the general law into particular actions. In the natural case, there seems to be no such mediator.

Second, because of the mediation of a deliberative intellect, legal and moral laws can be disobeyed. We can choose, after reflection, to ignore or break the laws. Even though laws might, like promises, be binding, we also have the freedom to choose to break them. This motivates a system of social sanctions and punishments for those who offend against the law. In the case of laws of nature, however, it is not possible to break the laws, even in the cases of laws that affect deliberative intellects. Hence, I can choose not to make a tax return, breaking the taxation laws of the land, but I cannot choose whether or not to break the 'law' of gravity. This also illustrates the first point: just because all my actions are consistent with the 'law' of gravity, that does not mean that I am obeying or complying with it. There are, of course, putative cases of laws with exceptions, such as *ceteris paribus* clauses. But on these cases, I follow many others in arguing that they do not violate the law.[3]

Third, legal laws are unquestionably contingent. They could be otherwise. (Moral laws may be contingent or necessary, depending upon one's preferred metaethics.[4]) There are many different systems of laws: indeed, the many different societies in our world exemplify many different systems of laws. Until recently, the law of nature metaphor was thought to be consistent with this. But increasingly, some form of necessitarianism is looking plausible. If things could not have behaved other than they do, the laws seem redundant. There is a point in making legal laws, because there are many possible legal systems. But would there be many possible systems of laws of nature? Theologians and philosophers have in the past thought so but this should be re-evaluated. I have supported a kind of necessitarianism in which properties are understood to be clusters of causal powers. Properties are thus tied necessarily with sets of (dispositional) behaviour. This contrasts with the Humean metaphysics in which the behaviour associated with a property was contingent and determined, in neo-Humeanism, only by the contingent laws of nature. Necessitarianism suggests that even God could not impose a set of laws that makes properties behave (dispositionally) other than they do. There are no alternate systems of laws for these properties. Laws are not imposed on any things, which they then govern.

The law metaphor really does break down when applied to nature. The last point seems a crucial one, however. It suggests not only that the metaphor of law is the wrong metaphor, but also that it might be a metaphysically misleading one.

12.3 Law as a harmful metaphor

There are a number of philosophically misleading suggestions and associations that come with a law of nature metaphor. These include:

1   that the world needs something that plays the role that laws are sup-
    posed to have;
2   that the world consists of discrete and inert units that stand in need of
    animation;[5]
3   that the Humean metaphysics is roughly correct at the basic, subve-
    nient level: there are no necessary connections between distinct exis-
    tences;
4   any compulsion there is in nature must be imposed by external and
    contingent laws;
5   the same elements that we have in our world could be rearranged to
    make a different picture (see §11.2, on the Humean mosaic).

Consider again the quotation from Trefil in §5.4.

> In principle, each object could behave according to its own set of laws,
> totally unrelated to the laws that govern all other objects. Such a uni-
> verse would be chaotic and difficult to understand, but it is logically
> possible. That we do not live in such a chaotic universe is, to a large
> extent, the result of the existence of natural laws.
>
> (2002: xxi)

Trefil states that a world without laws would be chaotic. He implies that
there needs to be something in the world that keeps the other things – the
objects, properties and kinds – in order. But this is to accept a 'solution',
and not a very good one, when the 'problem' should never have been conceded in the first place. The problem is the Humean denial of immanent
and internal necessity in nature. But there are good reasons to think that
Hume's denial was wrong, or at least that it generates so many problems
that it should not have been accepted. Laws of nature were a patch on this
faulty metaphysic. To accept the need for the patch is to accept the validity of the underlying metaphysic that it serves. If, instead, one rejects the
problem, replacing the discrete conception of the world with one that is
holistic and connected, one no longer has any use for the 'solution'.

There does not need to be anything that is added to the world to keep
it in order and regular. So the law metaphor provides no enlightenment.
The world is interconnected, self-regulated if you must, by the internal
relations of its properties. I am not making properties serve the role of
laws. Rather, the world leaves no such role to be filled by anything. The
nomological argument 'laws because order', and its contrapositive 'no
laws, therefore chaos', really do have no force. It would be impossible for
anyone and anything to subtract something from the world, leaving
behind its properties and kinds, and create chaos. This suggests that laws
are just not there at all, and nor is anything that can usefully be captured
by the metaphor of a law.

I invoke the notion of a power. This might also be a metaphorical term, perhaps originally from the notion of a human power to act. But here, the damaging associations seem harder to find. The ideas of being active and animated, while perhaps having their core use in relation to persons, seem to carry over to the non-mental realm without causing irresolvable metaphysical confusion. If we are to run with metaphors, therefore, this seems a more useful and appropriate one.

Whether or not the power metaphor is exact, I hope the case for abandoning the metaphor of laws in nature looks strong. Hence, I do not accept that an easy response is to give up realism about laws and claim instead that laws should be understood metaphorically. Even if law in nature is a metaphor, it is the wrong metaphor and a philosophically misleading one.

Notes

1 Laws in science and philosophy

1 Hume (1739–40) and Lewis (1986b: ix) are examples, though this claim will have to be explained and justified in greater detail later.

2 A philosopher who believes in laws is Armstrong (1983). A scientist who believes in laws is Feynman (1965). A belief in laws seems almost universal in science, though what the belief amounts to is not easy to say. For a survey, see Trefil (2002).

3 The value of G was first established by Henry Cavendish in 1798. See Feynman (1965: 28) for an explanation how.

4 See, for example, Ayer (1963), van Fraassen (1989) and Lange (1993 and 2000).

5 I am not ruling out the more credible case where one regularity explains a different regularity, for example, a specific regularity may be explained in terms of being an instance of a more general regularity.

6 Kuhn (1962) contains a detailed study of such revolutions.

7 For summaries of these, and other significant contributions to the debate, see Bird (1998a) and Ladyman (2002).

8 A detailed study of the problems of scientific realism, with possible solutions, is to be found in Psillos (1999).

9 Some deflationary accounts of laws would agree with the view that laws can be nothing more than statements. Such accounts will have to be tackled later. It is clear, however, that a statement could never determine or make a regularity. A law *qua* statement does not look a good candidate for something that explains its instances.

10 This claim is inspired by the Preface to Lange (2002a).

11 See Lowe (2002a: Ch. 1).

12 See Einstein (1920: Chs 8–10).

13 Statements might explain other statements. Therefore, if laws are statements, we might be able to say that one law explains another, as in n. 5, above. There is also a clear sense in which a statement can make something happen in the world, as when a General yells 'Charge!'. What seems more problematic, is the case of a statement explaining the instances within its scope. Can the statement 'all ravens are black' make this particular raven black?

14 Mill (1843, Bk III, Chs 4 and 5), Ramsey (1928, 1929) and Lewis (1973: 72–7 and 1986a).

15 Molnar (1969) summarizes some of the problems.

16 It has been suggested to me by Stathis Psillos that no one has ever seriously believed that laws are statements. But even if not, they have said things close enough to that view to make its contradiction worth asserting, if only to clarify the matter.

17 For a thorough, though appropriately philosophically opinionated, account of how science regards laws, see Lange (2000). Scientists may, as we have seen, believe in the reality of such laws when they allow themselves to indulge in ontology.

18 For a summary and critique of van Fraassen's constructive empiricism, see Ladyman (2002: 185–93).

19 Lewis admitted (1986a: viii) that he gave his theory a bad name. His position was realist about other worlds but anti-realist about the (intrinsic) modality of any of those worlds.

20 See also Lowe (1982) for a model of laws that have permissible exceptions.

21 Hume also has a semantic argument: that we cannot meaningfully refer to necessary connections in nature. For a modern version, the acquisition argument, see Mumford (1998a: §3.6).

22 This is not to suggest that one cannot be a singularist about causation *and* believe in laws. See Psillos (2002: §5.1, §6.3.3).

2 The lawless world

1 Here, as in a number of other places, I lean on Lewis's articulation of Humeanism (Lewis, 1986b, especially his Introduction).

2 Lewis likens the world to a mosaic: 'the world is a vast mosaic of local matters of particular fact, just one little thing and then another' (1986b: ix).

3 On internal and external relations, see Russell (1911).

4 Perhaps the mosaic-maker is like a lawmaker who dictates, from outside the mosaic, what the mosaic looks like. This is also a useful analogy but not one I wish to employ in relation to the lawless world. We could, therefore, remove the mosaic-maker from the analogy by imagining that the mosaic is a result of a random and indeterministic spreading of tiles, as discussed in the next section.

5 I support a tenseless theory of time, for example, see Mellor (1998).

6 Let us assume that they are all so conjoined, though them being so would be a simplification, as explained in §1.1.

7 The simplifying assumptions in this account of science are too numerous to list.

8 Cartwright (1983: 1) distinguishes two uses of the term 'phenomenological law'. Here I am following the first, philosophical use, pertaining to observables, rather than the second use, pertaining to fundamental laws.

9 See Ayer (1946: 72) on the likeness between Hume and logical positivism. See (1946: Ch. 1) for Ayer on the elimination of metaphysics. The work of David Lewis is a more metaphysics-friendly version of Humeanism.

10 This is a moot point, however. Ellis (2001), for example, argues that because these are metaphysical necessities in nature, they must be precisely natural laws. Ellis's view is discussed in detail in Chapter 7. But Armstrong has an objection against water = H_2O being a law, which could be extended to all essential truths about natural kinds.

11 See Chapter 1, n. 19. I use the term *modal realism* to mean the exact opposite of what David Lewis meant by it.

3 Regularities and best systems

1 See Lipton (1999) and Mumford (1998a: 224) for discussion of the meaning of the *ceteris paribus* clause.

2 Hence Psillos's formulation of Hume on causation might also be apt to mislead: 'causation is a species of regularity' (2002: 137). I follow a broadly traditional view of Hume on causation and laws, namely, that he held an error-theory that said we are grossly in error to think there are such things as causes

and laws in addition to regularities. Chapter 4 considers Hume's position in greater detail.

3 There is no reason why the regularity view cannot permit variants on (4), such as (4*) $\forall x \forall y$ $(Fx \rightarrow Gy)$, (4**) $\forall x$ $((Fx \ \& \ Gx) \rightarrow Hx)$, and a number of other possibilities.

4 For detailed surveys, see Armstrong (1983: Chs 2–5) and Psillos (2002: Ch. 5).

5 Notably, Ellis (2001) has done much to show the paucity of the metaphysics of discreta.

6 Psillos (2002: 137–8) misses a chance to make this point.

7 Most of the other objections to the regularity theory, to be discussed below, are to be found summarized in Armstrong (1983).

8 Here, and at various other places, I make use of a metaphysical notion of explanation in which some phenomenon explains another if it provides a metaphysical ground of it. This is the notion of explanation that I find best suited to the current investigation. But I accept that this might be a controversial account and that there are many other views of what constitutes explanation. See the various accounts in Psillos (2002: Pt. III) and Ruben (1993).

9 For an account of four-dimensional metaphysics, see Sider (2001).

10 It does not matter that (6) contains a 'local' predicate, that brings restrictions as to times or places, as in 'my pocket'. As Psillos shows (2002: 140–1), there are apparently acceptable laws, such as Kepler's first, that has a spatiotemporally limited scope. And there can be true statements of unlimited scope that are still not regarded as laws, for instance that 'all gold cubes are smaller than one cubic mile' (from Reichenbach 1947: 368).

11 For philosophical theories of probability, see Gillies (2000), notably, Chapter 4 on subjective theories, Chapter 5 on frequentism and Chapter 8 on the intersubjective approach. The account of real, single-case probabilities, such as the case of the half-life of a single particle, is based on a propensity theory, discussed by Gillies in Chapters 6 and 7.

12 Lewis's own footnote: 'I doubt that our standards of simplicity would permit an infinite ascent of better and better systems; but if they do, we should say that a law must appear as a theorem in all sufficiently good true systems.'

13 To get a flavour of the concerns, such as the danger of relativism, see Engel (2002).

14 This may be asked of the speculative version of the Ramsey–Lewis theory alluded to by Psillos (2002: 154). Laws are still said to be systematizable regularities but they are nevertheless grounded in the world's objective nomological structure. This seems to be moving away from a Humean theory towards a form of nomological realism.

15 This quotation contains a corrected typing error: 'then' instead of 'than'.

16 Even here, the determination need not be exact. If the history shows a frequency close to 50/50, Lewis allows us to conclude a probabilistic law of exactly 50:50. Such an account is simpler and nearly fits the facts. But the world might not be simple after all. There might be some probabilities that are 51/49, as instanced by a slightly weighted coin. Lewis's systematization of the world will not allow this, though. The system aims for simplicity even if the world is not simple.

17 Lewis himself rules out, as a 'blind alley', counterfactual evidence in these cases, where probabilities of one world are determined by probabilities of another world in which these atoms are more abundant. So I shall do the same.

4 Hume's argument

1 There are exceptions, for example, in the 1748 *Enquiry*: Part VII, p. 70, on the occasionalists. In the rest of this chapter references to the 1739–40 *Treatise* and 1748 *Enquiry* will be given as 'T' and 'E' respectively, followed by page number.

2 'Principle of Order' comes from Hume's *Dialogues*: (1779: 200).

3 This is not to suggest that (4.1) is straightforwardly true, however, nor that there is nothing of interest in discussing it. There is a vast literature on *ceteris paribus* laws (see Lange, 2002b, for example). One may, in the light of it, be obliged to say that constant conjunctions are rarer than it might be supposed or that they occur mainly only *ceteris paribus*. But the dispute between Humeans and anti-Humeans is unlikely to be settled on the issue of the truth of (4.1).

4 This follows Molnar's (2003: 116–24) formulation of Hume.

5 Metaphysics can show the possibility of necessity in nature (Lowe 1998: Ch. 1) but that there is some actual such thing is plausibly an a posteriori matter.

6 There remain defenders of the conceivability test, for example, Sidelle, who speaks of 'appeals to imagination as the basic method of modal inquiry' (2002: 310).

7 This argument is repeated at (T: 161–2).

8 See (T: I, I, VI), especially: 'We have therefore no idea of substance, distinct from that of a collection of particular entities, nor have we any other meaning when we either talk or reason concerning it' (T: 16).

9 For example, the relata of causal relations are usually viewed by Hume as being events (see E: 74), yet he is happy to use the term 'object' in his definitions of cause, for example at (E: 76 and 77) and (T: 172).

10 There appears to be an unfortunate typographical error in Lewis (1986b: ix). Lewis's text reads: Humean supervenience is named in honor of the *greater* denier of necessary connections' (italic added). Lewis might have intended to say *greater* instead of *great*, even though it appears awkward. But confidence in this view is undermined by an obvious typographical error on the following page (1986b: x).

11 Russell had formerly been under the influence of the Meinongian-inference: see his very confusing account of *Being* in (1903: §427).

12 See also Mumford (1998a: §3.6).

13 The quotation that is supposed to support this interpretation ('Chance has no place, on any Hypothesis, sceptical or religious', Hume 1779: 200–1) is another ambiguous one and does not conclusively support the view that Hume believed there was a Principle of Order.

14 This is not to suggest that there is no metaphysical contribution to be made to our understanding of the world (see §1.2).

15 For an account of deductivism, see Stove (1970).

16 Molnar argues (2003: 122–3) that Hume's response to his 'missing shade of blue' case (T: 5–6) – that a person could recognize the gap and infer the missing shade – fails to meet the deductive standards of proof that Hume demands of his realist opponents.

5 The nomological argument

1 Is there not a self-evident argument for the existence of mind? Descartes thought so (1637: 127), but his argument 'je pense, donc je suis' only assumed that there was a mind. The best that could be made of the argument is 'thought, therefore something', which is merely an instance of the above argument 'there is something'.

2 An empiricist may nevertheless allow that there are some modal-values in the

trivial cases that follow from the axioms of possibility and necessity: namely, if P is true, then P is (trivially) possible and if P is false, then P is (trivially) not necessary.

3 I leave the meaning of an ontological ground undefined, for the moment. It would be for those who positively advocate something like NA to offer a precise account of how a law grounds such features. The difficulties in providing such an account will be an issue considered in Chapters 6, 7 and 9.

4 The example of the accidentally true universal generalization originates in Reichenbach, who gives 'all gold cubes are smaller than one cubic mile' (1947: 368).

5 This idea occurs much earlier, though Carroll makes no reference to it, in Sellars (1948).

6 Of course, Lewis attempted to make sense of modal concepts in a world that was metaphysically free of modal facts. Hence, his 1986a account effectively allowed that there were modal and nomic concepts but, if he was right, they were gained only by invoking relations with other worlds. In this sense, there were legitimate inter-world modal concepts but no legitimate intra-world modal concepts.

It should be noted also that Lewis was not entirely successful. As Black (2000) argues, Lewis seems to ignore the intrinsically modal character of properties. Carroll may have a point, therefore, but as I argue below, his point only shows the centrality of the modal, not the centrality of the nomic.

7 This is directed against Cartwright's (1983) denial of the truth of fundamental laws.

8 James Ladyman articulated this approach to me, in discussion.

9 A weaker version of D would suffice, where $x =$ a single law of nature. Presumably, each individual law grounds at least some regularity, order, universality, and so on.

10 Following Quine (1953), I wish to leave open the possibility that a proposition might become analytic when formerly it was not.

11 Such necessity is not supposed to be merely analytic. This is to invoke a form of Ellis's (2001) essentialism. Ellis's view is not accepted uncritically: see Chapter 7.

6   Natural necessitation relations

1 Hochberg (1999) has argued that the DTA theory appears also in McTaggart and arguably in Broad and Husserl.

2 Dretske (1977: 253) gives the form of a law simply as F-ness $\rightarrow$ G-ness, where the connective $\rightarrow$ can mean different things for different laws. Tooley favours a Ramsey sentence approach for expressing laws (1977: 674), as developed by Lewis (1972), though a simplified version can be given in terms of a relation of nomic necessitation between properties (T 1977: 676). Neither of these proposals can be seen as a major departure from the core theory. Armstrong himself has later said that N(F,G) underdescribes the nomic relation (1997: 228–30), which is better understood as a relation between state of affairs types.

3 Now that Armstrong sees the nomic relation as a relation between state of affairs types (see n. 1, above), he is prepared to allow laws that involve the same universal twice: where like causes like in a lawlike way (Armstrong 1997: 228). Hence, we can allow cases where a being F causes b being F. Indeed, a being F may cause the next temporal part of a to be F (ibid.: 229).

4 Both the relation N and a law, N(F,G), are understood to be universals.

5 Armstrong has subsequently revised his view of uninstantiated or alien properties. See Armstrong (2004b).

6 If I think there are no (instantiated) laws, perhaps I should judge that there are no uninstantiated laws either. But might I be better to judge instead that all laws are uninstantiated? Is this decision no more than spoils to the victor? I am not so sure. If one were to say that all laws are uninstantiated, then it might be thought that it allows some possible world in which those laws are instantiated. The lawless view to be developed in Part III suggests, in contrast, that nothing could be a law, based on the core metaphysical understanding of laws. The Central Dilemma suggests that real laws are impossible so there is no possible world in which they are instantiated.

7 There might be some derived exclusion laws. A derived law is simply a deduction from another law. There need be no special problem of the instantiation of a derived exclusion law because it is deduced from instantiated laws. Armstrong's worry, therefore, concerns only the instantiation of underived exclusion laws.

8 Only Lowe (1980, 1982, 1989) makes use of a similar analogy.

9 This last claim is not strictly true. In a complicated way, there could be a law in which H figures though its possibility raises further difficulties for DTA. There could be a probabilistic law that N(G,H) where G has been instantiated but, by chance, H has not. The further difficulty this raises concerns what counts as the instantiation of a probabilistic law.

10 Prompted by Baxter (2001), Armstrong has given up this view. He now thinks that all instantiation is necessary, with the consequence that he no longer thinks laws are contingent.

11 Armstrong is not, of course, a realist about other such worlds so would construe these possibilities combinatorially.

12 This may be another commitment that Armstrong would revise in the light of Baxter (2001).

13 See Ellis (2001), though it was Eugenio Lombardo, in conversation, who converted me to this view.

14 Instead of 'revive', it seems highly apposite to speak of the doctrine of internal relations being 'exhumed' (From *The Philosophical Lexicon*, D. Dennett (1987): 'hume, pron. . . . To commit to the flames, bury, or otherwise destroy a philosophical position, as in "That theory was humed in the 1920s." Hence, *exhume*, v. to revive a position generally believed to [be] humed'.)

15 One such view is essentialism (Ellis 2001), which is the topic of the next chapter.

16 Tooley does not anticipate Armstrong's argument that the transitivity of laws would entail the possibility of overdetermination (A 1983: 156). There may be a law N(F,G) and a law that N(G,H). If these two laws entailed that there was a law N(F,H), then whenever F was instantiated, H would be overdetermined. F would nomically necessitate G and G would nomically necessitate H but, if N(F,H) is also a law, H would also be nomically necessitated by F alone. Armstrong prefers to say that all that N(F,G) and N(G,H) would together entail is the counterfactual F → H, which does not entail a law N(F,H).

17 I will not quote Lewis's joke at Armstrong's expense, as it is already well known and Armstrong, no doubt, is already sick of seeing it.

18 Note that the following does not apply to Tooley's version of DTA, as it lacks Armstrong's instantiation requirement.

19 Combinatorialism does not permit the converse inference: if F is not instantiated, it is not a property and it is not even a possible property. See Chapter 10 for more on combinatorialism.

20 It is safe to assume that there is no other law, other than N(F,G), that can determine that F is instantiated. As F is uninstantiated, it figures in no law, though see n. 9 for a complication. As it is atomic, it cannot be derived

from the instantiation of other universals. So how could any law make F be instantiated?
21 The availability of this view to Tooley, who does not endorse immanent realism, should not be seen as much comfort to him.
22 The discarded ladder is no doubt Wittgensteinian (Wittgenstein 1921: §6.54)

7 Necessitarian essentialism

1 My thanks to James Ladyman for explaining to me the virtues of an object-free ontology. I do not want to rule out, however, that a field might itself count as an object.
2 This is my extrapolation from a point Ellis makes briefly (2001: 75).
3 See Ellis's *essentiality requirement* (2001: 21): 'natural kinds are distinguished from other sorts of things by their associations with *essential properties* and *real essences*' (italics in original).
4 For example, possession of one determinate value of a determinable property (as Armstrong says) or species of a general spectral kind (as Ellis says) excludes possession of all other determinates of the same determinable or all other species of the same spectral kind. For a more concrete example, having a charge −1 excludes having any other charge.
5 'what is wrong is the inherent nominalism of the whole program of analysis that gives rise to possible worlds semantics' (Ellis 2001: 274).
6 Drewery (2004) questions whether Ellis's essences are ontologically prior to his laws. If true, the first horn is indeed the danger.
7 Though all of them do commit to forms of essentialism at some point.
8 Elder (1994) has a similar position though his argument for necessity is based mainly on the weaknesses of the contingency account of laws.
9 See Drewery (2004), which argues that Ellis has not shown his essential properties to be anything more than necessary properties.

8 Are natural laws a natural kind?

1 This occurred before finding Trefil's amusing and engaging work (2002).
2 This is not to suggest that no one has offered a theory of which facts are the laws. Lange (2000: 47–55), for example, has argued that the laws are those facts that remain true under all physically possible counterfactual suppositions. But I contend that no such account of which facts are the nomological facts is uncontroversially acceptable. For criticism of Lange, see Psillos (2002: 203–6).
3 We have seen that Armstrong made this claim (1997: 227).
4 See Molnar (2003: 21–2) on the Lockean division of labour in philosophy.
5 I am assuming, however, that natural kinds are not in some sense ontologically posterior to natural laws. One might think they were if one believed that natural kinds are distinguished essentially by the different nomological roles they occupy. But while we might think that kinds would figure in natural laws (if there are any laws), I do not accept that laws are more fundamental existents than kinds.
6 This sets aside the possibility that Cartwright admits of a nomological machine occurring naturally. Whether one does so is a contingent matter.
7 This is not to deny that, at least in Ellis's version of the theory, which employs a wide sense of natural kinds, there is an attempt to account for the things classically called laws. Ellis allows that there are natural kinds of process and his essentialist analysis applied to such processes yields a theory of causal laws.
8 There is a disappearance theory of truth that says that 'it is true that P' says nothing more than 'P'. This suggests a disappearance theory of laws. What more, if anything, does 'it is a law of nature that X' say that 'X' does not?

9 I recognize that this may be dangerous territory for a philosopher to enter. This is not just due to ignorance of science but also due to the relative absence of discussion on the topic by those engaged in science.

9 The Central Dilemma

1 See the already quoted Trefil (2002: xxi).
2 It should be obvious that there is a Euthyphro problem lurking here, but I cannot be diverted by its details.
3 The parallel between Newton's view of laws and the *best system* laws of the Ramsey–Lewis theory should not go unnoticed.
4 Newton's attempt to prove the universality of the 'inverse square law' was motivated, at least in part, by the Royal Society's offer of a prize for a proof that such a law could explain the planetary motions described by Kepler. See Densmore (1995: xix).
5 If, instead, you take a Platonic approach, as Tooley (1977) does, then you have the difficulty of how laws *qua* Platonic forms relate to their instances. Platonic forms are also supernatural, like the Newtonian laws just considered. The problem of how a transcendent form relates to its instances is one of the oldest in philosophy.
6 In Chapter 6 it was shown that only laws that relate properties, rather than particulars, would produce the realists' required necessity for laws.
7 This statement need not be cast in past tense and it may also be cast in terms of possible worlds, where this entails no commitment to their reality.
8 Though quidditism would seem to allow something like this as the characterizing attribute could be replaced by one that played exactly the same role. So much the worse for quidditism.
9 See Wittgenstein (1953: §271) 'a wheel that can be turned though nothing else moves with it, is not part of the mechanism'.
10 See Mumford (2000a) on concerns about the normative account.
11 An attempted accurate representation of Newton's view in the General Scholium is that the laws are what bind the actions of the spirits (rather than directly what bind the behaviour of bodies). The spirits are God's minions and the laws are his instructions to them, which they cannot disobey. Newton's laws, are thus, far closer to the old, legal, notion of a law rather than the modern, natural conception. Newton's God is thus like the vice-chancellor of a university who tells his lecturers how they should run their courses. In bringing this legal notion of law to the natural world, Newton availed himself of the idea of the generality of law. A legal law, for instance, says that *anyone* convicted of dropping litter will be fined. In doing this, Newton instigated the search for the sources of natural generality and necessity.

10 Modal properties

1 Swoyer's essentialism differs from the others cited in that is concerns specifically the essences of properties rather than of kinds. It will be clear, later in this chapter, that I find such a view more persuasive than kind essentialism.
2 In less simple terms, formal logical necessities are true under all substitutions of their non-logical terms (Ellis 2001: 11). Hence, formal logical contradictions are false under all substitutions of their non-logical terms. Formal logical possibilities are true under some such substitutions (and false under others, where the possibility is less than a necessity).
3 For another example of the conflation of modes of necessity, see Ellis's claim (2002: 37, 71) that miracles are impossible. Even God could not have created a

square circle or a positively charged electron, we are told, because no such thing exists. But this does not show that that miracles are logically impossible, only that they are naturally or metaphysically impossible if you accept essentialism. A positively charged electron is not supposed to be a logical impossibility (an impossibility grounded in form) but only a metaphysical one. The essentialist position requires, at its core, that such metaphysical necessities, possibilities and impossibilities are not reducible to analytic or logical ones. There is certainly no proof here, therefore, of the logical impossibility of miracles, only their natural impossibility. But given that, for a miracle, we must have a *supernatural* cause of a natural event (Mumford 2001), their natural impossibility is already granted.

4 This claim is made *purely* on the basis of extension, rather than being a metaphysical claim about the groundings of the relevant necessities and possibilities.

5 I am making no attempt to generalize this claim to identities, the core Kripkean concern. I am saying only that *some* truths might be of this category.

6 Modes of necessity must be higher-order modes. Necessity and contingency are themselves modes (hence the term *modal*) in that they are ways propositions might be or modifications of propositions ($\Diamond$p, $\Box$p, $\neg\Box$p, etc.). Modes of necessity (and possibility) would thus modify the modifiers, for example, $<\Diamond_L\neg p \ \& \ \Box_N p>$ is consistent where the subscript $_L$ indicates the logical mode and $_N$ indicates the natural or metaphysical mode of possibility and necessity (see Mumford 2001: 198).

7 In this, I am taking a lead from Molnar (2003: 206–10).

8 I am allowing that there can be shape in two dimensions; that is, that a straight line is a shape.

9 One might have to rephrase this as stating that property tropes are distinct existences or as stating that property instances are.

10 When W. E. Johnson made the determinable/determinate distinction (1921: Ch. 11), he stipulated that a particular having a determinate property entailed that it also had the determinable of that determinate. An instance of being 2 grams in mass would entail being an instance of mass, on this view, so the case does not rule instantly in Ellis's favour.

11 A particular could instantiate two different determinates under the same determinable where they are of different levels of determinacy. For example, a coloured thing could be both red and scarlet where red is at an intermediate level of determinacy between the determinable coloured and the determinate scarlet (see Armstrong 1978b: 112).

12 See Armstrong (1978b: 112–13) for discussion and reservations.

13 For the details of this attack, see Mumford (1998a: Ch. 6).

14 For the functional analysis, see Mumford (1998a: Ch. 9). For the physical intentionality account see Molnar (2003: Ch. 3). On the intentionality account, the essences of powers are provided by the properties to which they are directed.

15 This assumes the truth of truthmaker theory rather than being an argument for it. It says that if there are truthmakers for modal truths, then properties are among them.

16 On the truthmakers of *formally* necessary truths, see Armstrong (2003).

17 I am grateful to Stephen Barker for impressing this third option on me.

18 Note that an analogous question can be asked about substantival alternatives to the theory of particulars that treats them as clusters of properties. We might query what such 'underlying substrata' really are and why we need them. The situations might not be entirely analogous, however. The substantivalist argues that two distinct things might coincide in all their properties (even their rela-

tional properties, given the possibility of a limited symmetrical world). We can only say that we really have distinct things, in such cases, if we allow a separate category of particularity in addition to properties. Can the same move be made against the exhaustion of properties by powers? Perhaps it can against trope theory, as such tropes are particularized properties. But it is then the substance-likeness of tropes that is in need of particularity, not their property-likeness.

19 Molnar (2003: 174–9) considers the attempt to make a vicious regress out of this argument and concludes that the attempt is unsuccessful.

20 Prior *et al.* (1982) have a position directly opposed to this: dispositions are impotent but their non-dispositional base is causal. I have argued against this elsewhere (Mumford 1998a: Ch. 5).

21 As suggested by Eugenio Lombardo (2002 and in discussion). The idea of the grid representation of restricted combinatorialism is largely due to Lombardo, though via Armstrong.

22 Note that we may also perform the ordinary truth-functional operations on our statements of connection between universals, such as $<X \& Y>$.

23 These are taken to be natural incompatibilities. One might try to argue that they are also logical incompatibilities. Being square means being non-triangular so we may reach logical incompatibility via analytic incompatibility. But this kind of argument, that transforms *de re* necessity into logical necessity has already been rejected. To say that being square means being non-triangular is highly problematic. Being square could not mean just being non-triangular as, by parity of reasoning, we would also have to say that it meant being non-circular, non-rhomboid and so on for every other shape. As there is an infinity of shapes, being square would be indefinable. In general, the strategy of defining something in terms of what it is not looks an incompletable task. Far simpler is to say that squareness and triangularity are metaphysically incompatible as they are two determinates under the determinable *shape*.

24 I am not denying that a shattered object might have its parts reassembled and thereby come back into existence. While shattered, however, it is plausible to say that it no longer exists as a substance or object.

11 Objections and replies

1 I am indebted for comments received when I have presented papers to audiences at Edinburgh, Birmingham Alabama, Lund, Bristol, Oxford, Macquarie, ANU at Canberra, Athens and York. I am grateful to David Armstrong and Stephen Barker for extended discussion and to Stathis Psillos for detailed comments.

2 There is a logical possibility of a world in which there are two or more systems of interconnected properties, where properties in one system have no connections with any properties in another system. If one were a non-interactionist dualist, one might think that the world is like this: with one system of interconnected physical properties and another system of interconnected mental properties but no connections between the two systems.

3 There is a consequence with a Leibnizian flavour that ought to be acknowledged (E. J. Lowe has identified the consequence). A possible world that appeared to have all the same fundamental properties as ours, but had one additional fundamental property X, would thereby have none of the properties from our world. Why so? Because, in that world, our properties would bear relations to X that were additional to their relations in our world, they would thereby become different properties as such relations fix the identities of the properties. Hence, our F would now be the slightly different property F^X. So

change one property and we change all the properties. Is this right? I think it is certainly not an incoherent consequence and I hope to show that the value of the theory makes the acceptance of the consequence worthwhile.

4 Properties are classes of *possibilia*; that is, classes of actual and otherworldly discrete particulars (Lewis 1983).

5 It must be kept in mind that the argument against recombination is against recombination of properties as they are related to other properties. I do not argue against the possibility of recombination of properties with particulars, as in Armstrong's already discussed combinatorial theory of possibility (1989). Hence, *a* could have the property F that *a* does not, in fact have.

6 This kind of objection may be what led Shoemaker to reject his former (1980) view that a property *is* a cluster of powers (1998: 412). Identity suggests reductionism, which is not possible because we must refer to further properties in specifying the identity of powers. Hence, properties are not reducible to powers. Instead, Shoemaker makes only the more modest claims that the causal features of a property are essential to it, and properties with the same causal features are identical (1998: 413, 1999: 297–8).

7 According to Armstrong's a posteriori realism about universals, our world may have a number of real universals as few as this. This is mainly because determinables are not to be counted as real universals (1978b: Ch. 22, §1), so the real universals would be those determinates that science identifies as real.

8 A perspective on the world giving us an idea within a relative system is also to be found in the case of position. We have a point of view on the world, from somewhere, which allows us to gain an idea of position even though all positions are relative.

9 Earlier cautionary notes on essentialism apply. I am not adding any more content to being essential than is gained from being necessary.

10 Molnar adds to this list temporal orientation and numerical identity of parts (2003: 160), which I will set aside on account of their obscurity. The response I give to the objection is not affected by them.

11 Alexander Bird has emphasized this point to me.

12 This is called the causal criterion of property existence in Mumford (1998a: 122). The circumstances *C* are actual or possible.

13 These relations between relations have a look of a priori necessity about them, rather than *de re* necessity. My restricted combinatorial grid (Figure 10.1) concerns necessary connections between universals and I could remain fairly neutral on the source of that necessity. Some of the connections between universals will be a priori but I do not want to allow that all are, certainly not the dispositional ones, for that would be to fall into the hands of neo-Humeanism as articulated, for example, in Ayer's (1946) logical positivism.

14 'This theory [Meinong's] regards any grammatically correct denoting phrase as standing for an object. Thus "the present King of France", "the round square", etc., are supposed to be genuine objects', Russell (1905: 418).

15 Subsistence was Meinong's term for an object that was real but not concrete, such as the relation of *being equal to*. He did not think the golden mountain subsisted. He did, however, think the golden mountain to be both golden and a mountain, even though it neither existed nor subsisted.

16 Why not all? Laws are supposed to deliver all of *S*, in the nomological argument NA (§5.3). It is not clear that a single category could (or even should) deliver all of *S*, not even powers. Natural kinds and other facts in the world may provide some of the other things for which we wanted laws.

17 I follow Armstrong (1997) in taking a state of affairs to be something in the world – a particular bearing a property – rather than a linguistic item.

18 This is the story for physical or natural possibility and necessity only. I am

happy to follow Ellis (2001: 37) in allowing logical possibility and necessity that is grounded in logical form alone and analytic possibility and necessity that is grounded in meaning.

19 If one is an immanent realist about universals, one will require that the universal be instantiated at least once, though not necessarily by this very power.

20 If we have a power specifically to dissolve at p_1t_1, then this becomes a complex universal to which the power is manifested and which is instantiated in the manifestation, perhaps with further contingent features.

21 Thanks to James Ladyman and Peter Menzies who have put this objection to me with the greatest force.

22 Alice Drewery put the objection to me this way.

23 Michael Smith voiced this response to me.

24 This question was first put to me by Jessica Brown and subsequently by others.

25 Christian Piller put something like this to me.

26 Though I concede that reductionism might have been my hope in Mumford (1998b).

27 Peter Clark has made this point to me in discussion, accompanied with the claim that powers indeed are no better understood.

28 See Martin (1994) and the debate it provoked in Mumford (1996), Lewis (1997), as well as Bird (1998b).

29 Cartwright (1999: 70–4) argues for a position in which a law can be known through a single instance. This can be maintained, however, only because she gives an account of laws in terms of powers.

12 Conclusion: law and metaphor

1 See Ruby (1986: 289), which includes other references.

2 The nature and workings of metaphor have a complexity that the above has barely touched. For an introduction, with further references, see McArthur (1992: 653–5).

3 Lowe's analysis of exception to laws is an alternative to the *ceteris paribus* approach. See Mumford (2000a).

4 If one thinks that moral laws are necessary, and perhaps discoverable a priori, one might draw the following contrasts. A. Legal laws are contingent and can be disobeyed. B. Moral laws are necessary but can be disobeyed. C. Natural laws are necessary and cannot be disobeyed.

5 See Ellis's excellent characterization of Humean metaphysics in his (2001) work particularly p. 7.

Bibliography

Anscombe, G. E. M. (1971) 'Causality and determinism', in *Metaphysics and the Philosophy of Mind*, Oxford: Blackwell, 1981, pp. 133–47.

Aquinas, T. (1964–81) *Summa Theologiae*, London: Blackfriars/Eyre and Spottiswoode, 61 vols.

Armstrong, D. M. (1968) *A Materialist Theory of the Mind*, rev. edn, 1993, London: Routledge.

—— (1978a) *Nominalism and Realism*, Cambridge: Cambridge University Press.

—— (1978b) *A Theory of Universals*, Cambridge: Cambridge University Press.

—— (1983) *What is a Law of Nature?*, Cambridge: Cambridge University Press.

—— (1989) *A Combinatorial Theory of Possibility*, Cambridge: Cambridge University Press.

—— (1997) *A World of States of Affairs*, Cambridge: Cambridge University Press.

—— (1999) 'The open door', in H. Sankey (ed.) *Causation and the Laws of Nature*, Dordrecht: Kluwer, pp. 175–85.

—— (2003) 'Truthmakers for necessary truths', in H. Lillehammer and G. Rodriguez-Pereyra (eds), *Real Metaphysics: Essays in Honour of D. H. Mellor*, London: Routledge, pp. 12–24.

—— (2004a) 'Four disputes about properties', *Synthese*, forthcoming.

—— (2004b) *Truth and Truthmakers*, Cambridge: Cambridge University Press, forthcoming.

—— (2004c) 'Combinatorialism revisited', in J-M. Monnoyer (ed.), *La structure du monde*, forthcoming.

—— (2004d) 'Going through the open door again', in J. Collins, N. Hall and L. Paul (eds), *Causation and Counterfactuals*, Cambridge, MA: MIT Press, forthcoming.

Ayer, A. J. (1946) *Language, Truth and Logic*, 2nd edn, London: Penguin.

—— (1963) 'What is a law of nature?', in *The Concept of a Person and Other Essays*, London: Macmillan, pp. 209–34.

Baxter, D. (2001) 'Instantiation as partial identity', *Australasian Journal of Philosophy*, 79: 449–64.

Bealer, G. (1992) 'The incoherence of empiricism', *Proceedings of the Aristotelian Society*, Supp. vol. 66: 99–138.

Bigelow, J., Ellis, B. and Lierse, C. (1992) 'The world as one of a kind: natural necessity and laws of nature', *British Journal for the Philosophy of Science*, 43: 371–88.

Bird, A. (1998a) *Philosophy of Science*, London: UCL Press.

—— (1998b) 'Dispositions and antidotes', *Philosophical Quarterly*, 48: 227–34.

—— (2001) 'Necessarily, salt dissolves in water', *Analysis*, 61: 267–74.

—— (2002) 'On whether some laws are necessary', *Analysis*, 62: 257–70.

Black, R. (2000) 'Against Quidditism', *Australasian Journal of Philosophy*, 78: 87–104.

Blackburn, S. (1990) 'Hume and thick connexions', in *Essays in Quasi-realism*, Oxford: Oxford University Press, 1993, pp. 94–107.

Boyle, R. (1686) 'A free enquiry into the vulgarly received notion of nature', in M. A. Stewart (ed.), *Selected Philosophical Papers of Robert Boyle*, Manchester: Manchester University Press, 1979, pp. 176–91.

Braithwaite, R. B. (1953) *Scientific Explanation*, Cambridge: Cambridge University Press.

Carroll, J. (1994) *Laws of Nature*, Cambridge: Cambridge University Press.

Cartwright, N. (1983) *How the Laws of Physics Lie*, Oxford: Clarendon Press.

—— (1989) *Nature's Capacities and Their Measurement*, Oxford: Clarendon Press.

—— (1993) 'In defence of "this worldy" causality: comments on van Fraassen's *Laws and Symmetry*', *Philosophy and Phenomenological Research*, 53: 423–9.

—— (1999) *The Dappled World*, Cambridge: Cambridge University Press.

Chalmers, A. (1999) 'Making sense of laws of physics', in H. Sankey (ed.) *Causation and Laws of Nature*, Dordrecht: Kluwer, pp. 3–16.

Craig, E. (1987) *The Mind of God and the Works of Man*, Oxford: Clarendon Press.

—— (2000) 'Hume on causality: projectivist and realist?', in R. Read (ed.), *The New Hume Debate*, London: Routledge, pp. 113–21.

—— (2002) 'The idea of necessary connexion', in P. Millican (ed.), *Reading Hume on Human Understanding*, Oxford: Clarendon Press, pp. 211–29.

Davies, P. C. W. (1986) *The Forces of Nature*, 2nd edn, Cambridge: Cambridge University Press.

Dennett, D. (ed.) (1987) *The Philosophical Lexicon*, 8th edn, Oxford: Blackwell.

Densmore, D. (1995) *Newton's Principia: The Central Argument, Translation, Notes and Expanded Proofs* (translation and diagrams by W. H. Donahue), Santa Fe, New Mexico: Green Lion Press.

Descartes, R. (1637) 'Discourse on the method', in J. Cottingham, R. Stoothoff and D. Murdoch (eds), *The Philosophical Writings of Descartes* I, Cambridge: Cambridge University Press, 1985, pp. 111–51.

—— (1644) 'Principles of Philosophy', in J. Cottingham, R. Stoothoff and D. Murdoch (eds), *The Philosophical Writings of Descartes* I, Cambridge: Cambridge University Press, 1985, pp. 177–291.

Dretske, F. (1977) 'Laws of nature', *Philosophy of Science*, 44: 248–68.

Drewery, A. (2004) 'Laws, dispositions and necessity', *Synthese*, forthcoming.

Dupré, J. (1993) *The Disorder of Things*, Cambridge, MA: Harvard University Press.

Earman, J. (1993) 'In defense of laws: reflections on Bas van Fraassen's *Laws and Symmetry*', *Philosophy and Phenomenological Research*, 53: 412–19.

Einstein, A. (1920) *Relativity: the Special and the General Theory*, London: Methuen.

Elder, C. (1994) 'Laws, necessities, and contingent necessities', *Philosophy and Phenomenological Research*, 54: 649–67.

Ellis, B. (2001) *Scientific Essentialism*, Cambridge: Cambridge University Press.

—— (2002) *The Philosophy of Nature: A Guide to the New Essentialism*, Chesham: Acumen.

Ellis, B. and Lierse, C. (1994) 'Dispositional essentialism', *Australasian Journal of Philosophy*, 72: 27–45.

Engel, P. (2002) *Truth*, Chesham: Acumen.

Feyerabend, P. (1977) *Against Method*, 3rd edn, London: Verso, 1993.

Feynman, R. P. (1965) *The Character of Physical Law*, London: Penguin, 1992.

Fodor, J. A. (1974) 'Special sciences, or the disunity of science as a working hypothesis', *Synthese*, 28: 97–115.

Gendler, T. S. and Hawthorne, J. (eds) (2002) *Conceivability and Possibility*, Oxford: Oxford University Press.

Giere, R. N. (1999) *Science Without Laws*, Chicago: University of Chicago Press.

Gillies, D. (2000) *Philosophical Theories of Probability*, London: Routledge.

Goodman N. (1965) *Fact, Fiction and Forecast*, 2nd edn, Indianapolis: Bobbs-Merrill Co.

Haavelmo, T. (1944) 'The probability approach to econometrics', *Econometrica*, 12 (suppl.): 1–117.

Handfield, T. (2002) 'Armstrong, Meinong, and dispositionalism'. Online. Available HTTP: http://home.iprimus.com.au/than/toby/am&d.pdf (accessed 19 December 2003).

Harré, R. (2001) 'Active powers and powerful actors', *Philosophy*, 76 (suppl.): 91–109.

Harré, R. and Madden, E. H. (1973) 'Natural powers and powerful natures', *Philosophy*, 48: 209–30.

—— (1975) *Causal Powers: A Theory of Natural Necessity*, Oxford: Blackwell.

Heathcote, A. and Armstrong, D. M. (1991) 'Causes and laws', *Noûs*, 25: 63–73.

Hochberg, H. (1999) 'Review of *A World of States of Affairs*', *Noûs*, 33: 473–95.

Hoffman, J. and Rosenkrantz, G. (1997) *Substance: Its Nature and Existence*, London: Routledge.

Huby, P. (1969) 'Family resemblance', *Philosophical Quarterly*, 18: 66–7.

Hume, D. (1739–40) *A Treatise of Human Nature*, L. A. Selby-Bigge (ed.), Oxford: Clarendon Press, 1888.

—— (1748) *An Enquiry Concerning Human Understanding*, in *Enquiries Concerning Human Understanding and Concerning the Principles of Morals*, L. A. Selby-Bigge (ed.), 3rd edn rev. P. H. Nidditch, Oxford: Clarendon Press, 1975.

—— (1779) *Dialogues Concerning Natural Religion*, N. Pike (ed.), Indianapolis: Bobbs-Merrill, 1970.

Issacs, A. (ed.) (2000) *Oxford Dictionary of Physics*, 4th edn, Oxford: Oxford University Press.

Johnson, W. E. (1921) *Logic* I, Cambridge: Cambridge University Press.

Kim, J. (1976) 'Events as property exemplifications', in *Supervenience and Mind*, Cambridge: Cambridge University Press, 1993, pp. 33–52.

Kripke, S. A. (1972) 'Naming and necessity' in G. Harman and D. Davidson (eds) *Semantics of Natural Language*, Dordrecht: Reidel, pp. 253–355.

—— (1980) *Naming and Necessity*, Oxford: Blackwell.

Kuhn, T. (1962) *The Structure of Scientific Revolutions*, 2nd edn, Chicago, IL: University of Chicago Press, 1970.

Ladyman, J. (2002) *Understanding Philosophy of Science*, London: Routledge.

Lakatos, I. (1970) 'Falsification and the methodology of scientific research programmes', in I. Lakatos and A. Musgrave (eds), *Criticism and the Growth of Knowledge*, Cambridge: Cambridge University Press, pp. 91–196.

Lange, M. (1993) 'Lawlikeness', *Noûs*, 27: 1–21.

—— (2000) *Natural Laws in Scientific Practice*, Oxford: Oxford University Press.

—— (2002a) *An Introduction to The Philosophy of Physics: Locality, Fields, Energy, and Mass*, Oxford: Blackwell.

—— (2002b) 'Who's afraid of ceteris-paribus laws? Or: how I learned to stop worrying and love them', *Erkenntnis*, 57: 407–23.

Langton, R. (1998) *Kantian Humility: Our Ignorance of Things in Themselves*, Oxford: Oxford University Press.

Lewis, D. (1972) 'Psychophysical and theoretical identifications', in *Papers in Metaphysics and Epistemology*, Cambridge: Cambridge University Press, 1999, pp. 248–61.

—— (1973) *Counterfactuals*, Oxford: Blackwell.

—— (1983) 'New work for a theory of universals', in *Papers in Metaphysics and Epistemology*, Cambridge: Cambridge University Press, 1999, pp. 8–55.

—— (1986a) *On the Plurality of Worlds*, Oxford: Blackwell.

—— (1986b) *Philosophical Papers II*, Oxford: Oxford University Press.

—— (1986c) 'A subjectivist's guide to objective chance' with Postscript, in D. Lewis *Philosophical Papers II*, Oxford: Oxford University Press, pp. 83–132.

—— (1994) 'Humean supervenience debugged', in *Papers in Metaphysics and Epistemology*, Cambridge: Cambridge University Press, 1999, pp. 224–47.

—— (1997) 'Finkish dispositions', *Philosophical Quarterly*, 47: 143–58.

Lipton, P. (1999) 'All else being equal', *Philosophy*, 74: 155–68.

Llewellyn, J. (1969) 'Family resemblance', *Philosophical Quarterly*, 18: 344–6.

Locke, J. (1690) *An Essay Concerning Human Understanding*, P. H. Nidditch (ed.), Oxford: Clarendon Press, 1975.

Lombard, L. (1986) *Events*, London: Routledge and Kegan Paul.

Lombardo, E. (2002) 'Analogical versus discrete theories of possibility', *Australasian Journal of Philosophy*, 80: 307–20.

Lowe, E. J. (1980) 'Sortal terms and natural laws', *American Philosophical Quarterly*, 17: 253–60.

—— (1982) 'Laws, dispositions and sortal logic', *American Philosophical Quarterly*, 19: 41–50.

—— (1987a) 'What is the "problem of induction"?', *Philosophy*, 62: 325–40.

—— (1987b) 'Miracles and laws of nature', *Religious Studies*, 23: 263–78.

—— (1989) *Kinds of Being*, Oxford: Blackwell.

—— (1998) *The Possibility of Metaphysics: Substance, Identity, and Time*, Oxford: Clarendon Press.

—— (2002a) *A Survey of Metaphysics*, Oxford: Oxford University Press.

—— (2002b) 'A defence of the four-category ontology', in *Argument und Analyse*, Paderborn: Mentis-Verlag, pp. 225–40.

McArthur, T. (ed.) (1992) *The Oxford Companion to the English Language*, Oxford: Oxford University Press.

McKitrick, J. (2003) 'The bare metaphysical possibility of bare dispositions', *Philosophy and Phenomenological Research*, 66: 349–69.

Martin, C. B. (1994) 'Dispositions and conditionals', *Philosophical Quarterly*, 44: 1–8.

Meinong, A. (1902) *On Assumptions*, J. Heanue (trans.), Berkeley, CA: University of California Press, 1983.

—— (1904) 'Über Gegenstandstheorie', trans. 'On the theory of objects', in R. M. Chisholm *et. al.* (eds), *Realism and the Background of Phenomenology*, New York: The Free Press, 1960, pp. 76–117.

Mellor, D. H. (1971) *The Matter of Chance*, Cambridge: Cambridge University Press.

—— (1977) 'Natural kinds', in D. H. Mellor, *Matters of Metaphysics*, Cambridge: Cambridge University Press, pp. 123–35.

—— (1980) 'Necessities and universals in natural laws', in D. H. Mellor, *Matters of Metaphysics*, Cambridge: Cambridge University Press, pp. 136–53.

—— (1991) *Matters of Metaphysics*, Cambridge: Cambridge University Press.

—— (1998) *Real Time II*, London: Routledge.

Mill, J. S. (1843) *A System of Logic*, London: Parker.

Molnar, G. (1969) 'Kneale's argument revisited', *Philosophical Review*, 78: 79–89.

—— (2003) *Powers: A Study in Metaphysics*, S. Mumford (ed.), Oxford: Oxford University Press.

Mumford, S. (1996) 'Conditionals, functional essences and Martin on dispositions', *Philosophical Quarterly*, 46: 86–92.

—— (1998a) *Dispositions*, Oxford: Clarendon Press.

—— (1998b) 'Laws of nature outlawed', *Dialectica*, 52: 83–101.

—— (2000a) 'Normative and natural laws', *Philosophy*, 75: 265–82.

—— (2000b) 'Review of *The Dappled World*', *Philosophy*, 75: 613–16.

—— (2001) 'Miracles: metaphysics and modality', *Religious Studies*, 37: 191–202.

—— (2004) 'L'état des lois', in J-M. Monnoyer (ed.), *La structure du monde*, forthcoming.

Nagel, E. (1961) *The Structure of Science: Problems in the Logic of Scientific Explanation*, London: Routledge and Kegan Paul.

Newton, I. (1687) *Philosophiae Naturalis Principia Mathematica*, A. Motte Trans., *Mathematical Principles of Natural Philosophy*, 1729, revised by F. Cajori, Cambridge: Cambridge University Press, 1934.

—— (1978) (*De gravitatio*) *De gravitatio et aequipondio fluidorum*, in *Unpublished Scientific Papers of Isaac Newton*, A. R. Hall and M. Boas Hall (eds) Cambridge: Cambridge University Press, 1978, pp. 89–156.

O'Hear, A. (1985) *What Philosophy Is: An Introduction to Contemporary Philosophy*, Harmondsworth: Penguin.

Pap, A. (1962) *An Introduction to the Philosophy of Science*, Glencoe, IL: Free Press.

Plato (1961a) *Phaedo*, in *The Collected Dialogues of Plato*, E. Hamilton and H. Cairns (eds), Princeton, NJ: Princeton University Press, 1961, pp. 40–98.

—— (1961b) *Sophist*, in *The Collected Dialogues of Plato*, E. Hamilton and H. Cairns (eds), Princeton, NJ: Princeton University Press, 1961, pp. 957–1017.

Pompa, L. (1967) 'Family resemblance', *Philosophical Quarterly*, 17: 63–9.

Popper, K. R. (1957) 'The propensity interpretation of the calculus of probability, and the quantum theory', in S. Körner (ed.), *Observation and Interpretation*, London: Butterworth, pp. 65–70.

—— (1959) *The Logic of Scientific Discovery*, London: Hutchinson.

—— (1971) 'Conjectural knowledge: my solution to the problem of induction', in *Objective Knowledge*, 2nd edn, Oxford, Clarendon Press, 1979, pp. 1–31.

Prior, E., Pargetter, R. and Jackson, F. (1982) 'Three theses about dispositions', *American Philosophical Quarterly*, 19: 251–7.

Psillos, S. (1999) *Scientific Realism: How Science Tracks Truth*, London: Routledge.

—— (2002) *Causation and Explanation*, Chesham: Acumen.

Purcell, E. M. (1965) *Electricity and Magnetism*, New York: McGraw-Hill.

Putnam, H. (1975) 'The meaning of "meaning"', in *Mind, Language and Reality: Philosophical Papers II*, Cambridge, Cambridge University Press, 1975, pp. 215–71.

Quine, W. v. O. (1953) 'Two dogmas of empiricism', in *From a Logical Point of View*, Cambridge, MA: Harvard University Press, pp. 20–46.

—— (1960) *Word and Object*, Cambridge, MA: MIT Press.

—— (1969) 'Natural kinds', in *Ontological Relativity and Other Essays*, New York: Colombia University Press, pp. 114–38.

Ramsey, F. P. (1928) 'Universals of law and of fact', in D. H. Mellor (ed.), *Philosophical Papers*, Cambridge: Cambridge University Press, pp. 140–4.

—— (1929) 'General propositions and causality', in D. H. Mellor (ed.), *Philosophical Papers*, Cambridge: Cambridge University Press, pp.145–63.

Reichenbach, H. (1947) *Elements of Symbolic Logic*, New York: Macmillan.

Robinson, H. (1982) *Matter and Sense*, Cambridge: Cambridge University Press.

Ruben, D-H. (ed.) (1993) *Explanation*, Oxford: Oxford University Press.

Ruby, J. (1986) 'The origins of scientific "law"', in F. Weinert (ed.), *Laws of Nature: Essays on the Philosophical, Scientific and Historical Dimensions*, Berlin: de Gruyter, 1995, pp. 289–315.

Russell, B. A. W. (1903) *The Principles of Mathematics*, London: George Allen and Unwin.

—— (1905) 'On Denoting', in *The Collected Papers of Bertrand Russell* 4, London: Routledge, 1994, pp. 415–27.

—— (1911) 'The basis of realism', in S. Mumford (ed.), *Russell on Metaphysics*, London: Routledge, 2003, pp. 85–90.

—— (1927a) *The Analysis of Matter*, London: Kegan Paul, Trench, Trubner & Co.

—— (1927b) *An Outline of Philosophy*, London: George Allen and Unwin.

—— (1948) *Human Knowledge: Its Scope and Limits*, London: George Allen and Unwin.

Salmon, N. U. (1982) *Reference and Essence*, Oxford: Blackwell.

Sankey, H. (ed.) (1999) *Causation and Laws of Nature*, Dordrecht: Kluwer.

Schiffer, S. (1991) '*Ceteris paribus* laws', *Mind*, 100: 1–17.

Sellars, W. (1948) 'Concepts as involving laws and inconceivable without them', *Philosophy of Science*, 15: 287–315.

Shoemaker, S. (1980) 'Causality and properties', in *Identity, Cause and Mind*, expanded edn, Oxford: Oxford University Press, 2003, pp. 206–33.

—— (1998) 'Causal and metaphysical necessity', in *Identity, Cause and Mind*, expanded edn, Oxford: Oxford University Press, 2003, 1984, pp. 407–26.

—— (1999) 'Self, body, and coincidence', *Proceedings of the Aristotelian Society*, supp. vol. 73, pp. 287–306.

Sidelle, A. (2002) 'On the metaphysical contingency of laws of nature', in T. S. Gendler and J. Hawthorne (eds), *Conceivability and Possibility*, Oxford: Oxford University Press, pp. 309–36.

Sider, T. (2001) *Four Dimensionalism: An Ontology of Persistence and Time*, Oxford: Oxford University Press.

Stein, H. (1995) 'Newton, Isaac', in J. Kim and E. Sosa (eds), *A Companion to Metaphysics*, Oxford: Blackwell, pp. 353–6.

Stevens, P. S. (1974) *Real Patterns*, London: Penguin.

Stove, D. C. (1970) 'Deductivism', *Australasian Journal of Philosophy*, 48: 76–98.

Strawson, G. (1989) *The Secret Connexion: Causation, Realism, and David Hume*, Oxford: Clarendon Press.

Stroud, B. (1977) *Hume*, London: Routledge.

Swartz, N. (1985) *The Concept of Physical Law*, Cambridge: Cambridge University Press.

Swoyer, C. (1982) 'The nature of natural laws', *Australasian Journal of Philosophy*, 60: 203–23.

Tooley, M. (1977) 'The nature of laws', *Canadian Journal of Philosophy*, 74: 667–98.

Trefil, J. (2002) *Cassell's Laws of Nature*, London: Cassell.

van Fraassen, B. C. (1980) *The Scientific Image*, Oxford: Clarendon Press.

—— (1989) *Laws and Symmetry*, Oxford: Clarendon Press.

Wilkerson, T. E. (1995) *Natural Kinds*, Aldershot: Avebury.

Wittgenstein, L. (1921) *Tractatus Logico-Philosophicus*, trans. 1961, London: Routledge and Kegan Paul.

—— (1953) *Philosophical Investigations*, Oxford, Blackwell.

—— (1958) *The Blue and Brown Books: Preliminary Studies for the 'Philosophical Investigations'*, Oxford: Blackwell.

Woodward, J. (1992) 'Realism about laws', *Erkenntnis*, 36: 181–218.

—— (1997) 'Explanation, invariance and intervention', *Philosophy of Science*, 64 (proceedings): S26–41.

—— (2000) 'Explanation and invariance in the special sciences', *British Journal for the Philosophy of Science*, 51: 197–254.

Wright, J. (1983) *The Sceptical Realism of David Hume*, Manchester: Manchester University Press.

Index

NOTTINGHAM UNIVERSITY LIBRARY

eBooks – at www.eBookstore.tandf.co.uk

A library at your fingertips!

eBooks are electronic versions of printed books. You can store them on your PC/laptop or browse them online.

They have advantages for anyone needing rapid access to a wide variety of published, copyright information.

eBooks can help your research by enabling you to bookmark chapters, annotate text and use instant searches to find specific words or phrases. Several eBook files would fit on even a small laptop or PDA.

NEW: Save money by eSubscribing: cheap, online access to any eBook for as long as you need it.

Annual subscription packages

We now offer special low-cost bulk subscriptions to packages of eBooks in certain subject areas. These are available to libraries or to individuals.

For more information please contact webmaster.ebooks@tandf.co.uk

We're continually developing the eBook concept, so keep up to date by visiting the website.

www.eBookstore.tandf.co.uk